J. P. Brock

Criticism of feminism

Why the Dialogue is in Danger of Failing

J. P. Brock

# Criticism of feminism

Why the Dialogue is in Danger of Failing

Publisher: BoD · Books on Demand GmbH, Überseering 33, 22297 Hamburg, bod@bod.de

Printing: Libri Plureos GmbH, Friedensallee 273, 22763 Hamburg

ISBN: 978-3-8192-1347-2

# Foreword

Feminism has triggered social progress: women now work in professions that were previously closed to them, violence in partnerships is addressed, and equality is a central concern of public debates. At the same time, this progress raises new questions – and not all of them are heard in the current discourse. This book is dedicated to those blind spots that have so far remained underilluminated.

Modern feminist currents such as intersectional feminism claim to integrate as many perspectives as possible. However, the focus is often primarily on women and marginalized groups, while male perspectives – despite their own problems – are hardly given any space. This is not due to malice, but often to historical patterns of interpretation and political attributions of power.

This creates an area of tension: While feminist theories seek to uncover patriarchal structures, there is sometimes a lack of willingness to critically examine new inequalities – especially when men are affected. While women's shelters are state-funded (rightly so), there are only about 50 shelters for men fleeing domestic violence in the whole of Germany. While young women in Great Britain now earn more on average than their male peers, the economic downward spiral of many men is hardly discussed.

## Objective of the book

This book is not a compulsive rejection of feminist concerns – some of them are legitimate and necessary. Rather, it wants to contribute to plurality: feminist arguments, which have already been dealt with in detail in mainstream publications, are deliberately kept short here. To this end, perspectives are to become visible that would otherwise be lost

– such as the psychological stress caused by general suspicion, grade discrimination of boys or gender-specific stereotypes in the judiciary.

## Methodological note

When this book speaks of "men" or "women", it does not mean absolute statements. This refers to statistical accumulations, recurring patterns or social constructions. The book does not claim to depict all perspectives. Rather, it is about an impulse: to open up spaces for debate, not to close them.

## One-sided warning

The one-sidedness of the perspective is methodical: the aim is to shed light on underrepresented aspects – in full knowledge that this itself can be a distortion. The book shares this attitude with many feminist theories, which in turn focus on certain experiences. I invite readers to read these thoughts not as the final truth, but as a contribution to dialogue.

## Feminist counter-positions

Many of the grievances criticized here – such as men as victims of violence or the educational crisis of young men – are certainly addressed by feminist theorists. A differentiated reception of feminist sources can help to avoid misunderstandings. The title says criticism of feminism, but I doubt that even one of the criticisms applies to feminism as a whole. Radical feminism and hobby feminism on social media are probably predominantly criticized. In other places, there is talk of mainstream feminism. What is meant is a presumed majority in feminism, without shedding light on exactly who exactly. From a logical point of view, one can say: If I criticize circumstance A and feminist groups B and C promote circumstance A, then I probably also criticize groups B and C and not the rest. Even statements like, "Feminism promotes X and Y", will probably only speak of a majority and never of the totality. You always have to keep in mind: There are numerous opinions within feminism, some of which differ so widely that one group sees the other as anti-feminist.

## Recommendation for self-reflection

Finally, it should be remembered that criticism of other groups – as justified as it may be in parts – can be psychologically stressful. A permanent "victim mindset" undermines the ability to be self-effective and rarely leads to viable solutions. Studies show that constructive goal orientation and a "creator mindset" lead to more resilience, self-esteem and social connectivity.[1]

Justified criticism of social groups can easily be perceived as one-sided and lead to the reciprocal game of "victim card" and counter-reaction: When one side emphasizes its victim role, the other party often reacts with the same pattern in order to gain attention as well. This creates a vicious circle of misunderstanding and mistrust that makes dialogue difficult.

Experience has shown that a sober, fact-based approach, in which statistics and studies from reliable sources are carefully examined, helps in order to focus on factual issues. At the same time, a deliberate change of perspective – the adoption of possible opposing positions – promotes the understanding of all parties involved and prevents polarization. My personal impression when writing this book was how quickly you fall into a defensive posture when you encounter well-known narratives. Only through continuous self-reflection and the effort to make constructive suggestions could a more balanced basis for discussion be created that acknowledges individualized experiences without forcing them into collective role clichés.

I mention it here because, even if I criticize it, this book will reproduce certain patterns from the subject matter and the culture of debate alone.

---

[1] https://youtu.be/6w_96Hnz8JM?si=4aOrJAA19owxvOkt

## Technical notes

Yes, links are suboptimal for a book, but quite practical for an e-book. I can only advise everyone with the book version to take a picture of the link and read it out with an image to text program or ChatGPT can do it too.

If a link does not work, the page can often be accessed via a web archive – for example, the Wayback Machine under https://web.archive.org . As of May 2025, all links should be available.

This book was originally written in German. To make its content accessible to a broader international audience, the initial translation into English was performed using Artificial Intelligence. While great care has been taken to review and refine the text for accuracy and clarity, some stylistic nuances typical of a human translation may differ. The comprehensive research and extensive bibliography, with over 600 verifiable sources, remain the core strength of this work.

"Enlightenment is man's emergence from his self-imposed immaturity. ... Have courage to use your own understanding!"

– Kant

# I. *Critical Theory* vs. *Traditional Theory*

*First*: Feminist references to *Critical Theory* can be found both in radical feminism and in the fourth wave, albeit in different intensity and expression.

Horkheimer, for example, first clarifies fundamental questions in his book.[2]

## What is a theory?

A theory is an ordered collection of statements about a topic; the fewer basic principles it requires, the more concise it is.

## How is their validity checked?

Theory and observation must agree; in the event of deviations, both shall be re-examined.

## Theory remains preliminary

That's why every theory is actually only a preliminary assumption – you have to be ready to change it at any time if weaknesses become visible. In the end, theory is accumulated knowledge, prepared in such a way that it helps to describe the world as precisely as possible.

One question that this book deals with is whether we are not at a point where weaknesses are slowly becoming visible.

---

[2] https://tinyurl.com/eba3syby

# 1. Foundations and Origins

## 1.1 *Traditional Theory*

**Traditional Theory**, as described by Max Horkheimer in his essay *Traditional and Critical Theory* (1937), portrays social institutions largely as they are, without normative evaluation or intent to change them. In line with the positivist tradition, it assumes that valid knowledge derives from sensory-empirical, measurable facts, and that other sources of insight—such as intuition or belief—are considered irrelevant.[3]

## 1.2 *Critical Theory*

**Critical Theory** emerged in the 1930s at the Frankfurt School and defines itself as a participatory, normatively critical practice that not only describes reality but also seeks to have an emancipatory effect. Its aim is to uncover and transform existing power and domination structures, recognizing that knowledge itself is socially mediated and shaped by interests.[4] [5]

# 2. Power and oppression

*Critical Theory* focuses on power as fundamental: social structures are not neutral, but privilege certain groups and oppress others. *Traditional theory,* on the other hand, tends to take such inequalities for granted or to grasp them only descriptively without questioning them normatively.

In critical analysis, oppression is understood not only as economic exploitation, but as a multi-layered network of racism, sexism, class dominance and other forms of domination.

---

[3] https://en.wikipedia.org/wiki/Positivism
[4] https://en.wikipedia.org/wiki/Critical_theory
[5] https://plato.stanford.edu/entries/critical-theory/

# 3. Value vs. Truth

**Traditional Theory** promotes the ideal of value-freedom (value-neutrality), which holds that research and theory should be conducted independently of normative intentions and values.[6]

**Critical Theory**, by contrast, views research as always influenced by values.[7]

On the other hand, scientific facts represent only one possible form of objectivity. All empirical findings can be falsified, and Karl Popper argued that this should apply to theories as well.[8] If something cannot be falsified, it does not meet the criteria of scientific inquiry.

# 4. Objectivity vs. Subjectivity

*Traditional Theory* strives for the most objective and universally valid consideration of phenomena and is based on quantifiable methods and formal logic.

*Critical Theory,* on the other hand, argues that any "objectivity" is always colored by prevailing discourses and power relations and argues for reflexive research that reveals one's own positioning and interests.

**What does this mean for research?**

**Susan Haack[9]**

In The Feminist Methodology Muddle and later works, Haack criticizes that feminist methodologies propagate the deliberate politicization of research – they do not primarily aim at unbiased knowledge acquisition,

---

[6] https://tinyurl.com/3ra65a3j
[7] https://en.wikipedia.org/wiki/Critical_theory
[8] https://plato.stanford.edu/entries/popper/#BasiStatFalsConv
[9] https://papers.ssrn.com/sol3/papers.cfm?abstract_id=3467041

but at the active promotion of feminist goals. This entails a mixture of honest investigation and disguised lobbying, comparable to the catastrophes of Nazi physics or Soviet biology.

## Pinnick, Koertge & Almeder vs. Anderson[10]

Critics claim that feminist epistemology is "politically correct" by prioritizing political criteria over scientific evidence. In addition, she is "tribalist" in that she assumes a uniform, "feminine" way of thinking for all women and postulates their superiority.

## Refutation: Defense by Elizabeth Anderson

Feminist epistemologists call for empirical verifiability and objectivity through a variety of critical interactions. Political values influence the discovery of research questions, not the truth of the results.

The idea of a unified "feminine" way of thinking is outdated and rejected within feminist research. The focus is on methodological pluralism and viewpoint theory, which emphasizes knowledge achieved from marginalized perspectives, without automatic privileges or global claims.

## Sandra Harding[11]

Harding herself makes no secret of the fact that good feminist research must be an explicitly emancipatory and political project: In An Invitation to Feminist Research, she argues that objective positive methods are part of patriarchal power relations that must be actively broken up.

---

[10] https://public.websites.umich.edu/~eandersn/hownotreview.html
[11] https://books.google.de/books?id=w2gzw6zz4fIC

## Stanford Encyclopedia of Philosophy[12]

The entry on feminist epistemology emphasizes that feminists consciously integrate values and political goals into their research and reject neutral-value-free research concepts. Critics like Haack, however, see this as a challenge to scientific objectivity.

Official positions of feminist science policy demand that science and research be managed in such a way that hierarchical structures are broken up and gender policy goals are supported – research thus becomes an instrument of emancipatory agenda work.

Let us take this book as an example: it clearly pursues a political agenda and presents the subject matter from a noticeably one-sided perspective. Of course, Critical Theory can be a useful tool for drawing attention to real social grievances. The crucial question, however, is what happens when this theory is no longer treated merely as a tool but is elevated to the status of a scientific principle. Could it not be the case that, forty years from now, someone might knock on your door and ask: What underrepresentation are you still talking about? Women's issues have long been overrepresented by a factor of 2.25 to 1.[13]

# 5. Biology vs. Socialization

Biological approaches emphasize that human behavior and identity are primarily determined by genetic and evolutionary factors.[14] [15] [16]

Perspectives on socialization theory counter that identity and behavior are constructed to a large extent socially, for example through culture, education, and historical contexts.[17]

---

[12] https://plato.stanford.edu/archIves/sum2023/entries/feminism-epistemology/
[13] https://direct.mit.edu/qss/article/3/1/244/108658/Researching-women-and-men-1996-2020-Is
[14] https://pmc.ncbi.nlm.nih.gov/articles/PMC5751942/
[15] https://pmc.ncbi.nlm.nih.gov/articles/PMC10691233/
[16] https://tinyurl.com/4jhwjz7j
[17] https://www.frontiersin.org/journals/psychology/articles/10.3389/fpsyg.2020.00609/full

In current debates, an integrative approach is sometimes called for, which understands biological and social determinants as mutually determined.

# 6. Reflection

By its own logic, *Critical Theory* would have to question itself as soon as it is in a position to make a difference, i.e. from a position of power. We may see in this book that this doesn't work so well.

# II. Sexism and feminism

## 1. Discrimination vs. disadvantage

The terms "discrimination" and "disadvantage" are often mixed, but they can be clearly distinguished:

**Discrimination**

- Discrimination refers to active unequal treatment or disparagement of persons on the basis of a certain characteristic (e.g. gender, origin, religion).
- It can be conscious or unconscious and is often associated with prejudice.
- Discrimination can be prosecuted if it violates equal treatment or anti-discrimination laws.

**Disadvantage**

- Disadvantage describes a worse starting position or negative consequences that can result from social structures or individual circumstances.

- It does not necessarily have to be associated with discrimination, but can also arise from historical, economic or biological factors.
- Discrimination can exist without targeted discrimination having taken place.

Discrimination is always a form of disadvantage, but not every disadvantage is always discrimination. While discrimination is often intentional, disadvantage also arises from seemingly neutral rules – such as pension models or care work. This dynamic is later exemplified in education policy or access to shelters

## Constitution

Article 3 of the Basic Law: "Men and women have equal rights. The state promotes the actual implementation of equal rights for women and men and works towards the elimination of existing disadvantages."[18]

## Recognizing structural disadvantage

To check whether discrimination is *structural*, ask yourself the following questions:

## Does it affect entire groups, not individuals?

→ Structural disadvantage affects *system groups* (e.g., all women, people of color, people with disabilities).
*Example:* If only 5% of professors in a country are women, although 50% of graduates are female, this may be a systemic problem – not an isolated case.

## Is there a historical continuity?

→ Inequality has existed for generations and is shaped by historical events (colonialism, patriarchy, class systems).

---

[18] https://tinyurl.com/5b8f88u3

*Example:* Racist housing policy in the USA ("redlining") led to today's wealth inequality between black and white families.

### Is discrimination anchored in institutions?

→ laws, rules or practices of authorities, companies or educational institutions favor certain groups.

*Example:* Textbooks that only teach European perspectives indirectly disadvantage children with a migrant background.

### Is inequality automatically reproduced?

→ The system ensures that disadvantaged people will continue to have worse opportunities in the future ("vicious circle").

*Example:* Children from poor families often attend poorer schools → lower educational qualifications → lower incomes.

### Are there "neutral" rules that seem unfair?

→ requirements that seem fair at first glance indirectly disadvantage certain groups.

*Example:* A job posting requires "fluent German" for a job where language is irrelevant → excludes refugees.

### Is there a lack of data or representation?

→ affected groups are underrepresented in decision-making positions, the media or research.

*Example:* Medical studies test drugs mainly on men → dosages often have a different effect on women.

### Equality

- **Definition:** *Every person has the same rights, regardless of gender, origin, or belief.*[19]

---

[19] https://tinyurl.com/nhcfta82

- **Critical note:** Legal equality does not automatically guarantee actual equality in daily life or in the labor market. Without accompanying measures, inequalities often persist.

## Equal Opportunities[20]

- **Definition:** *Equal opportunities aim to ensure that no one is disadvantaged because of their gender, origin, or social background.*
- **EU Charter of Fundamental Rights (Art. 21):** Discrimination based on sex, among other factors, is prohibited.

## Gender Equality[21]

- **Definition:**[22] *Equal rights, duties, and opportunities for women and men, girls and boys.* Furthermore, it says: Moreover, it states in essence that gender equality does not mean that women and men must be identical in every respect, but that their rights, duties, and opportunities should not depend on the sex assigned to them at birth. Gender equality involves taking into account the interests, needs, and priorities of both women and men equally—while also recognizing the diversity within each group. Gender equality is not merely a "women's issue"; it also concerns men and should actively include both genders. The equality of women and men is both a human rights issue and a fundamental prerequisite and indicator of sustainable, people-centered development and democratic societies.
- **BMFSFJ Objective:** "Gender equality is one of the key challenges for making life in our country sustainable and fair for the future. To achieve this, women and men must have equal opportunities throughout their entire lives—personally,

---

[20] https://tinyurl.com/3txtpxd9
[21] https://www.bmfsfj.de/bmfsfj/themen/gleichstellung
[22] https://tinyurl.com/bp6ta5ym

professionally, and within the family." This essentially describes equal opportunities.

## Note

**Instrumentalization:** Gender equality policy is sometimes criticized as a "female bonus" because it tends to emphasize the promotion of women specifically rather than broader family-friendly policies.

## Parity[23]

- **Definition:** *The term means equivalence, equality, or numerical equality. However, it is used in various fields to describe different concepts.*

## Critical Note

- **Conflict of freedom:** Complete parity can be perceived as an infringement on citizens' freedom of choice and creates tension between representative fairness and individual autonomy.[24]
- **Birth deficit and subject preferences:** There are imbalances already at birth and in the choice of study fields that cannot simply be leveled out through parity.

Fundamentally, there is a conflict within these definitions: *Gender equality* is intended to mean *equal opportunities*, while *parity* refers to *equality* and *numerical balance*. (Personally, I will use "parity" strictly in the sense of numerical equality.)

However, equal opportunity is not the same as numerical equality. Suppose we are looking for six people who are over two meters tall, and there are 100 male applicants and 3 female applicants. Equal opportunity would mean selecting six at random from all 103 applicants.

---

[23] https://www.politische-bildung-brandenburg.de/lexikon/paritaet-parite
[24] https://tinyurl.com/mr29cd3u

Numerical equality would mean taking three from each group. In that case, the women would have a 100% chance of being selected, while the men would have a 3% chance. These chances are clearly not equal.

# 2. Definition of Sexism

Sexism is generally defined as discrimination based on sex or gender. In the broadest sense, it encompasses all forms of prejudice, stereotyping, and disadvantage arising from belonging to a particular gender.

According to Wikipedia,[25] sexism is an umbrella term for a wide range of phenomena — both conscious and unconscious discrimination that stems from socially shared gender prejudices and implicit gender theories. This definition in principle includes all genders, as any person can be discriminated against on the basis of their sex.

A distinction is often made between:

- **Traditional (overt) sexism:** Open, explicit gender-based discrimination.
- **Modern sexism:** The denial of discrimination and the rejection of measures aimed at reducing social inequalities.
- **Neosexism and ambivalent sexism:** Forms in which negative attitudes and benevolent stereotypes are intertwined.

**General / Lexical Definitions:**
   These definitions are neutral and describe sexism as any form of gender-based discrimination.

- **Oxford English Dictionary:** *"Prejudice, stereotyping, or discrimination, typically against women, on the basis of sex."*
   → *Condition:* Any discrimination based on sex, regardless of the sex of those affected.

---

[25] https://de.wikipedia.org/wiki/Sexismus

- **Duden:** *"The notion that one gender is naturally superior, and the [therefore considered justified] discrimination, oppression, marginalization, or disadvantage of people, especially women, based on their gender."*
  → *Condition:* Both genders can be victims of sexism.

## UN Convention (CEDAW):

Definition of discrimination against women: *Any distinction, exclusion, or restriction made on the basis of sex which has the effect or purpose of impairing or nullifying the recognition, enjoyment, or exercise by women of human rights and fundamental freedoms in the political, economic, social, cultural, or civil fields on a basis of equality with men.*

# 3. Understanding sexism

In feminist discourse, sexism is not a mere insult for individual disadvantage, but a system that has cemented power relations over thousands of years. Its core lies in patriarchy: a social structure that elevated masculinity to the norm and marked femininity as deviation. This dynamic is reflected not only in open discrimination, but also in invisible structures – from wage inequality to care work to the underrepresentation of women in leadership positions. Even if Angela Merkel ruled Germany for 16 years, sexism against women remains a systemic problem. After all, a female chancellor, a female board member or a Nobel Prize winner are exceptions, not evidence of a change in power. They prove that women can overcome barriers – not that the barriers have fallen.

The patriarchy acts like a river that has furrowed into its bed for centuries: even if individual stones are removed, the water continues to flow in the same direction. The 16% wage gap, the dominance of men on DAX boards or the fact that women still do most of the unpaid care work – these are all after-effects of the patriarchal legacy. Institutions, laws and cultural norms bear the traces of past power relations, even if formal equality prevails today.

But what does this mean for men who feel discriminated against? Feminist theory rejects the term "sexism against men" – even in extreme scenarios. Let's assume that there were widespread laws in a society that prohibit men from entering certain professions and public offices and discriminate against them in all schools: From a feminist point of view, this would not be sexism, but a reactive act of power historically directed against patriarchy. Sexism, by definition, remains tied to the maintenance of male power. Even if all men suffer in this scenario, the suffering lacks the historically deep-rooted structural anchoring that constitutes sexism. In this case, exclusion would not be a system for consolidating male supremacy, but a new form of discrimination – comparable to a legally sanctioned exclusion regime that plays social groups off against each other.

This creates an area of tension: While feminism recognizes intersectional discrimination (e.g., racism + sexism), male suffering is categorically excluded from the sexism debate. The reasoning is political, not logical: the term "sexism" is intended to serve as a tool to unmask patriarchal structures – not to describe all gender-related injustices.

## 3.1 Why this definition is deliberately biased

The feminist definition of sexism is not a value-free research tool, but deliberately politically exaggerated: it aims to expose patriarchy as a power structure, not to treat all gender-related disadvantages equally. If male suffering were also to be included under "sexism", there would be a danger of watering down debates and relativising central feminist demands – for example with objections such as "But men also have a hard time!".

By linking sexism by definition to male domination, men are generally excluded as perpetrators. This blocks a dialogue that recognizes both sexes as victims of structural constraints. Even if men are discriminated against in certain situations – for example, as victims of domestic violence or through persistent educational disadvantage – they are considered in this narrative as "collateral damage" of a higher-level system of rule.

This is precisely where the problem lies: the narrowing may make tactical sense in order to make feminist concerns visible. However, it leads to male suffering being institutionally overlooked or assigned to other power structures. Empirical findings show how long some disadvantages have existed: According to Voyer & Voyer (2014), a school grade gap between boys and girls has existed for over a hundred years. In the Federal Republic of Germany, it took until 1980 for girls to catch up with the boys and graduate from high school at about the same rate – but since 1985 they have been in the fast lane unhindered.

In order to achieve an inclusive gender equality policy, such partisan definitions do not belong in politics.

## Other reviews

Prof. Dr. Christian Rieck's critique is probably not so different from what I mean.[26] If there is a power imbalance, then it must first be documented and then continuously reviewed. It is precisely this point that I will go into in more detail under the keyword indices.

Every countermeasure – no matter how well-intentioned it may be – is ultimately an expression of power. What Rieck addresses is essentially the principle of positive discrimination. This is generally permissible under German and European law. The purpose is to compensate for structural disadvantages or gender-specific socialization patterns – with the aim of achieving equal rights or equal opportunities (or parity).

---

[26] https://youtu.be/ayxgHMu3bwU?si=lPq5KXHjT3273Rj4

At first glance, this sounds reasonable and fair – but: In order for it to actually be positive discrimination legally and ethically, two central conditions must be met:

1. There is a demonstrable *disadvantage in advance*;
2. As a result, the measure leads to an *improvement in terms of equality* – and not to a new form of disadvantage.

Take the Bundestag, for example – in 1998, the proportion of women rose above 30% for the first time and since then it has been between 30% and 36[27]%. Is socialization and hurdles really being dismantled here or does this simply reflect the (current) interest of women in politics? One hurdle that is always real is being a mother and I am absolutely in favor of making working conditions more mother-friendly, but that has little to do with women's quotas in politics. Let's take a look at party members of large parties by gender and their seats in the Bundestag.

Party/Seats in the Bundestag(A)[28]/ Proportion of women among the members of the party(B)[29] [30] (Use statista as a source, as the data is newer)/Real share[31]/ AxB

| | A | B | | AxB |
|---|---|---|---|---|
| • CDU | 164 | 26.6% | 22.6% | 43.6 |
| • CSU | 44 | 21.6% | 25% | 9.5 |
| • AfD | 152 | 18.7% | 11.8% | 28.4 |
| • SPD | 120 | 33.1% | 41.7% | 39.7 |
| • Alliance 90/The Greens | 85 | 42.3% | 61.2% | 36 |
| • Die Linke | 64 | 36.8% | 56.2% | 23.6 |
| • Non-attached Members[32] | 1 | 0 % | 0 % | 0 |

[27] https://tinyurl.com/39b8axzd
[28] https://tinyurl.com/2wrtxbrt
[29] https://tinyurl.com/3ywx6yyt
[30] https://www.statista.com/statistics/955972/women-share-political-party-members-germany/
[31] https://www.bundestag.de/dokumente/textarchiv/2025/kw09-wahlergebnis-statistik-1055550
[32] https://de.wikipedia.org/wiki/Liste_fraktionsloser_Mitglieder_des_Deutschen_Bundestags

The sum of the woman that would result if the party seats were calculated according to the proportion of women in the membership (AxB; rounded before sum) results in 182. In reality, there are 204 women in the Bundestag.

The Federal Foundation for Gender Equality states the following for the low quota of women in the Bundestag:[33] structural disadvantages, outdated role models of the 19th century and the difficult advancement of women within parties "that are often culturally strongly male and characterized by discrimination".

I do not know. To me, it looks more like interest minus *Motherhood penalty*[34] plus odds that lead to this result. Becoming a member of a party doesn't have any major hurdles for me now.[35] [36] [37]

One could argue that this model greatly simplifies reality – and that is true to a certain extent. In fact, here and elsewhere, I am concerned with determining the potential for candidacies, or determining the size of the group that fits the profile: If 20% of all politically interested people are women, it stands to reason that around 20% of party entries also come from women. If this proportion of women in the membership corresponds to 20%, 20% of potential candidates follow – and in the end, 20% of the Bundestag seats would be occupied by women. This calculation is based on the basic assumption of pure equality of opportunity. That's just one factor that works now, odds and *motherhood penalties* are different. If my simplification fully explained the actual distribution of seats – which it does not, since I have so far ignored factors such as the "motherhood penalty" or internal quotas – this would not mean that there are no intra-party disadvantages. Rather, there would inevitably have to be at least one other, hitherto unknown positive factor that compensates for any disadvantage. This must be

---

[33] https://tinyurl.com/389r5bfd
[34] https://en.wikipedia.org/wiki/Motherhood_penalty
[35] https://www.cdu-deutschlands.de/mitglied-werden
[36] https://www.spd.de/unterstuetzen/mitglied-werden
[37] https://www.gruene.de/mitglied-werden

logical, because at this point it is basically an equation, and we know the intermediate result and the final result, and in my particular case, the intermediate result was already the result.

Back to interest: You need interest, yes and that can be socialized, but you don't arouse interest with quotas, but by bringing women in society closer to politics. And something like that already exists. *Motherhood penalty* may be partly socialized, but also partly personal preference. The *gender-equality paradox*[38] basically shows that the more equal countries are, the more traditionally women make decisions. This does not automatically confirm traditional role models, because this decision can also be shaped by social influences – it just shows that the pressure to decide against one's own priorities disappears with the falling financial pressure. Some studies, on the other hand, suggest that it could have partly biological reasons.[39] [40] My whole calculation does not necessarily prove discrimination, especially since quota rules are party internal affairs, but it is a counterargument against legally fixed quotas, as they are believed to already exist in France. The fact that it is a debatable topic is also addressed in the source of the Federal Foundation for Gender Equality below. Ironically, they call Article 3, paragraph 2 of the Basic Law the principle of equality. "Men and women have equal rights. The state promotes the actual implementation of equal rights for women and men and works towards the elimination of existing disadvantages." But there is talk of equality. And I think I have tried to suggest quite extensively that equality does not have to be parity, the striving for a 50/50 quota.

Back to the topic: The fact that quotas dissolve socializations should also be checked, otherwise it is only discrimination. Basically, there is a lack of an impartial authority or institution that checks something like this for us. Perhaps impartial is only a theoretical term and one can rather put men's rights activists and feminists in parity there.

---

[38] https://en.wikipedia.org/wiki/Gender-equality_paradox
[39] https://ifstudies.org/blog/of-boys-and-toys
[40] https://pmc.ncbi.nlm.nih.gov/articles/PMC7002030/

## 3.2 Individual responsibility vs. socialization

As soon as discrimination becomes obvious, the question immediately arises: How do we deal with it, and who bears what responsibility? To what extent is it up to the individual to take his or her fate into his or her own hands, and to what extent are we all shaped by socialization processes and social structures? In feminist discourse, discrimination against women is usually explained in terms of precisely these external factors: unequal power relations, role models, institutional hurdles. Any emphasis on individual responsibility is quickly perceived as victim blaming, because it distracts attention from the systemic causes.

With men, however, the tables are often turned: Here, the focus is more on personal responsibility. Where women point to structural barriers, men are often expected to change their situation themselves. This asymmetrical expectation shows how unequally the power of interpretation is distributed and how much we still think in seemingly "neutral" patterns that in reality reproduce very concrete gender stereotypes and norms.

**Examples:**

- **Gender pay gap:** Women are sometimes advised to pursue lucrative professions or management positions. Feminist perspectives, on the other hand, emphasize that social expectations and structural hurdles shape career paths at an early stage.
- **Leadership positions:** Men dominate top positions (e.g. 69% in Germany). A 50/50 distribution is sometimes stated as a goal, although it is objectively difficult to say what would be "fair". Factors such as education, IQ distribution and interests are hardly considered in a differentiated way in this debate – although they could play relevant roles without being the sole determinant.[41]
- **Care work:** The fact that women take on significantly more care work is sometimes interpreted as a free decision. At the same time,

---

[41] https://tinyurl.com/597hymju

social norms and economic incentives shape this distribution – which limits real choice.

- **Safety behavior:** Women should often behave particularly carefully in public spaces. This can be read as a shift in responsibility, but it does not hide the fact that structural dangers really exist. **Beauty ideals:** On the one hand, women are criticized for their fixation on external appearance, on the other hand, these norms arise from media and cultural attributions that elude individual control.
- **Political engagement:** Women are less likely to be politically engaged. This is sometimes seen as a lack of interest, without taking into account that hostility in public spaces and structural hurdles can have a deterrent effect.

## Double standards?

In men, on the other hand, structural explanations are sought less frequently:

- **Incel phenomenon:** Belonging to misogynistic online groups is primarily seen as an individual failure. Social exclusion, lack of economic prospects or problematic images of masculinity are rarely discussed as contributing causes.
- **Male violence:** Responsibility for the perpetrator is usually in the foreground. Structural or social backgrounds – such as upbringing, violent socialisation or the lack of emotional role models – are addressed in individual cases, but less often systematically.
- **Disadvantage in school and health:** Boys are often rated worse in the education system, men have a lower life expectancy – but here reference is often made to individual deficits ("they live unhealthier", "they learn worse"), while structural issues hardly play a role.[42]

---

[42] https://tinyurl.com/ycfkytf9

The debate about responsibility is often ideologically charged. In feminist discourses, women's individual responsibility tends to be relativized – with reference to structural barriers. In men, on the other hand, it is emphasized, sometimes independently of social conditions. In the case of violence against women, it is sometimes even criticized as trivialization.

A balanced view would have to consider both levels – structures and the individual – for all genders, without falling into protective claims or general suspicion. Otherwise, double standards will arise that ultimately do justice to neither women nor men.

# 4. Definition of feminism and historical functions

At its core, feminism refers to the movement and theory that advocates equal rights for women. Originally created as a reaction to the systematic discrimination of women in political, economic and social areas, its aim was to reduce existing inequalities and enable access to equal rights and opportunities.

**Historical Functions of Feminism**

- **Emancipatory function:**
  The first wave fought above all for women's suffrage and access to education and work.
- **Gender equality:**
  The second wave expanded the focus on sexual self-determination, labor market opportunities and social role models.

It is also worth mentioning that feminism is a movement that has many different groups and views. There is no classic hierarchy, even if there is such a thing as an information hierarchy.

**Liberal Feminism**

- Focused on legal equality and equal opportunities.
- Emphasizes individual rights and freedoms.
- The liberal-feminist focus on suffrage and education initially privileged white, middle-class women. It was not until the third wave that intersectional struggles – such as those of black feminists like Audre Lorde – came to the fore. These tensions continue to shape debates today about who is recognized as a 'victim'.

**Radical feminism**

- Sees patriarchal structures as the core of the oppression of women.
- Criticizes gender roles and norms.

**Socialist Feminism**

- Combines gender inequality with economic inequalities.
- Analyzes the role of capitalism in the oppression of women.

**Intersectional Feminism**

- Considers the interactions of different forms of discrimination (e.g. gender, ethnicity, class).
- Emphasizes that women have different experiences.

# 5. Critical perspectives

A central point of criticism of today's feminism concerns its self-perception as the sole authority for equality. Nowadays, it is often claimed that feminism alone can ensure that everyone is equal – but this is more of a misunderstanding of the actual function and actions that you often hear on social media. Feminism promotes the betterment of women.

## 5.1 Misunderstood function

The original purpose of feminism was to overcome the structural disadvantage of women – a goal that has already been realized in many areas. However, problems that affect men are usually not perceived in this discourse as an integral part of the feminine awakening, and they obviously are not. The equality of all is simply instrumentalized here as a driving force for the enforcement of women's interests. This is not absolute, neither for people nor for the actions.

## 5.2 Overcompensation instead of equality

Measures such as the expansion of women's shelters or targeted offers of help are used as proof of progress. However, it is often ignored that such measures further expand existing disadvantages of men , at least proportionately. Instead of achieving balanced equality, this results in a relative improvement in the position of women – which distorts the claim to real equality.

# 6. Why male discrimination is often overlooked

## 6.1 What is oppression?

Oppression means that a person or group is systematically prevented from fully exercising their rights, freedoms or opportunities. This can happen through violence, laws, social norms or economic dependencies.

**Characteristics of Suppression:**

- Power imbalance: One group or institution is in control of another.
- Restriction of rights: Certain people are not allowed to do what others are allowed to do.
- Forced adaptation: The oppressed must abide by rules that are not in their interest.

- Systematic disadvantages: The affected group has permanently worse chances.

**Examples of suppression:**

- Political: dictatorships in which members of the opposition are persecuted.
- Economic: Low wages and a lack of social security for certain groups.
- Social: Discrimination based on origin, gender or religion.

However, "oppression" is sometimes overused – not every disadvantage is automatically oppression. It depends on whether there is a structural, deliberate restriction behind it.

# 6.2 Discrimination as oppression

A central narrative claims that discrimination is inextricably linked to oppression – and since men have historically been dominant in most areas, there can be no systematic discrimination against them. This view leads to the fact that male suffering is often dismissed as "reverse sexism". The term implies that the victim discriminates against the perpetrator, which makes the debate about male discrimination linguistically and structurally difficult.

This narrative alone is already problematic, as it makes male victims invisible:

- **Ignorance of male discrimination**: The narrative ignores the fact that men are disadvantaged in certain contexts – such as in custody disputes, domestic violence or in the education system.
- **Lack of recognition of male victims**:
  By dismissing discrimination against men as "reverse sexism", it makes male victims invisible and prevents their needs from being taken seriously.

- **Narrow Understanding of Discrimination**: The narrative is based on a narrow understanding of discrimination that considers historical oppression as a prerequisite. This ignores the fact that discrimination can also occur in other contexts – for example, through social expectations or institutional structures.

These points are not to be understood as absolute.

## 6.3 The Normative Burden of Patriarchy for Men

It is rarely considered that men were also enormously burdened by the normative requirements of patriarchy. Historically, many social norms have been inherited from egalitarian origins – not because they were created exclusively to the detriment of women, but because they were functional and obliged men to take on risky tasks.

For example, in over 99% of human history, men have lived in hunter-gatherer cultures in which they acted as primary risk-takers – a role that continued in patriarchy. This historical burden shows that patriarchy forced not only women but also men into rigid roles, or, to put it more concretely, never liberated them.

Another point is that in patriarchy, rights always go hand in hand with duties. It seems contradictory to view predominantly male leaders as an expression of discrimination, while at the same time ignoring the harshness in the school evaluation of boys. Reality shows that patriarchy educates men to bear high burdens – and that these burdens also result in entitlements to benefits.

# 7. Examples of discrimination against men

## 7.1 Men's shelters

A particularly clear example of structural discrimination against men is the systematic refusal to create men's shelters on a comparable scale to women's shelters. Studies show that men are also victims of domestic violence − often by their partners − and yet there are hardly any protection offers for them.

As early as 2000, the then Federal Minister for Family Affairs, Christine Bergmann (SPD), was asked whether there were plans for men's shelters. Her answer was: "No, I don't think that's necessary. If men don't use violence, they don't need places of refuge."[43] This statement implies that men can only exist as perpetrators, but not as victims. It reveals a sexism that makes male victims of violence invisible and denies them the same help that female victims are naturally entitled to.

In 2004, the Federal Ministry of Family Affairs published the pilot study "Violence against Men", which showed that 11% of the men surveyed stated that they had been physically attacked by their partner. Despite these findings, the ministry continued to say: "The issue of domestic violence against men is not one that is a priority for us."

Today, there are 15 shelters for men with 49 places available nationwide (as of 03.2025), while the BFKM recommends at least one family place for men and their children per 200,000 inhabitants.[44] (Which would be at least 420 with 84 million people. I assume that the real need was estimated here on the basis of inquiries. If you assume that men are informed about the offer, destigmatized and men are persuaded to accept help in the rate like women, then 20% men share the victim

---

[43] https://tinyurl.com/yfptkcs3
[44] https://www.maennergewaltschutz.de/maennerschutz-und-beratung/bedarf/

share and 7700 places for women, more like 1925 places, would be fair. If we assume a number of unreported cases of 33%, then even 3850.)

## 7.1.1 The former Ministry of Family Affairs

This ignorance is no coincidence. The refusal to finance men's shelters is happening in a political climate that is strongly influenced by feminist actors. Since 1985, every Federal Minister for Family Affairs has been female. This means that the ministry, which is responsible for equality with regard to the family, has been in the hands of a single gender group for over 40 years, predominantly feminist.

The insufficient consideration of male victims of violence in policy measures raises questions about the balance of gender equality policies.

## 7.1.2 How can the political restraint be explained?

Although numerous studies and reports indicate that men are also victims of domestic violence, the Bundestag has so far hardly reacted to this problem. The question arises as to why there are no clear impulses at the political level to improve the support structure for affected men. If equality is a central goal of German politics, why does this issue receive so little attention?

One possible explanation lies in the political influence of established interest groups, for example from the field of gender equality policy, which is traditionally focused on female victims. While women's shelters are considered indispensable facilities, men's shelters are still only supported to a limited extent – despite comparable needs. On the conservative side, too, the social image of male victims seems to find little support, which could further weaken political will.

This leads to a structural disadvantage of male victims of violence. The lack of provision of shelters for men is not merely an expression of institutional inertia, but reflects deep-rooted normative ideas about gender and vulnerability. It is striking that it is precisely where equality is propagated that existing imbalances are perpetuated – for example, by adhering to gender-specific care structures. Political implementation does not yet seem to be able to extend the principle of equal treatment to all affected groups equally.

## 7.1.3 Violence Assistance Act 2025

In January 2025, two central initiatives for the protection against violence were adopted in the German Bundestag:[45]

- **Act to strengthen structures against sexual violence against children and adolescents**
  This draft law of the Federal Government aims to improve the protection of children and adolescents from sexual violence.
- **Violence Assistance Act**
  Introduced by the parliamentary groups of the SPD and Bündnis 90/Die Grünen, this law focuses on the expansion and safeguarding of protection and counselling services for victims of gender-based and domestic violence.

The Assistance in Violence Act establishes an individual legal entitlement to protection and counselling after the help system has been expanded accordingly. The aim is to better protect women and their children from gender-based and domestic violence and to offer them support.

The law does not mention male victims – it was initially, but went too far for the CDU/CSU[46] (I would have liked to quote Dorothee Bär of the CSU in this context, but the subtitle does not correspond to what was said, which is why I refrain from doing so. If you like, you can watch her speech, which is linked in the footnote.[47]) – a continuation of the existing

---

[45] https://www.bundestag.de/dokumente/textarchiv/2025/kw05-de-sexuelle-gewalt-1042042
[46] https://www.deutschlandfunk.de/gewalthilfegesetz-100.html
[47] https://tinyurl.com/bd5zfxzs

practice in which assistance is provided almost exclusively for women. This further expands structural unequal treatment.

Media reactions were mixed. Deutschlandfunk criticized: "... However, this does not apply to male victims of domestic violence. Transphobic violence is also excluded from the law."[48] Another example is the reaction of journalist Anja Reschke,[49] who criticized the failure of the planned Protection against Violence Act – not because of the lack of support for male victims in the Violence Assistance Act, but because, in her view, necessary measures against male perpetrators were not implemented in the Protection against Violence Act.

## 7.2 Federal Anti-Discrimination Agency (ADS)

According to § 27 and § 29 AGG, the Federal Anti-Discrimination Agency has the task of strengthening protection against discrimination, in particular by promoting cooperation between different actors – such as organisations – and by raising public awareness. Nevertheless, examples such as Manndat and her interest in cases of male discrimination, especially in the field of education, show that according to Manndat these are not sufficiently taken into account by the ADS:

### Open letter to the ADS (27.01.2014):[50]

An association that sees itself as "critical of feminism", Manndat, which campaigns for the elimination of disadvantages against boys, fathers and men, criticized the attitude of the ADS in an open letter. The letter points out that boys systematically receive lower grades for the same school performance and are less likely to be recommended to secondary schools than girls. Despite several independent studies, including those by the Federal Ministry of Education, the ADS rejects the

---

[48] https://www.deutschlandfunk.de/gewalthilfegesetz-100.html
[49] https://www.instagram.com/reel/DHA8KrnsQ9O/
[50]
https://manndat.de/jungen/antidiskriminierungsstelle-fuer-jungen-nicht-zustaendig.html

request with changing reasons – once with the statement that the AGG does not apply to boys in the education sector, another time it has to wait for its own studies.

## Education policy and gender-specific support measures

In the education sector, there are also clear indications of one-sided funding:

## Grading differences:

Numerous studies, including the meta-analysis by Voyer & Voyer (2014), show that girls are rated on average about 0.39 standard deviations (Cohen's d) better than boys (school types that allow students to study) with identical subject-specific competencies. This difference is perceived as a systematic distortion that can have long-term effects on the educational path and career opportunities of boys.

## Unequal funding offer:

A striking example can be found in state-funded educational support: for about 94 STEM girls' promotion projects, there are only four state-supported boys' reading promotion projects, of which only one is directly supported by a Ministry of Education. This discrepancy leads to a massive educational disadvantage of boys, which can be explained not only by the role model, but also by the targeted exclusion of male concerns from the statistical record. (As of 2012)[51]

## Statistical bias:

Most education statistics from the federal and state governments only collect data for girls and women, while the data situation on boys is often complicated by indirect calculations. This reinforces the impression

---

[51] https://jungenleseliste.de/stand-der-jungenlesefoerderung-in-den-bundeslandern/

that the focus is only on the interests of girls – an approach that violates the principles of gender mainstreaming.

## Effects on the example of England

In England, the first pay gap to the disadvantage of young men has been revealed. New research from the UK shows that young women (aged 16 to 24) working full-time now earn an average of £2,200 more a year than their male peers – a significant reversal from two years ago, when men were paid better. According to the Centre for Social Justice (CSJ), this shift reflects a growing crisis among young and young men, who are increasingly falling behind in education, career opportunities and income. For example, the average annual salary of young women is around £26,500, while that of men is £24,300 – a male pay gap of 9.

The study also shows that since the beginning of the pandemic, the number of 16-24-year-old men who are considered "NEETs" (not in education, employment or training) has increased by 40%, compared to only 7% for young women. Miriam Cates, Senior Fellow at the CSJ, attributes this trend in part to the decline of traditionally male-dominated industries such as manufacturing, where stable and well-paid jobs for non-university graduates are increasingly disappearing.

However, problems begin early in life: by the age of five, 74% of girls achieve their early learning goals, compared to only 60% of boys. Up to A-level, girls perform better by more than one and a half grades, and boys are twice as likely to be excluded from school. Andy Burnham, the Labour Mayor of Greater Manchester, warns that young men in their teenage years are increasingly losing hope if they do not follow the traditional path from school to university.

In the face of stagnating economic growth, politics and business in the UK are faced with the urgent task of breaking down barriers to male participation, skills development and career opportunities. If this trend is not reversed, there is a risk not only of disruptions in the labor market, but also of long-term social problems that go hand in hand with the disappointment of young men.[52]

## Political double standards and lack of inclusion

The examples described above show a striking political double standard:

## Lack of cooperation:

The ADS works more frequently with women's rights organizations, while requests from men's rights organizations are repeatedly rejected. This makes it clear that it could be that male concerns are systematically excluded in practice.

## Inadmissible use of discretion(?):

The ADS invokes discretionary powers to reject responsibility for discrimination against boys. The law (e.g. §29 AGG) is interpreted in such a way that only specific individual cases are relevant – a procedure that leads to unequal treatment. As a result, male educational discrimination is deliberately neglected.

The Manndat sees it similarly with equal opportunity officers.[53] [54] [55]

(I can't judge that personally.)

---

[52] https://tinyurl.com/3kmsfptp
[53] https://tinyurl.com/mr47f2vv
[54] https://tinyurl.com/bdf2n9nt
[55] https://tinyurl.com/bdd7225z

**Political passivity:**

Despite clear data – such as the significantly higher youth unemployment among young people (a male gap of 20, in some regions even over 40) – the Bundestag remains rather passive on this issue .[56]

(Source for development up to 2019)[57]

In 2025, it will be 11% among girls and 15% among boys, i.e. a male gap of 36 across Germany.[58]

## 7.3 The case of Zaunegger v. Germany (2009)

In 2009, the Zaunegger v. Germany case brought a crucial aspect of gender-specific discrimination in family law into the public debate. Unmarried fathers, represented by Mr. Zaunegger, complained to the European Court of Justice that the legislation on custody at the time systematically disadvantaged them. The Court found that unmarried fathers were discriminated against by the existing legal situation and forced Germany to adapt the regulations.

In 2014, a reform was implemented that strengthened the rights of unmarried fathers and thus aimed at a non-discriminatory custody regime. It is striking that this problem was largely overlooked by the responsible experts up to this point.

---

[56] https://manndat.de/jungen/antidiskriminierungsstelle-fuer-jungen-nicht-zustaendig.html
[57] https://tinyurl.com/3u99wpra
[58] https://www.instagram.com/p/DH_K_MsKUu8/

# 7.4 Indexes that calculate disadvantages

## 7.4.1 A simplified approach to measuring national gender inequality[59]

Feminists measure the disadvantages of women, men's rights activists that of men. There is little that tries to compare both groups transparently in order to present a fair and differentiated state of affairs. Here, however, we have such an attempt. Their conclusion is:

Our simplified measure of gender inequality correlates well with national differences in human development and speaks to its validity and usefulness. It apparently provides a more nuanced picture of inequality than commonly used indicators such as the Global Gender Gap Index (GGGI). We are not necessarily saying that indices such as the GGGI should not be used, but that the inclusion of the BIGI in relevant studies provides additional and different information and thus allows for a more complete assessment of gender equality.

Our overall results suggest that many countries today have achieved historically high levels of gender parity. Nevertheless, addressing gender inequality alone is not enough for all people to reach their full potential; full gender parity does not necessarily mean that both men and women have equal opportunities everywhere, as both may experience a lack of opportunities in different areas.

Internationally, improvements in gender parity can be achieved by focusing on education in the least developed countries and on preventive health measures, such as drug and alcohol abuse, in medium and advanced countries.

## Summary of the BIGI results (2012–2016) for Europe and Germany

---

[59] https://journals.plos.org/plosone/article?id=10.1371/journal.pone.0205349

The Basic Index of Gender Inequality (BIGI) analysis for 134 countries (data 2012–2016) shows that in 91 out of 131 countries, men are on average more disadvantaged than women (BIGI < 0). Among the very highly developed countries (HDI > 0.8), to which Germany belongs, the values typically differ in favor of women, i.e. men are more disadvantaged there overall. For Germany, the average BIGI score (2012–2016) shows a negative deviation of about -2%, reflecting the combined effect of shorter healthy life expectancy and slightly lower life satisfaction for men. These data show that men are already experiencing more disadvantages in many highly developed countries and that public debate often takes these aspects insufficiently into account.

Of course, there is criticism of the BIGI, as there is of all indices that try to show the disadvantage of a group in a representative way.

## 7.4.2 Gender Development Index

The Gender Development Index (GDI) measures gender gaps in key dimensions of human development – health, education and income – by calculating the ratio of women's Human Development Index (HDI) to men's HDI. For Germany, the GDI was most recently 0.968 (as of 2018), which means that women achieve an average of 96.8% of men's human development achievements. This puts Germany in the middle of the field (72nd) of the UN member states and shows a remaining gap of just under 3.2% in favor of men.[60]

## 7.4.3 Other indexes

There are other indices such as GII[61] or *Global Gender Gap Report*[62] (GGGR), but these are specifically geared towards women's issues or engage in truncation and do not even indicate male disadvantages.

---

[60] https://de.wikipedia.org/wiki/Index_der_geschlechtsspezifischen_Entwicklung
[61] https://de.wikipedia.org/wiki/Index_der_geschlechtsspezifischen_Ungleichheit
[62] https://de.wikipedia.org/wiki/Global_Gender_Gap_Report

## Gender Equality Index (GEI)[63]

In addition, I looked at the GEI. For education, he has a score of 57.1. You only look at tertiary education here.

What does the OECD say about tertiary education: By almost all available measures, girls and women achieve better educational outcomes than boys and men, and in many cases this gap continues to grow. This is reflected in the gender-specific differences in educational attainment. In all OECD member countries, women aged 25–34 are as or more likely than their male peers to hold tertiary qualifications (54% vs. 41% on average across OECD countries). In Germany, the tertiary education completion rate is 41% for women and 36% for men, which is much smaller than the OECD average.[64]

One might think that he would report the discrimination of men. No, he points out inequalities and does not offset them against the sexes. This is not about discrimination, but about gender roles.

## 7.4.4 What's missing?

A meaningful gender equality index must be fair, comprehensive and realistic. Existing models such as the GDI or BIGI are already trend-setting at their core, but they neglect essential living conditions: None of the common indices adequately reflects family income, although it is precisely household alliances and tax regulations – keyword spousal splitting – that strongly shape financial reality.

One possible solution would be to divide the joint income fairly between the two partners: This would create two values that act as an upper and lower limit and thus make the scope of household income transparent. On this basis, indicators for time expenditure and participation could then be determined – analogous to common

---

[63] https://eige.europa.eu/gender-equality-index/2024/DE
[64] https://tinyurl.com/2s4bbw4u

education or participation indicators. Especially in countries with educational policy hurdles for women, this procedure provides valid results. In Germany, however, it is currently leading to apparent disadvantages for women, because boys invest more time on average in school performance and achieve poorer qualifications. In this case, it would make more sense not to spend time, but to take educational qualifications directly as a benchmark.

There is also a lack of an impartial body that reliably coordinates indicator development, data collection and evaluation. Perhaps the Federal Statistical Office would be a candidate for implementation, supported by a neutral panel of experts made up of representatives of women's and men's rights organisations. Together, they could systematically identify disadvantages, define suitable metrics and finally publish an index that reflects the actual state of equality in all its facets.

# 8. Power in democracies through networks

In democracies, power is less concentrated in individuals than tied up in networks of actors, institutions and transnational alliances. Feminist networks—from transnational gender mainstreaming alliances to specialized policy networks in governments and universities—have thus gained a disproportionate prerogative of interpretation, occupying issues and discourses. Male disadvantages (e.g. educational, health and judicial disadvantages), on the other hand, remain largely invisible due to the lack of comparable advocacy networks, which explains a persistent power imbalance in favor of well-connected feminist actors in these cases.

# 8.1 Power networks in democracies

## 8.1.1 Theoretical basics

- Democracies are characterized by the fact that decision-making power **is distributed among large "winning coalitions"** that expect public goods, in contrast to autocratic systems with small cliques of private favors.[65]
- Michael Mann's approach emphasizes four intersecting networks of power—ideological, economic, military, and political—that interact dynamically in democracies, thus enabling decentralized control.[66]

## 8.1.2 Network and Policy Analysis

- **Feminist foreign policies** (FFP) have brought women's and gender-informed foreign policy and governance to the forefront of international politics. The source describes how networks in the Global South in particular have created the foundations and pathways for gender-inclusive and feminist-informed foreign policy and governance to flourish. In doing so, it shows that such policies are based on the knowledge foundation of transnational feminist networks.[67]
- **Social network analysis** highlights that it is not only formal offices that count, but informal connections in the media, NGOs and think tanks that bundle agenda-setting power. Those who have visibility have the power of interpretation.[68]

---

[65] https://en.wikipedia.org/wiki/Selectorate_theory
[66] https://academic.oup.com/isq/article-abstract/45/1/27/1792550
[67] https://bristoluniversitypressdigital.com/edcollchap/book/9781529239492/ch005.xml
[68] https://wac.colostate.edu/docs/books/positionality/chapter6.pdf

## 8.2 Feminist Networks as a Prerogative of Interpretation

### 8.2.1 Transnational Gender Mainstreaming Alliances

The spread of gender mainstreaming mechanisms in the EU and UN was largely driven by transnational feminist networks.[69]

### 8.2.2 Political Networks and Think Tanks

- Rutgers University's CAWP project documents how women's political power is increasing through coordinated networks in U.S. states — bipartisan and multiracial.[70]
- The Wilson Center Guide to Women's Political Networks shows best practices on how networks support women in elections and government.[71]

### 8.2.3 Internal GE Units in Organizations

Internal Gender Equality Units at universities use networks to convert research, teaching and administration to gender-equitable practices ("internal networks supporting GE processes").[72]

---

[69] https://academic.oup.com/isq/article-abstract/45/1/27/1792550
[70] https://cawp.rutgers.edu/news-media/press-releases/rethinking-womens-political-power
[71] https://tinyurl.com/53vppx5z
[72] https://academic.oup.com/sp/advance-article/doi/10.1093/sp/jxae019/7900929

## 8.3 Male Discrimination and Lack of Networks

### 8.3.1 Lack of Advocacy Alliances

In contrast to feminist alliances, there are hardly any transnational or policy-oriented networks that systematically address men's disadvantages and represent them politically.

### 8.3.2 Media Networking

Feminist media productions create participatory platforms on which gender issues are prominently negotiated,[73] while male victims and disadvantaged people are hardly addressed. (e.g. [74])

## 8.4 Why networks generate power

### 8.4.1 Resource Mobilization

Closely networked actors can efficiently pool funds, expertise and political support and thus shape legislative processes and public perception.[75]

### 8.4.2 Agenda Setting and Discourse Control

Networks determine which topics are on the agenda. Feminist gender mainstreaming alliances have thus largely prevented debates about male discrimination and violence prevention for boys and men.[76] Not necessarily out of malice, but rather as a by-product of one's own representation of interests and because there is no serious counterweight.

---

[73] https://tinyurl.com/mwk7pj58
[74] https://www.kas.de/en/single-title/-/content/frauen-maenner-und-kaum-unterschiede
[75] https://bristoluniversitypressdigital.com/edcollchap/book/9781529239492/ch005.xml
[76] https://academic.oup.com/isq/article-abstract/45/1/27/1792550

### 8.4.3 Networks versus individual positions

Power in democracies lies less in formal offices than in the ability to establish and activate cooperative networks of NGOs, media and politics.[77]

## 8.5 Conclusion

The dominance of feminist networks explains why male discrimination hardly becomes part of the public discourse despite empirical evidence. Without comparable advocacy and policy networks for men, a public interest gap remains. A balanced political landscape would therefore have to build and strengthen men's networks in order to negotiate issues such as boys' education, men's health and male victims' rights on an equal footing. One should also criticize any demonization of men. These create or expand an empathy bias that prevents people from taking men's problems seriously.

# 9. Power in partnerships

## 9.1 Terms: Hard Power vs. Soft Power

- **Hard power** refers to direct means of power: formal authority, money, legal or physical means of coercion (cf. French-Raven sources of power).[78]
- **Soft power** encompasses subtle forms of influence: social rewards or sanctions, emotional conviction, moral sovereignty of interpretation and indirect manipulation within relationships.[79] (So not only: networks are also to be understood as soft power.)

---

[77] https://wac.colostate.edu/docs/books/positionality/chapter6.pdf
[78] https://tinyurl.com/5fzpvm7c
[79] https://tinyurl.com/2k68fd53

## 9.2 Theoretical foundations

### 9.2.1 Expectation theory

Women in groups declared as "high status" perceived legitimate authority, but were reluctant to enforce it aggressively – an indication of restrained but existing soft power. To be fair, it's worth mentioning that if they try to use hard power, it doesn't go down well with the group, especially men, than if a man does it.[80]

### 9.2.2 Sociopsychological perspective

Power is the central organizing principle of social interactions and remains permanently effective in close relationships; partners, especially women, use relational influence to influence decisions on financial, sexual or family issues.[81]

## 9.3 Decisions in Daily Life and Relationships

### 9.3.1 Household and Family

Studies in Bangladesh show that women often only formally "co-decide" on questions of family planning and household expenses, but de facto tip the scales through soft channels of influence – more autonomy for women did not necessarily lead to improved reproductive health.[82]

### 9.3.2 Partnership and intimacy

- In a study of 181 couples, Körner & Schütz found that the subjective feeling of personal agency/decision-making power

---

[80] https://tinyurl.com/5ajn69kn
[81] https://tinyurl.com/5fzpvm7c
[82] https://pmc.ncbi.nlm.nih.gov/articles/PMC5680601/

correlates significantly with relationship satisfaction – and although men had more *hard power*, this did not reduce happiness. Indication that the subjective sensation takes *soft power* into account.[83]

- The Myth of Mutuality study shows that while couples ideologically emphasize mutual equality, in practice women are more likely to steer "the key issues" inconspicuously, e.g., through emotional appeals and promises.[84]

### 9.3.3 Influence Styles and Communication

- Women are more likely to use **community-oriented** strategies of influence (e.g., cooperation, relationship building), while men prefer more direct tactics; both sexes achieve their goals comparably often.[85]
- Traditional gender roles often anchor in women the expectation of being an "emotional manager" and thus a central mediator in everyday relationships.[86]

## 9.4 Hard Power Equals Income

Income can be reliably collected and is considered a proxy for who is "solvent" and thus dictates economic conditions (e.g. mortgages, major purchases). Even if money formally belongs to both partners, a higher individual or family income increases the **moral legitimacy** to decide on larger expenses.

---

[83] https://neurosciencenews.com/power-dynamics-happiness-relationships-18829/
[84] https://journals.sagepub.com/doi/10.1177/08912432241230555
[85] https://en.wikipedia.org/wiki/Expectation_states_theory
[86] https://tinyurl.com/bdhmjwrv

## 9.5 Soft Power: Control of Household Spending

- **NielsenIQ (2024):** Women worldwide influence 70–80% of all consumer spending, especially on everyday and discretionary expenditures.[87]
- **Girlpower Marketing** reports that women in the U.S. control **85%** of purchasing decisions, including food, clothing, and health spending.[88]

## 9.6 Overall balance of decision-making power[89]

- A **Pew Research** survey found that in **43%** of heterosexual couples, the woman makes the decisions in more areas, in **26%** the man has the dominant role and **31%** make equal decisions.
- In dual-income households, this pattern remains stable: women are more likely to have the upper hand, regardless of who earns more.

## 9.7 Conclusion

It seems that there are numerous studies that show that women often have more soft power than men in many "normal issues" of everyday life – from household decisions to intimate relationship dynamics. These research results invalidate the common narrative of an exclusively male-dominated power structure and highlight the importance of subtle, relational strategies of influence. Formal equality therefore requires not only criticism of hard power distribution, but also an awareness of soft power within relationships.

---

[87] https://tinyurl.com/3zvd258h
[88] https://girlpowermarketing.com/statistics-purchasing-power-women/
[89] https://tinyurl.com/bdhah3tk

# 10. Gender Equality Overview

## 10.1 Historical development

Gender equality work arose at a time when women really had structural disadvantages (e.g. 1950–1970: suffrage, education, property rights). In Germany, Article 3 (2) sentence 2 of the Basic Law states: "Men and women have equal rights. The state promotes the actual implementation of equal rights for women and men and works towards the elimination of existing disadvantages."[90]

In practice and politics, however, this phrase has almost always been applied only to women. Even when women no longer had systematic disadvantages (e.g. in education[91]), the paradigm remained.

## 10.2 Institutional self-protection

Institutions such as equality bodies, funding programs, or specialized chairs usually pursue a specific agenda – and their continued existence often depends on the underlying problem continuing to be considered relevant. When the problem is solved, they lose budget, power and jobs. Power leads to abuse of power and there doesn't even have to be any evil intent behind it. When a problem is solved, the focus – out of habit and through the prevailing political narrative – turns back to the next women's issue. As a result, I have heard more often about the room temperature, which is supposedly geared towards male well-being, than about the systematic discrimination of boys in school grades. There is a lack of control mechanisms and, as already mentioned, of a fair and meaningful index that indicates the direction of where equality is going at all, for each issue individually and for society as a whole.

---

[90] https://tinyurl.com/3vjehnmb
[91] https://tinyurl.com/2vkx9pp8  Kapitel 5.1

## 10.3 Why are they allowed to do it?

**Because there is no counterweight.**

- There are no powerful men's lobby groups.
- Boys and men are politically weakly organized.
- Many men do not see themselves as "victims" at all, but swallow the disadvantages ("It's your own fault" / "You just have to work harder").
- In addition, many politicians, university administrators, etc. shy away from openly addressing men's problems – for fear of being perceived as "misogynistic". One example, which I will discuss in more detail later, illustrates this dynamic particularly well: At a university, a planned event for International Men's Day was canceled to draw attention to the high suicide rate among men – among other things, because a fellow student had taken his own life. Around 200 students, mostly from the feminist spectrum, had protested against the event and collected signatures. The event was cancelled and although there were over 1000 countersignatures, the cancellation remained. The question arises: Why was a smaller group able to prevail? One possible explanation – and here I am deliberately entering the realm of speculation – lies in the structural balance of power. Behind the 200 protesters there may be a well-organized network. If a university management is publicly branded as "misogynistic", there is a risk not only of reputational losses, but in the worst case also of professional consequences. For a manager, this could mean losing his or her job – and possibly not finding a new one at the university. Of course, it is not possible to say with certainty from the outside which factors specifically led to the decision. Nevertheless, this example shows how real or perceived social pressure mechanisms can work – and why men's concerns are often hardly heard in public discourse.

## 10.5 How the Response Is Going

Instead of taking this perception seriously, it is very often devalued or ridiculed, according to the pattern:

- This is just whining[92]
- You only cry because you lose your privileges![93]
- Now you can see how women have always felt!
- As men, you can't be discriminated against at all.[94]
- Are men discriminated against more than women? Forum discussion – Only answers that fit into the feminist narrative have been attached, but if you read further, many people come up who say yes.[95]
- Articles like: "It is patriarchy that harms both men and women."[96] It starts promisingly and draws attention to real disadvantages of men. As the film progresses, however, the author loses herself in feminist narrative patterns, with men's problems receding further and further into the background. Real equality is far from being achieved. The underlying idea is true – just differently than she argues. Absolute equality remains an unattainable ideal: one could analyze every area of life down to the smallest detail – for example, the ceiling height in living rooms – in order to theoretically build houses for women ten centimeters lower and thus save heating costs. Even after you have theoretically adjusted everything, priorities can shift or completely new topics can arise, for example due to technological progress such as AI. Equality is therefore an eternal, ongoing process. The cited GGGR study also does not provide a point in time for when equality will be achieved, but only a prognosis as to when the examined disadvantages of women could be equalized – and it does not record any male disadvantages from the outset. Originally, the argumentation began with the topic

---

[92] https://tinyurl.com/3tjjkejb
[93] https://www.instagram.com/p/DI-6fiyuIIs/
[94] https://tinyurl.com/bddjmsfs
[95] https://tinyurl.com/5cvn98j4
[96] https://mads.de/feminismus-als-problem-wieso-sich-maenner-benachteiligt-fuehlen/

of discrimination against men, but soon the buzzword "equality" was used to focus exclusively on women's problems. Instead of considering all concerns equally and developing solutions for all those affected, from then on almost exclusively women's issues came to the fore. In the end, patriarchy remains as a scapegoat – and thus feminism seems to be the remedy. But if you are serious about equality, you have to dedicate yourself equally to all forms of discrimination. Feminism, as her own text shows, is partisan.

In this and another way, any serious debate about male discrimination is nipped in the bud.

## 10.6 Patriarchy is to blame[97]

A well-known narrative:

- Although men have historically often been considered "powerful", "privileged" or "oppressors", this has long since ceased to be relevant in the reality of most people's lives today – but this is not taken into account.
- That is why every complaint about today's disadvantages is not seen as new problems, but is dismissed as a just punishment or howling about lost supremacy or self-inflicted.

In short:

By definition, men are not allowed to be victims in this worldview. However, this idea alone is already sexism.

## 10.7 Why it's dangerous

When half of a population group experiences structural disadvantages but has no way of expressing it socially, the result is:

---

[97] https://tinyurl.com/bddjmsfs

- political alienation
- Radicalization tendencies (e.g. among young men)
- Severe mental health problems (e.g., depression, suicide — male-to-female suicide rate: 3:1 or worse)
- And no one talks honestly about it, because men are still allowed to "show no weakness" in the public perception.

A perfect vicious circle. Men who experience discrimination are doubly discriminated against by social devaluation.

## 10.8 Solution

As long as men do not collectively build up political pressure (as women's movements have done since the 60s), nothing will change, because as long as equality = "women's advancement" will remain — even if that is de facto sexism against boys and men.

## 11. Equality — What do we think?

There are now solid surveys that show:

Around 50% of men (varies slightly depending on the country and study)[98] [99] feel disadvantaged or unfairly treated, especially when it comes to issues such as:

- Education
- Custody
- Gender equality
- Social pressure of expectations
- Dating (I almost didn't want to write it down, because feminism only ever shows misogynistic dating coaches here, but still, it is important to us men and hypergamy is an outdated role model that

---

[98] https://tinyurl.com/34v2vyzw
[99] https://www.20min.ch/story/jeder-zweite-mann-fuehlt-sich-diskriminiert-358528104146

the boys rightly criticize. And parts of feminism try to defend it at *bare minimum*.)

## Ipsos study[100]

- Younger generations (Gen Z & Millennials) are less fortunate with gender equality policies than older generations (Gen X, baby boomers).
- There are strong differences of opinion between men and women within the young generations.
- The idea that men are disadvantaged by equality is particularly widespread among young men.

## Key results (worldwide, 31 countries):

## Attitude towards equality

- 60% of Gen Z men think equality discriminates against men (vs. 40% of Gen Z women).
- 57% (Gen Z) / 60% (Millennials) think enough has already been done for women's rights, vs. 43% of baby boomers.
- 54-57% of younger people think that too much is expected of men to promote equality.

## Role model and masculinity

- 31% of Gen Z men believe that a man who cares for children is less masculine.
- Only 11% of baby boomer men share this opinion

## Long-term trends (24-country average, 2019–2024):

- Approval of "too much is expected of men": 41% (2019) → 52% (2023/24)

---

[100] https://tinyurl.com/yt7hy8m2

- Approval of "Equality has gone far enough": 41% (2019) → 54% (2023/24)
- Percentage of people who identify as feminists: 33% (2019) → 39% (2023/24)

## Male Allies & Room for Maneuver

- 65% believe that equality needs active support from men.
- 64% think they can personally contribute to equality.

## Executives & Gender

- No preference for the gender of the manager (politics/profession): → ~70% neutral if experience with both genders is available.

- Those who have only experienced men/women tend to prefer the familiar sex.
- Own gender preferred: → 22% of women want female bosses, 26% of men want male bosses.

## Skills of Politicians (f/m)

Majority believes: both sexes equally competent in:

- Economy (43%)
- Security (43%)
- Fight against crime (42%)
- Governance (55%)

# 12. Result

Historically, feminism has made a significant contribution to making structural disadvantages of women visible and reducing them — for example through women's suffrage, the opening up of educational and professional opportunities or the fight against violence. These achievements are undisputed and remain relevant in many parts of the world today.

But modern feminist discourse shows weaknesses when it comes to acknowledging or addressing systematic discrimination against men . As far as addressing or solving these problems is concerned, however, feminism is not responsible at all.

There is a lack of a movement that takes up men's concerns and has real soft power. Such a movement from the political center could start right here – perhaps quotas would be a helpful starting point.

Institutions that are supposed to promote equality – such as the Federal Anti-Discrimination Agency – often act one-sidedly and thus perhaps reproduce unequal treatment themselves.

## II. The Men's Rights Movements

## 1. Representatives of the men's rights movement

The Men's Rights Movement (MRM) is a heterogeneous movement that advocates for men's rights and concerns. Its representatives come from different social and political camps. Among the most influential figures are:

- **Warren Farrell**: Former member of the National Organization for Women (NOW) who later distanced himself from the feminist movement and wrote books such as *The Myth of Male Power*. He argues that men experience just as much systematic discrimination as women.
- **Paul Elam**: Founder of the website *A Voice for Men*, one of the most well-known platforms for men's rights activism. His positions are sometimes controversial, as he cultivates an aggressive rhetoric towards feminism.

- **Christina Hoff Sommers**: A feminist herself, but a critic of modern feminism, who advocates an "equity feminism" position and argues in *The War Against Boys How Misguided Feminism Is Harming Our Young Men*[101] how education systems disadvantage boys. In her book, Christina Hoff Sommers shows that, despite common assumptions, American boys lag behind girls in reading and writing and are less likely to go to university. Nevertheless, the best-known studies and experts focus almost exclusively on an alleged "girl crisis" that no longer existed. This exaggerated portrayal has led to profound changes in schools, politics and education – often to the detriment of boys. Sommers criticizes that feminism artificially inflates the problems of girls while ignoring the growing challenges of young men. Today, what she said 21 years ago is at least recognized, but the achievements of the boys have also continued to fall.
- **Karen Straughan**: YouTuber and blogger who challenges feminist myths about gender inequality.
- **Erin Pizzey** was a British activist and feminist who founded the world's first women's shelter in the 1970s. Her work against domestic violence led her to the realization that violence is often reciprocal (I will show later in the chapter on violence that her observation is completely correct) – so women were just as capable of violence as men. This view brought her into direct conflict with the feminist movement, of which she reports that she was sent death and bomb threats, especially by militant feminists. These threats, as well as systematic exclusion, led to her having to go into exile, while her original contributions to the women's shelter movement were erased from official history.[102] [103] [104]

---

[101] https://www.amazon.com/WAR-AGAINST-BOYS-Misguided-Feminism/dp/0684849577
[102] https://tinyurl.com/5n8er2au
[103] https://en.wikipedia.org/wiki/Erin_Pizzey
[104] https://search.worldcat.org/de/title/829180547

## 2. Misunderstandings of the men's rights movement

The men's rights movement is often portrayed as anti-feminist or even misogynistic. This perception is based on several factors:

- Mixing with extreme fringe groups: Some groups within the MRM use radical, misogynistic rhetoric, which puts the entire movement in a bad light.
- Misconceptions about the movement's concerns: While feminists often advocate for equality, men's rights activists often emphasize that equality does not mean that men do not experience specific disadvantages.
- Media coverage: Media reports on men's rights movements often focus on polarizing statements by individual activists and ignore moderate or academic voices.
- Lack of differentiation: Many critics equate men's rights activists with the "red pill" movement or the "inceldom", although there are clear differences.

Maybe I've mentioned this before, but not all people are the same – everyone is an individual.

## 3. Why men's rights don't have to be anti-feminist

A widespread narrative is that men's rights and feminism are incompatible. In fact, however, there are numerous interfaces:

- **Common goals**: Both movements fight against rigid gender roles. Feminists, for example, criticize "patriarchy," which also forces men to remain in traditional roles.
- **Gender discrimination affects both sides**: While feminist concerns often focus on discrimination against women, MRM shows

that men also experience structural disadvantages (e.g. in family law or education).

- **Potential for collaboration**: Feminism and the men's rights movement could work together on issues such as domestic violence, gender-equitable education policies, or mental health.
- **"Equality" vs. "Equal opportunities" vs. "Parity"**: Many men's rights activists demand equality in the legal sense, while some feminist currents advocate parity. Maybe they meet at equal opportunities?

## 4. Conclusion

The men's rights movement is a diverse movement with legitimate concerns that is often misunderstood or deliberately misrepresented. Instead of viewing feminism and men's rights as opposites, it would make sense to recognize the intersections of both movements and develop common solutions.

# III A little history

## 1. Egalitarian societies

30,000 years ago, somewhere in the icy tundra of Siberia: A group of hunter-gatherers shares the prey of a slain mammoth. Among them is Anuka, a young woman with furrowed skin and well-trained arms. She threw the spear that hit the animal – not because she had to, but because she is the best thrower in the group. Her brother Kiran, who is actually responsible for hunting, stays around the campfire today and looks after the children. It's not an act of rebellion, but pure pragmatism: Kiran sprained his ankle while tripping over a tree root, Anuka is faster.

This is how egalitarian societies work: **flexibility instead of dogma**. Archaeologists found the grave of a 9,000-year-old huntress in Peru, surrounded by stone spikes and the bones of a giant sloth. The Stone Age was not a feminist utopia, but neither was it a patriarchy. It was a struggle for survival, in which roles were based on necessity, not gender.[105]

**Why do I still write "Hunt men, gather women"?**

One study (Anderson et al., 2023) claims that this division is a myth – because women also hunt in some groups. But a closer examination shows that in most hunter-gatherer societies, men are the main hunters. (Instead of 80% of all communities also hunted women, more likely to hunt 5.5% or 13.5% depending on the question) Women collect more often or hunt smaller animals, especially when caring for children (Venkataraman et al., 2024).[106] [107]

# 1.1 The biology of the grass root

But why did men hunt more often in the first place?[108] The answer lies in evolution and culture, not in oppression:

- **Testosterone** made men more willing to take risks – a survival advantage when it came to circling a rhino or venturing into unfamiliar territory.
- **Muscle mass**: An average Stone Age man could muster more strength than a woman – crucial when throwing a javelin or carrying heavy prey.[109]

But these differences were statistics, not fate.

---

[105] https://tinyurl.com/y5m6uexa
[106] https://www.sciencedirect.com/science/article/abs/pii/S1090513824000497
[107] https://www.vivekvenkataraman.com/blog/2023/7/5/debunking-a-debunking
[108] https://science.orf.at/stories/3220047/
[109] https://tinyurl.com/42sy8e8b

Many hunter-gatherer groups show remarkable flexibility in women's hunting strategies. Researchers found that women are more adaptable than men overall: "Women use a greater variety of options both in their choice of weapons and in their hunting strategies." An example of this is the Akha, an ethnic group from Southeast Asia whose women hunt with nets, spears, machetes and crossbows. The situation is similar with the Agta, a collective term for indigenous peoples in the Philippines: While some women use knives exclusively for hunting, others use bows and arrows or combine different weapons.[110]

In another article, it says: The research team also investigated whether anatomical and physiological differences between men and women prevented women from hunting. They found that men have an advantage in activities that require speed and strength – such as sprinting and throwing. Women, on the other hand, have an advantage in activities that require endurance, such as long-distance running. Both skills were crucial in prehistoric hunting.[111] However, this statement can be put into perspective. Looking at today's athletic performance, it can be seen that men are on average about eleven percent faster in marathon running. Only at even longer distances do women compensate for this difference and finally surpass men in endurance performance.[112] This means that women could not score points everywhere in endurance hunting through endurance.

- Up to 40 hours hunting a large kudu antelope[113]
- Up to 35 km when hunting antelope such as kudus in the Kalahari Desert[114]
- The animal endures several hours, often from sunrise to the afternoon, until sunset, then it survives[115]

---

[110] https://tinyurl.com/y5m6uexa
[111] https://phys.org/news/2023-10-prehistoric-gender-roles-women-hunters.html
[112] https://tinyurl.com/bdhmwc3s
[113] https://www.markus-bussmann.com/2013/07/ausdauerjagd.html
[114] https://deutsch.wikibrief.org/wiki/Persistence_hunting
[115] https://de.wikipedia.org/wiki/Hetzjagd

## 1.2 The Silent Price of Hunting

But the Stone Age was not a paradise. While feminists today like to invoke the "equality" of this time, there was certainly a bloody tribute, which men in particular paid:

- **Genetic heritage**: DNA analyses show that more **women than men lived** in the Stone Age. Why? Because many men died — silent evidence of asymmetric risks.[116]
- Hunting can be fatal[117] [118] [119]
- In addition to hunting, violence among each other seems to be a main cause of death for humans and Neanderthals.[120] [121] Most disputes there arise from disputes about the abduction of women and the preservation of the "good reputation" within the community. Often the origin lies in the suspicion that someone has practiced black magic or violated moral norms. Such conflicts can sometimes end in blood.[122] In rare cases, it is assumed that it is a conflict with another group.[123] Observations of modern hunter-gatherer communities suggest that diseases are still a common cause.[124]

Books such as 'The Invention of Inequality' romanticize this period as the 'golden age of equality'. But they ignore the fact that the pragmatic distribution of roles was not a conscious act of emancipation, but a survival mechanism — at high cost: many men died young from hunting accidents or violent conflicts, often triggered by rivalry among themselves or the pressure to survive as providers. At the same time, the groups benefited from the fact that women hunted, gathered or

---

[116] https://www.biomedcentral.com/about/press-centre/science-press-releases/24-sep-2014-
[117] https://de.wikipedia.org/wiki/Hadza
[118] https://tinyurl.com/yth5zyk2
[119] https://johnhawks.net/weblog/high-adult-mortality-in-some-contemporary-hunter-gatherers/
[120] https://www.sciencedirect.com/science/article/abs/pii/S030544031200297X
[121] https://tinyurl.com/33uxucc3
[122] https://de.wikipedia.org/wiki/J%C3%A4ger_und_Sammler
[123] https://tinyurl.com/y7tjhmc7
[124] https://johnhawks.net/weblog/high-adult-mortality-in-some-contemporary-hunter-gatherers/

cared for children depending on the situation – a flexibility that did not correspond to a modern ideal, but ensured survival.

# 2. Patriarchy

## 2.1 The seeds of inequality

10,000 years ago, in the Fertile Crescent, a farmer named Kurush crumbled grains of wheat between his hands for the first time. He has no idea that he is triggering a revolution: **agriculture**. With the first harvests came the first inheritance debate: *Who owns the land? Who will inherit me?*

The answer was brutally simple: only children whose paternity was guaranteed were allowed to inherit. And how did you guarantee that? By controlling women. In the Codex Hammurapi, one of the oldest collections of laws (1750 BC), it was written: "*Suppose the wife of one man is caught lying with another man, she will be bound and thrown into the water. Suppose the husband wants his wife to live, the king will leave his slave alive.*"[125] It was not morality, but economics – the protection of lineages.

## 2.2 The farm quota

Let's jump to medieval Europe: Henry, a serf in the Rhineland of the 12th century, stands in front of his burned-down farm. The harvest has been destroyed, but the farm quota – the annual levy to the landlord – remains. Heinrich knows: If he does not meet the quota, he will lose his country. His daughter Gisela is married to the master, his son Konrad is sold as a servant.

The irony? Women like Gisela were exempt from the court quota – not out of privilege, but because they were legally considered

---

[125] https://www.koeblergerhard.de/Fontes/CodexHammurapi_de.htm

"underage". The burden of responsibility was on the men, who received no power in return. A system that degraded men to debt slaves and women to bargaining chips. This is no exception, women were usually punished less harshly or not at all, except for adultery, immoral behavior and witchcraft.

## 2.3 Cannon Fodder: The Forgotten Victims of Wars

In the mud of the Battle of Waterloo (1815) lies Jean-Luc, a 19-year-old French soldier. Next to him, 50,000 men bleed to death in nine hours – a bloodbath that no woman had to share. Meanwhile, Jean-Luc's sister Marie works in a Parisian munitions factory. She earns a third of a man, but her life is safe.

This pattern runs through history:

- **Antiquity**: In the Battle of Cannae (216 BC), 50,000 Romans died – all men.
- **Industrialization**: In the English mines of the 19th century, 90% of the fatalities are men. Boys die in shafts, girls weave at home.
- **Modernity**: Even today, the suicide rate among men is almost **3 times higher** than among women – a silent cry for help.
- **Today**: 96% of fatal accidents at work affect men

**Patriarchy was not a gift to men** – it was a devil's pact. Men were allowed to "rule" as long as they sacrificed themselves. A farmer who "controlled" his wife was himself a slave of the feudal lord.

# 3. Ancient Paradoxes: Rome and Sparta

## 3.1 Livia Drusilla

Rome, 14 AD: Livia, widow of Emperor Augustus, stands in the marble hall of her palace. Papyrus scrolls are piled up in front of her –

tax lists, reports from the provinces, petitions from senators. Officially, Livia has no office. Unofficially, she decides on the succession of her son Tiberius, administers the patrimonium Caesaris (imperial treasury) and has temples built that bear her name. When she dies, she is declared a goddess – an honor bestowed on only a few men.

But Livia was no exception. In the shadow of the toga, women such as:

- **Eumachia**: The "Wool Queen" of Pompeii, who donated a public building – her inscription (*"Eumachia, daughter of Lucius, for the people")* is still emblazoned at the entrance today.
- **Turia**: A Roman woman who went to court in the 1st century BC to secure her murdered father's legacy.

Feminists emphasize the legal immaturity of Roman women, (since men did politics) but ignore the fact that the household was a center of power. Whoever controlled supplies, slaves and children controlled the family – and thus a nucleus of Roman power. Roman women were neither powerless nor equal. Their influence was invisible but real – tied to family, wealth, and the ability to skillfully circumvent social norms. Livia, Eumachia and Turia stand for a "silent power" that helped shape the history of Rome, but was rarely recorded in inscriptions or chronicles.

If we compare ancient Rome with today's matrilineal Mosuo society in China – which is often described as matriarchal – the primary difference lies in the succession. In the case of the Mosuo, descent occurs through the maternal line, and the biological father does not take responsibility for his own children. Instead, he raises his sister's children, as they belong to the female line of his family. Apart from that, there are some interesting parallels: In both systems, women play a central role in the domestic sphere as women of the house, while men are primarily active in politics or in public spheres and a similar division of labor prevails as in patriarchal societies. Of course, this account is simplified – the Mosuo society comprises about 50,000 people, while Rome, as an ancient world empire, had a completely different cultural and structural complexity.[126]

## 3.2 Sparta

Sparta, 480 BC: Lysandra, 18, trains javelin throw in the olive grove. Next to her, a group of young women are practicing the sprint – not out of joy, but because the state orders it. Sparta needs strong mothers who give birth to healthy sons. Lysandra is allowed to own land, manage crops and train in high school. Her brother Leonidas, on the other hand, has lived in the barracks since he was 7 years old. He is not allowed to marry until he is 30, can only secretly visit his wife and later dies at Thermopylae – a hero whom no one asked if he wanted to be.

The Spartan paradox: a military dictatorship, of all things, granted women more freedom than "democratic" Athens. Sparta's women were not feminists, they were important to society.

## 4. Result

Patriarchy is the cradle of our civilization, which gave birth to democracy and human rights, but also what the feminists say. Above all, however, it is history in our latitude. Learn from this, but stop trying to attribute every wrong to it or to justify new ones with it.

# VI. Education and schools[127]

Several studies indicate that boys are systematically disadvantaged in many school systems. This disadvantage manifests itself in various aspects that go far beyond individual achievements.

---

[126] https://en.wikipedia.org/wiki/Mosuo
[127] https://tinyurl.com/53kksf68

## Mirror[128]

Der Spiegel just reported that 55% of high school graduates will be female in 2023. The first qualification after the 9th grade was again achieved by 59% of the boys. 56% of repeaters are male. 15% of men up to the age of 24 have not completed vocational training and 11% of girls. This is basically not a new development, because girls have been leading the grammar school since 1980.[129] The reactions could hardly be more different: Some express fundamental discomfort with this development, others see above all a "women's problem" and ask why women are then paid less or move up to the coveted CEO positions less often. Still others accept that boys with reading difficulties will become potential long-term unemployed, incel supporters, suicidal people, homeless people, red-pill supporters or supporters of extremist groups – often out of frustration over the surplus of male managers, etc. This, too, can be interpreted as a facet of feminist debates, although not all feminists share this perspective.

## Meta-Analysis von Voyer & Voyer (2014)[130]

The meta-analysis by Voyer & Voyer (2014) summarizes that girls consistently perform better than boys in school grades. This gender difference is evident across different disciplines and can be seen in all age groups and socioeconomic groups. The average effect size ($d = 0.23$) indicates a stable but small to moderate lead of the girls. This difference is particularly pronounced in school types with direct university admission (e.g. grammar schools), where the effect size increases to $d = 0.39$ – an indication that school performance requirements or selection mechanisms reinforce the gender effect. Even at universities, the lead of women remains unchanged at $d = 0.21$, albeit somewhat reduced.

---

[128] https://www.instagram.com/p/DH_K_MsKUu8/
[129] https://tinyurl.com/y6vn686s
[130] https://psycnet.apa.org/record/2014-15035-001

The analysis included data from over 30 countries and examined studies published between 1914 and 2011. The results suggest that girls' grade advantage is a robust, long-term phenomenon that has been confirmed over almost a century and in different cultural contexts. Possible reasons include differences in motivation, learning behavior and social background.

## Gender-specific grading

- **Italian study (2022)[131]**
  Boys receive lower grades than girls for equal performance in mathematics and languages. The study analyzed 38,957 10th grade students and showed that teachers systematically favored girls by an average of **0.4 grade points**.
- **OECD report (2015)[132]**
  In over 60 countries, girls are systematically graded better than boys, even if they have the same skills.

## Stereotyping and Self-Fulfilling Prophecies

**Studies by the University of Kent (2013)[133]**
Five studies show that children from the age of 7 internalize that boys are "worse students". These stereotypes lead to real performance deficits:

- **Study 1: Girls from 4 years old and boys from 7 years old** believed that adults believe that boys are worse than girls in school
- **Study 2:** Manipulated stereotype threat by telling children that boys are worse at school. This **worsened the performance of the boys**, but not that of the girls
- **Study 3**: Counteracted the stereotype by conveying that **boys and girls do equally well**. As a result**, the boys' performance improved** without affecting that of the girls

---

[131] https://www.tandfonline.com/doi/full/10.1080/01425692.2022.2122942
[132] https://www.bbc.com/news/education-31751672
[133] https://srcd.onlinelibrary.wiley.com/doi/10.1111/cdev.12079

## Additional difficulties[134]

- School is not adapted to the needs of boys[135]
- Boys have ADHD more often[136]
- Support programs focus mainly on girls[137]

| Indicator | Girls/Women | Boys/Men |
|---|---|---|
| Grade advantage girls (d-value, total) | 0.23 | N/A |
| Grade advantage girls (d-value, grammar school) | 0.39 | N/A |
| Proportion of Abitur graduates | 55 % | 45 % |
| Abi-Gap | - | 22 |
| First graduation after 9th grade | 41 % | 59 % |

[134] https://boys-up.de/jungen-im-bildungsabseits/
[135] https://youtu.be/ZuAaD33vW5k?si=spUQGGIliUZ3hJ7-
[136] https://pmc.ncbi.nlm.nih.gov/articles/PMC3101894/
[137] https://tinyurl.com/mrxffrsb Chapter 5.1

| | | |
|---|---|---|
| Retriever | 44 % | 56 % |
| Grade-Repeater-Gap | - | 27.2 |
| NEET-Rate (16-24 Jahre, England) | 7 % | 40 % |
| Funded projects (2012) | 94 | 4 |
| Support-Level-Gap | - | 2250 |
| Dropout[138] | 10.4 % | 15.2 % |
| Dropout-Gap | - | 46.2 |

On how the gaps work: They are similar to the gender pay gap. I have already determined whether a higher or lower value is to be considered positive – e.g. more support and fewer school dropouts are all positive. Since boys have the worst scores in both categories, the gap is on the side of boys in both indicators.

## The War Against Boys: How Misguided Feminism Is Harming Our Young Men

---

[138] https://tinyurl.com/8sy7zu25

Christina Hoff Sommers is a conservative philosopher and prominent representative of so-called "equity feminism". In The War Against Boys (2000), she argues that radical forms of feminism have influenced the education system in the USA (and beyond) to such an extent that boys are systematically disadvantaged.

- Girls have risen to become a "privileged gender elite" through feminist ideologies.
- Boys, on the other hand, are left behind at school, disciplined and morally delegitimized – "simply because they are boys".
- She sees the solution in a return to traditional values, discipline, authority and biologically based gender roles.

**Context on the State of Education in the U.S.**

| High School Dropouts in the U.S. in %[139] | | | | | |
|---|---|---|---|---|---|
| | 80 | 90 | 2000 | 2010 | 2020 |
| Guys | 15.1 | 11.9 | 12 | 8.5 | 6.2 |
| Girl | 13.8 | 11.8 | 9.9 | 6.3 | 4.4 |
| Dropout-Gap | 9.4 | 0.8 | 21.2 | 34.9 | 40.9 |

The dropout gap is the relative difference between the rates. We see that with a decreasing base rate and a relatively constant difference of one to two percent, the dropout gap increases and with it the nominal ratio of men to women. According to this, for every 100 abortions in women, there are 141 abortions in men. What the numbers tell us is that the problem is decreasing in society as a whole, but that gender-specific problems are increasing.

---

[139] https://www.smartick.com/data/charted-high-school-dropout-rates-in-the-united-states/

Other college degree sources. Women overtook men in the 90s.[140]
More data, but only up to 2010.[141]

High school diplomas don't have much difference.[142]

## Central points of criticism of Sommers' book according to Robert Menzies

### Ideologically motivated

- The book is ideologically motivated and permeated by moral absolutism, biological determinism and an elitist conservatism that looks back nostalgically on a "better" past.
- Sommers is a fellow of the right-wing conservative American Enterprise Institute, which underlines her political orientation.
- ➢ I think that's true so far.

### Surrealism of the depiction

- The portrayal of feminist influence seems exaggerated, caricature-esque and surreal in places.
- The idea of a school "matriarchy" that deliberately suppresses boys is a dramatization that does not correspond to reality.
- ➢ I don't know how surreal or real their depiction is. But what was and is quite real is the problem and that the performance of the boys is worse than that of the girls. I have already substantiated this for Germany and now for the USA.

### Apparent scientificity

- Sommers draws on a selection of studies and "Atrocity Tales", without systematic or balanced research.

---

[140] https://tinyurl.com/mtvbpvdn
[141] https://tinyurl.com/582wnh7v
[142] https://tinyurl.com/2zp498sf

- In particular, her attacks on Carol Gilligan are vitriolic and are based on an undifferentiated rejection of any gender-cultural theoretical approaches.
- The first three chapters set out Sommers' main thesis, which deals with the alleged tyranny of gender equality. She cites a wealth of sources to argue that boys are victims of a state-run educational machinery controlled by feminists. According to Sommers, a politically correct circle of authoritarian do-gooders...
- ➢ So, what Ms. Sommers describes here does sound a bit like what we now call wokeness. Back in 2000, perhaps still in its infancy — but by now, it's certainly nothing new. I can actually recommend an interesting video on this topic.[143]
- "... Embodied by organizations such as the American Association of University Women, the Wellesley Center for Research on Women, and the Women's Educational Equity Act Equity Resource Center—masculinity in schools, as elsewhere, is under siege. Various gruesome examples are selectively used to describe how equality-obsessed and gender-enthusiastic academics, researchers, and decision-makers have conspired to portray young men as culturally deficient and inherently abusive, and how they have made boys the target of vile brainwashing methods designed to plunge an entire generation of men into a state of androgynous ineptitude."
- ➢ Yes, even here. This is also no longer a marginal phenomenon of elitist circles whose existence can simply be denied. You see it regularly on social media. We have #killallmen, #menaretrash, bear-vs. male, and young men talking about men in reels as if evil were the most basic trait that describes men.

**Biological essentialism**

- Sommers' thesis that gender-specific behavior is biologically determined ("boys will be boys") reflects the same essentialism that

---

[143] https://youtu.be/sABcWG9OHOk?si=l5Q1DeWXxfkWn2pV

she herself accuses feminists of – only from the opposite direction (biologically rather than culturally based).

➢ Sommer is not the only one who argued this way at this time. In Germany, for example, there was Vera F. Birkenbihl, and this woman was a veritable walking collection of sources. Also, in my opinion, Ms. Birkenbihl's argumentation was less ideological, if at all.[144] [145] Sometimes the distinction between cultural and biological is not expedient – for example, when the decisive question is: What helps boys the most? In such cases, the current state itself often provides the best indications of effective approaches.

## Instrumentalization of the topic

- The book is not a neutral contribution to education policy, but an instrument of the "new right male agenda", i.e. part of a political retreat movement against feminist achievements.
- It is part of a broader "backlash" literature that tries to turn back the gender equality discourse.

➢ Personally, I deliberately stay out of whether gender equalization through socialization is fundamentally good or bad. Ultimately, it has neither been proven nor disproved – and we will probably only know when a society has realized this state of affairs over a longer period of time and adapted to it. At the same time, there are indications that make us skeptical: the so-called gender equality paradox[146] or that women in more egalitarian societies are sometimes more dissatisfied – for example, when men take over the entire household (and this triggers feelings of guilt in women).[147] The global trend of female mental health is also pointing downwards.[148] Studies suggest that conservative women are happier on average than liberal women (37% vs. 12%).[149] Of

---

[144] https://youtu.be/FLlc45TDx5I?si=S9dV8cabs9Lznxbc
[145] https://youtu.be/7A0ZfAoKPrA?si=4s6SiFGyZyG31EHi
[146] https://tinyurl.com/2p3p3wd8
[147] https://tinyurl.com/39ycxr5t
[148] https://www.science.org/doi/10.1126/sciadv.adt1646
[149] https://tinyurl.com/2p2sry6k

course, there are counter-studies, explanatory approaches and also research that proves positive effects of equality. That's why I deliberately tried to refrain from making a clear judgment in favor of traditional or progressive role models in the context of the book. Perhaps the answer also lies in the fact that you can choose your own way of life – without the constant ideological suggestion from the right or left.

## Neglect of structural problems

- Sommers ignores social, economic and racial inequalities and focuses solely on a moral crisis of the young.
- Causes such as poverty, racism, heterosexism or systematic discrimination are completely ignored.
- ➢ That also doesn't seem to be the main topic of the book — and logically, it's mostly irrelevant for a comparative gender analysis at this point, because such factors are likely to be found in roughly similar proportions among boys and girls alike. So, sure, one can look into this, but the comparison between boys and girls — and the fact that boys tend to come out worse — is mostly consistent (with the exception of Michigan, but I found the table there very clear).[150] Another source shows the ratio of men to women who complete a bachelor's degree, and it turns out that the imbalance is most severe precisely where I would expect to find the highest levels of racism. Maybe because the targeted support for women is actually working well?

## Proportion of women with bachlor[151]

- Black people: 65.2%
- People of Latin American origin: 62.3%
- White people: 57.3%
- Asians: 55.3%

---

[150] https://www.mlive.com/news/kalamazoo/2012/04/a_closer_look_at_the_gender_ga.html
[151] https://www.rsfjournal.org/content/11/1/154

- Another source speaks of 38% of all black women and 26% of black men. Which is still a ratio of 59.4% women, while the ratio for all is 56%.[152]
  - ➢ What does the single rate look like?

## Single rates (25–54 years)[153]

- Black men: 55%
- Black women: 62%
- Latin American: 38%
- Whiteness: 33%
- Asians: 29%

## Double standards in argumentation

- While Sommers dismisses feminist theories as ideological and anti-masculine, she herself pursues an ideological agenda – in the name of "true" equality, but with conservative-hierarchical gender roles.
- Zitat: "Sommers's arch-conservative politics of nostalgia, her hierarchical vision of gender relations, her caricature of 'gender feminism' as anti-male, and her identification with the 'men's rights' movement are all the more accentuated by her professed allegiance to 'real' feminist values."
- Their condemnation of ('radical' and 'authoritarian' versions) of feminism in the name of women and on behalf of men is just another tiresome elaboration of this chronically recurring theme in anti-feminist literature. Ultimately, apart from focusing attention on boys instead of men, and offering an imaginative critique of liberal education as a misogynistic establishment, The War against Boys is best seen as one of many backlash books that have flooded the academic and popular market over the past decade. So if Sommers is merely reworking old arguments, why should feminists and social

---

[152] https://tinyurl.com/4wskhkxm
[153] https://tinyurl.com/b76r2dr9

law scholars pay attention to The War against Boys and similar publications at all? Why should we give this politically outdated, scientifically questionable, and decidedly androcentric pamphlet space in the pages of the Canadian Journal of Women and the Law and other progressive academic forums? In my view, the actual content of The War against Boys, the rigor of Sommers' research, and the quality of its scholarship are ultimately secondary—perhaps even completely irrelevant—to this book's undeniable status as a contemporary feminist concern. Rather, the real impact and the associated danger of Sommers' writings lie in their instrumental and symbolic value as an ideological medium of the new right-wing men's agenda.

➢ In summary, you could say that it basically does the same thing as feminism – only in the opposite direction. And then it follows: So we should cancel it. Of course, this is a somewhat pointed example, but it was the first one I encountered. My reaction to this may be a bit sharp – especially since or precisely because I don't know the actual conditions at American universities or schools first-hand and can't go into them. Nevertheless, this reminds me a lot of what is presented in the YouTube video recommended above. And if we take stock today, some 20 years later, the basic trend seems to have continued.

## Leaky Pipeline

The buzzword "leaky pipeline" refers to the steady decline in the proportion of women in science and research along the qualification levels and career stages. Despite increasing educational qualifications among women, a wide range of support programs, gender equality policies and special initiatives in the STEM field – such as mentoring and gender mainstreaming – a comparatively low proportion of women can still be observed in many disciplines. Reference is made to continuing structural inequalities between men and women.[154]

---

[154] https://www.uni-paderborn.de/gleichstellung/genderportal/gender-glossar/leaky-pipeline

## Promotions

At the end of 2023, 204,900 doctoral candidates were enrolled at higher education institutions in Germany – 400 people, or 0.2%, fewer than in 2022. According to Destatis, the proportion of women remained unchanged at 47.22% (98,800) and the proportion of men at 51.78% (106,100).[155]

If you attribute the surplus of men among doctoral students to biological and demographic effects in isolation, you get:

1. **Pipeline loss due to maternity** was set by me to a male advantage of **+1.0 PP**
2. **Demographic cohort** at the typical doctoral age (25–34 years) results in a male advantage of **+3.4 pp**.
3. Greater male variability *leads to a male advantage of* +33.3 pp.

Together, this results in a ~37.2 PP male advantage → predicted male share ≈ **68.6** % vs. women ≈ 31.4%, and what we have in real terms is 54% men in doctorates in Germany.

## 1. Pipeline loss due to maternity

- **68.4%** of women aged 20–75 are mothers (2022 microcensus: 20.3 million out of 29.7 million women).[156]
- 7–8% of active graduate students in the U.S. have children[157]
- 13-14% of the 25,000 women in the U.S. who complete their PhDs are mothers[158]
- In Germany, 16.7% of women with doctoral studies are mothers[159]
- 42% of mothers and 15% of fathers in the U.S. give up full-time STEM jobs within three years of having a child[160]

---

[155] https://www.destatis.de/DE/Presse/Pressemitteilungen/2024/08/PD24_315_213.html
[156] https://tinyurl.com/mwapmasu
[157] https://journals.indianapolis.iu.edu/index.php/advancesinsocialwork/article/download/23220/23016
[158] https://ijds.org/Volume15/IJDSv15p089-110Mirick5906.pdf
[159] https://tinyurl.com/yc8v3wry
[160] https://tinyurl.com/53ysyae5

- Another 2011 study found that married women with children are about 35 percent less likely to enter a tenure-track position after completing their PhD than married men with children
- In addition, they are 27 percent less likely to achieve a tenure[161]
- The dropout rate among all PhD students is high in North America – it is estimated that 40% to 50% drop out.[162]
- Having children before working as a postdoctoral researcher leads to a 19 percent probability of men dropping out of college, compared to 32 percent for women. New children after starting postdoctoral work lead to a difference of 20 percent for men and 41 percent for women.[163]
- Recent mothers have given up their careers in the STEM field almost three times as often as fathers or childless colleagues.[164]

Apparently, due to the complex interactions of various factors, it is difficult to isolate an exact percentage of "pipeline abort" that is solely due to motherhood. It is often mentioned that motherhood does not fully explain the so-called pipeline leak, but it has a (large) share in it. This means significant in the lower academic levels, but in professorship and tenure it will be no or less.[165] Ironically, I would now propose more parental quotas to argue against women's quotas, but I am probably not the first to have come up with this. Quotas are not the only problem either. Being a parent, especially for mothers, makes research more difficult and there are structural hurdles here that should be removed. Here, too, one can have a discussion about socialization and a biologically explainable preference of the woman to prefer motherhood, and one will again come to no conclusion. Also, the overall rate of parenthood doesn't exactly suggest that students think it's a good time to have children.

[161] https://www.bu.edu/articles/2019/pregnant-and-phd/
[162] https://tinyurl.com/bdhy459j
[163] https://pmc.ncbi.nlm.nih.gov/articles/PMC3939045/
[164] https://awis.org/resource/motherhood-causing-critical-leak-stem-pipeline/
[165] https://www.sciencedirect.com/science/article/pii/S0277539524001407?#s0120

Since I didn't find any usable data here, I'll just take + 1 PP so 50.5% vs. 49.5% male advantage to demonstrate the calculation, but it's a bit more than that.

## 2. Demographic Cohort (25–34 years)

**Target group of doctoral candidates**: Mostly aged **25–34** years. In 2022, this age group in Germany lived:[166]

Men: 5,485,485; Women: 5,112,229; Total: 10,597,714

**Proportion of men**: 5,485,485 / (5,485,485 + 5,112,229) ≈ **51.76 %** → **+3.4 PP** male advantage.

## 3. Greater-Male-Variability[167]

- Meta-analyses confirm that men have a higher variance in cognitive tests (variability hypothesis). In the Wikipedia article linked above, there are numerous studies on this: Some attribute the differences to biological causes, others emphasize sociological factors above all – and to this day it remains controversial to what extent each of these explanatory approaches applies.
- PhD students have an IQ of 125.[168] [169] From 125 onwards, there is one woman with this IQ for every 2 men.[170] Which represents 67 vs. 33 or **+33.3 PP.**

Ok, I'd like to tend to just add it up, but then the overlap is missing.

- 666/333 x 517/483 x 505/495 = 2,184
- ➢ 2,184 + 1 = 3,184
- ➢ 1 / 3.184 = **0.314**

---

[166] https://ugeo.urbistat.com/AdminStat/de/de/demografia/eta/deutschland/276/1
[167] https://en.wikipedia.org/wiki/Variability_hypothesis
[168] https://academiainsider.com/iq-phd/
[169] https://www.religjournal.com/pdf/ijrr10001.pdf
[170] https://tinyurl.com/3pjs5wtk

> 0.314 x 2.184 = **0.686**
> 68.6 % vs. 31.4 %

The **biological-demographic forecast** of **68.6%** for men is thus slightly higher than the actual **54%** and could represent an underrepresentation of men. The reasons for this could be that structural disadvantages of boys in the school system have been overlooked and, at the same time, girls have been specifically promoted, and that women are given preference at some universities if places are limited and have the same qualifications.[171] [172] [173]

## The variability of extremes

The previous consideration of the distribution of doctoral students in Germany and the derivation of a forecast of 68.6% male doctoral students (based on demographic shifts, pipeline loss due to maternity and peak cognitive variance) raises important questions. In particular, the factor of *greater male variability*, which accounts for a significant share of the predicted discrepancy, probably needs further explanation to avoid misunderstandings.

## What is *Greater Male Variability?*

*Greater male variability* describes the empirically proven fact that the spread in certain cognitive abilities – such as standardized intelligence tests (IQ tests) – is greater in men than in women. The important thing is that this does not mean that men are more intelligent on average; the mean values of both groups can be very similar or identical. Rather, men are more likely to show extreme values (both very low and very high), while women tend to be more grouped around the mean.

[171] https://tinyurl.com/478uw9kk
[172] https://www.uni-due.de/physik/gleichstellung/gleichstellungsmassnahmen.php
[173] https://tinyurl.com/c2z7rcae

In psychometric research, the existence of this distribution is widely recognized.[174] Numerous meta-analyses and individual studies show that male samples have higher ranges of variation in IQ tests. The debate revolves more around the underlying causes (biological vs. social) of this greater dispersion and the implications for education and research. However, this is irrelevant for our calculation.

## Why is *greater male variability* relevant for our prognosis?

For the estimation of the expected gender distribution in doctorates, only the currently observed distribution counts, regardless of the reason why this is the case. A simple calculation example makes the principle clear: Imagine two groups, A and B. Group A is twice as large as group B. Both roll fair dice. Mathematically, it is to be expected that group A will roll almost twice as many "sixes" as group B – regardless of why group A is actually larger. This effect is caused solely by the different group sizes and the random process.

Applying this concept to IQ distributions, it is easy to understand why an IQ of 125 in absolute numbers is more common in men as soon as more men are represented in the initial population. In fact, analyses show that from an IQ cutoff of 125 onwards, a ratio of about 2 : 1 in favor of men arises. This means that among those who really achieve "extremely high" IQ scores (≥ 125), there are about twice as many men as women.

## Why a mere look at equal opportunities without taking variability into account would be misleading

A purely "ideal" assumption that assumes a 50:50 distribution with the same qualifications ignores the actual distribution of top cognitive profiles. The higher variance among men leads to more men accumulating at the margins (IQ ≥ 125), and thus the selection pools for doctoral scholarships and positions also have a different basis.

---

[174] https://tinyurl.com/2u53d65p

## Criticism

This reasoning is usually criticized on a few points, so let's address a few points.

- **Abbreviated presentation**
  - ➢ Absolutely, for this and other reasons, the current distribution would have to be recalculated regularly.
- **Biology vs. Sozialization**
  - ➢ Mathematically irrelevant for the current state, but sociology is one of the other reasons why the distribution has to be redetermined regularly.
- **Reduction of success to IQ**
  - ➢ Absolutely not. I am absolutely in favor of taking into account all relevant, measurable and calculable characteristics in order to get a profile that is as representative as possible.
- **Deviation in IQ assessment, methodology, etc.**
  - ➢ Absolutely, this is just a simplified approximation. If you want to apply this in practice, you probably need qualitative and representative data and someone who knows probability calculus.
- **Math is potentially simplistic**
  - ➢ The larger the basic set, the closer you will get to what should be fair in the understanding of equal opportunity. And you can certainly take other characteristics into account. It is not to be expected that it will be perfect; only the probability expert will probably calculate a range and not a point. There will also be characteristics that are not so easy to measure and calculate. However, I believe that what is found out here is fairer than ignoring it.
- **Maybe criticism of my understanding of equal opportunities**
  - ➢ Basically, this has already been explained when it came to the discussion about the 2-meter people, and the principle is not particularly different here. If you have two groups, 2000 people

in one and 1000 in the other, and now 300 people are to be selected for certain projects, then there is equality of opportunity if these 300 people are randomly selected from the total of 3000 people. What does not constitute equal opportunities, however, is the automatic selection of 150 people from each group just to establish numerical equality. Equal opportunities here refers to the equal possibility of access to the selection pool, which reflects the real distributions and proportions of the total population.

- **Quotas**
- ➢ This treatise has nothing to do with quotas. I will go into the topic of quotas in more detail in another chapter. Here, odds were only briefly mentioned in order to name them as a possible reason for deviations from the expected value. One point is, perhaps. It is worth mentioning that what has been called fair here does not have to be the same fair as I am talking about in the context of quotas, because socialization can play a role there.

## Professorships

At the end of 2023, there were 51,873 full-time professors employed in Germany, of whom 29% were women (approx. 14,934) and 71% were men (approx. 36,939).[175] Here, too, one could repeat the familiar argument: motherhood alone does not explain the gender difference, whereas the greater IQ variance among men — assuming an average IQ slightly above 125 — would contribute significantly. Taking both factors into account, one is once again faced with the question of how much of the difference is due to socialization and how much to biological causes.

## Result

The collected results show that the education system – although standardized tests often do not show significant gender differences –

---

[175] https://tinyurl.com/38tpxxvm

systematically disadvantages boys in everyday grading. This disadvantage manifests itself in lower grades, higher dropout rates and lower career opportunities in the long term, as well as reduced self-esteem. The numerous studies underline that this is a structural problem that is deeply rooted in the culturally shaped evaluation norms of the school system. This systematic disadvantage of boys contradicts the principles of a balanced education system and has far-reaching negative consequences for the future opportunities and self-confidence of the pupils concerned.

# VII. Economy, labor market and professional world

Specific challenges for men also emerge in the labor market, which often contradict the structures and expectations supported. More detailed analyses show that the unadjusted gender pay gap in Germany will be around 16% in 2024, but will be reduced to around 6% after taking into account occupation, education and working hours. Partial gaps arise, among other things, from differences in willingness to negotiate, career breaks due to parental leave and subtle discrimination in promotions. Paradoxically, the gap hardly shrinks in countries with high pay equality. In some cases, women earn more per hour than men (Luxembourg, 2023: −0.9%).[176] At the same time, meta-analyses show that women have stronger preferences for people-related activities on average (d = 0.93), while men are more interested in "things".[177]. These preferences remain stable even after targeted STEM support programs, and even increase in egalitarian countries (gender equality paradox).[178] Technological structural change is putting young men at a particular disadvantage: in the UK, full-time women (16-24) earn an average of £2,200 more than men, while their NEET rate has increased by 40%.[179]

[176] https://unric.org/en/gender-equality-smaller-pay-gaps-in-belgium-italy-and-luxembourg/
[177] https://pubmed.ncbi.nlm.nih.gov/19883140/
[178] https://journals.sagepub.com/doi/10.1177/0956797617741719
[179] https://www.centreforsocialjustice.org.uk/library/lost-boys

While the rate of early school-leaving in the EU is declining overall, reaching 9.5% in 2023, Germany recorded an increase over the same period: from 9.8% in 2013, the rate rose by 3 percentage points to 12.8% – well above the EU target of below 9%. The gender-specific difference is particularly striking: at 15.2%, the rate of young men is 4.8 percentage points higher than that of young women (10.4%). This difference has increased more than fivefold since 2013, when it was still 0.9 percentage points – mainly due to the significant increase among young men. There are also considerable disparities in the migration background: While 9.7% of 18- to 24-year-olds born in Germany left school early in 2023, the proportion of foreign-born children was around three times as high at 29.4%. Young people born outside the EU were particularly hard hit – with a rate of 33.5%.[180] Women work an average of 34.3 hours, men 40.2 hours per week. Despite egalitarian rhetoric, in most EU households the man remains the main breadwinner; Hypergamy intensifies role constraints.

# 1. Introduction

Economic inequalities cannot be traced back to discrimination monocausally, but result from the interaction of individual preferences, historical role specifications and current labor market conditions. While feminist discourses often address structural discrimination against women, educationally disadvantaged men suffer from job loss due to automation and training deficits. To facilitate a fair debate, we need to examine who loses or wins under what circumstances – and what policies can do justice to both groups.

# 2. Female leaders

Let's first take a look at the distribution of female executives. In 2022, barely one in three leadership positions was held by a woman (28.9 percent). In academic professions — for example, doctors,

---

[180] https://tinyurl.com/8sy7zu25

lawyers, or teachers — the proportion of women was significantly higher at 49.5 percent. This is a trend that has persisted for quite some time: since the 1990s, the share of women in academic professions has increased substantially — a notable contrast to the overall development of female leadership representation. The share of female executives is particularly high in the public sector (43 percent) and among NGOs (42 percent). In small and medium-sized enterprises (SMEs), however, executives are mostly male — the proportion of women here is only 16 percent.[181]

The point that clearly falls outside the scope of Greater Male Variability and the *Motherhood Penalty* is the low 16% figure for SMEs.

## How many executives are there? A question of definition.

- In 2013, it is estimated that just over four million salaried executives were employed in the German private sector, 29% of whom were women.[182]
- In the 2017 reporting year, the employment statistics indicated around 1,118,000 managers and 749,000 supervisors, while the microcensus projections showed 1,167,000 in management functions and 1,048,000 in supervisory functions.[183]

## More data:

- In 2022, around 99.3% of all enterprises (SMEs) belonged to the group of small and medium-sized enterprises (SMEs) with 3.1 million establishments.[184]
- It can be seen that the share of owner- and family-managed companies in the 2014 reporting year was 93.6%. (To all companies.)[185]

---

[181] https://www.academics.de/ratgeber/weibliche-fuehrungskraefte
[182] https://tinyurl.com/ynk2w52s
[183] https://tinyurl.com/mz7vtu3e
[184] https://tinyurl.com/3ef2tekb
[185] https://tinyurl.com/msxnj4a8

- Total private enterprises and businesses 3,228,000[186]
- Family-controlled businesses 2,919,000
- Owner-managed family businesses 2,838,000
- In 2023, around 602,000 small and medium-sized enterprises (SMEs) in Germany were led by women, which corresponds to a share of 15.8%. The basis of all SMEs here is 3.8 million.[187]
- The slight increase in the proportion of women in entrepreneurship so far can be explained primarily by the fact that women are less likely to start their own businesses overall – and this trend has even been declining recently. For many, traditional employment remains more attractive than entrepreneurship, so that women often decide against taking the step into self-employment.
- In women-led medium-sized companies, the proportion of women in management positions is 77% on average.
- In male-led SMEs, the proportion of women in management positions is only 16%.
- The "entrepreneur gender pay gap" was 44% in 2017.[188]

A large part of the problem of the low proportion of women in management positions seems to lie in small and medium-sized enterprises (SMEs). These companies make up the vast majority of the economy, but are often overlooked when it comes to gender equality issues. In order to ensure a better balance here, more start-ups by women would be an effective lever. Studies show that women in leadership roles tend to promote other women more often – an effect of so-called homosociality. Alternatively, one would have to try to change existing structures, for example by making male decision-makers aware of how strongly their choice of leadership is influenced by homosocial preferences – i.e. by the tendency to prefer similar people (in this case: men). However, it remains questionable how effective appeals against these deep-rooted, often unconscious patterns can be – and whether the

---

[186] https://tinyurl.com/mrukw9tm
[187] https://tinyurl.com/mtw8h9v6
[188] https://tinyurl.com/umzb482r

more sustainable way is not to strengthen more female networks and start-up structures.

# 3. Lack of support measures

In industries traditionally dominated by women — such as education, caregiving, or social work — there is often a lack of targeted support measures for men. Male quotas or special programs to encourage men to enter these fields are rare.[189] As a result, men who wish to work in these sectors frequently encounter structural barriers that put them at a disadvantage. However, this has improved somewhat in recent years: for example, the share of male childcare workers in Germany increased from 4.2% in 2012 to 7.9% in 2022.[190]

Germany ranks among the global leaders in promoting gender equality.[191]

# 4. Pressure of expectations

Men are often under considerable pressure of expectations in their professional lives. Society, they are required to prove themselves as "self-made" – i.e. to achieve success through their own performance alone. This idea, combined with the claim to define oneself through one's profession, leads to enormous inner tension in many men. It is not uncommon for this to push them to the limit of their resilience. As current surveys show, it is mainly self-imposed demands that cause stress for men – rather than external factors such as bosses or colleagues. This desire for perfection in the job can lead to burnout and mental illness in the long term.

[189] https://life-online.de/die-auswertung-fuer-den-girlsday-und-boysday-2024-ist-da/
[190] https://tinyurl.com/3pbh7dv4
[191] https://donortracker.org/donor_profiles/germany/gender

Even though men are less likely to classify themselves as "very stressed" than women, the consequences of professional pressure are still serious for them: permanent stress, emotional exhaustion and high absenteeism due to psychological stress are steadily increasing.

And yet: Women are more often exposed to severe stress overall (20% to 11% according to Forsa) – mainly because of the double burden of work and family. They are struggling not only with their own demands, but also with social role expectations: career, care work, perfect leisure time – all at the same time. So it's no wonder that women often suffer from adjustment disorders, burnout and depression.[192]

# 5. Structural change

Structural change in economies – the transition from industrial to service- and knowledge-based sectors – often hits men harder than women in traditional industries. While companies are increasingly relying on highly qualified specialists, men who work in classic industrial professions are disadvantaged by the change. This change leads to job losses and a shift in labor market demand, which poses major challenges for men in many regions.[193]

# 6. Gender-Pay-Gap

## 6.1 Unadjusted vs. Adjusted

The unadjusted gender pay gap indicates the general difference in average gross hourly earnings – in Germany, this was around 16% less for women in 2024. If education, work experience, industry and working hours are taken into account, an adjusted pay gap of around 6% remains, which is considered the upper limit of direct discrimination.[194]

---

[192] https://tinyurl.com/5k5rk9uw
[193] https://www.cream-migration.org/publ_uploads/CDP_13_23.pdf
[194] https://tinyurl.com/46k6k3t8

98

## 6.2 Explanatory factors[195]

- As an unadjusted indicator, the gender pay gap provides an overall picture of the income gap between men and women. In fact, parts of the income gap between men and women can be explained by (1) differences in the average characteristics of male and female employees and (2) differences in the financial return for the same characteristics.
- **Negative gaps:** In Luxembourg, a negative unadjusted gender pay gap in gross hourly earnings of −0.9% was recorded in 2023, which means that women earn more per hour worked than men on average.
- Among those under 25, negative gender pay gaps were observed in Belgium (−8.3%), Greece (−4.4%), France (−7.2%), Malta (−2.0%) and Finland (−0.5%) in 2023.
- In the 25–34 age group, Belgium (−5.0%) and Malta (−4.3%) also had a negative gender pay gap.
- Germany has 1.7% for those under 25.

## 6.3 Adjusted must be further adjusted

On the *Destatis* website, it also says under frequently asked questions: "It is important to take into account that the adjusted gender pay gap should not be equated with earnings discrimination, as not all relevant wage-determining characteristics are present in the earnings survey. For example, the earnings survey does not have information on career breaks (such as maternity leave or parental leave). If such information were available, the adjusted gender pay gap would be smaller. The adjusted gender pay gap is therefore considered an 'upper limit' for direct pay discrimination by the employer."[196]

Personally, I would like to see something more than just this hint. What is missing? Is it possible to make an approximate calculation?

[195] https://ec.europa.eu/eurostat/statistics-explained/index.php?title=Gender_pay_gap_statistics
[196] https://tinyurl.com/yxv3r554

Where is it all going? Now we have: is less than 6. Can be in the minus, can be in the plus, that says pretty much nothing about the gender debate. And then the clue is hidden far below. That's the clue I want to see right next to the number so that I can understand what it means.

# 7. Preferences, socialization and biology

## 7.1 Meta-analyses and interventions

In a meta-analysis, over 500,000 participants were analyzed and found that women showed strong social interests and a people-orientation (d = 0.93), while men were "things"-oriented. The study suggests that interests could play a crucial role in gender-specific career choices and gender inequality in STEM subjects.[197]

## 7.2 Gender-Equality-Paradox

International school performance data show that in two out of three countries, girls are as good or better at science than boys. Nevertheless, in almost all countries, fewer girls are enrolling in STEM courses than would actually be able to do so. Surprisingly, the differences in strengths and choice of study between the sexes increase the more equal a country is. An analysis suggests that in less equal countries, living conditions are more likely to encourage girls to enter STEM subjects.[198]

## 7.3 Biological aspects

In children aged 4 to 11 years, girls scored significantly higher in EQ-C, while boys scored significantly higher in SQ-C.[199]

---

[197] https://pubmed.ncbi.nlm.nih.gov/19883140/
[198] https://tinyurl.com/2p3p3wd8
[199] https://docs.autismresearchcentre.com/papers/2009_Auyeung_etal_ChildEQSQ_JADD.pdf

## 8. The man as the main breadwinner

Despite egalitarian rhetoric, 55% of US households have men as the main breadwinner, and 16% of households have a female primary breadwinner.[200] Hypergamy studies show that women often choose partners with higher status.[201]

## 9. Conclusion

The disadvantages in the labor market and in the professional world show that men often face specific challenges in areas that are considered "feminized" or that traditionally male-dominated professions come under pressure from structural changes. A lack of support measures, high pressure of expectations and the rapid change in economic structures contribute to men being disadvantaged in certain sectors – which can also have long-term effects on their professional development and social position.

# VIII. Family Law, Custody and Maintenance

In the field of family law, there are often specific challenges for men. Structural disadvantages become visible in custody disputes, alimony regulations and social expectations.

## 1. Custody disputes:

In the event of separations and divorces, mothers are more likely to receive custody of joint children, even if both parents appear equally suitable. This tendency is often based on traditional role models that see women as primary caregivers for children. Although both parents are legally equal and decisions are to be made in the best interests of the

---

[200] https://tinyurl.com/2p8xv7cv
[201] https://docs.iza.org/dp12185.pdf

child, statistics show that mothers in the US have custody about 65% of the time and fathers about 35%.[202] In Australia, the ratio is 80 to 10%.[203]

For biological reasons, mothers often take on the main responsibility in early childhood, for example through breastfeeding, and are often more involved in upbringing. In addition, existing prejudices in favor of the mother can further reinforce this trend. However, some voices claim that gender bias is a myth and court decisions are based on facts.[204] [205]

Interestingly, men take on about 40% (3.26:[4.81+3.26] source: Care work chapter), which indicates an increasingly even distribution. Nevertheless, fathers in the USA only get custody in about 35% of cases, which indicates possible imbalances and thus there are also critics.[206]

# 2. Maintenance arrangements

German maintenance law has its origins in the Civil Code of 1896 and has been reformed several times since then in order to do justice to social developments. Nevertheless, there is repeated criticism that men in particular are disadvantaged in the current system. Many voices complain that the regulations are often outdated, bureaucratic and unbalanced – especially at a time when care models have become more diverse and role models more flexible.

**Imbalance in maintenance obligations**

In practice, men are disproportionately often obliged to pay maintenance – even in shared care models. The underlying assumption that men, as the main breadwinner, must automatically bear financial

---

[202] https://www.wmtxlaw.com/divorce-and-custody-statistics-2024/
[203] https://melbournefamilylawyers.com.au/news/child-custody-statistics-by-gender
[204] https://melbournefamilylawyers.com.au/news/child-custody-statistics-by-gender
[205] https://ascentlawfirm.com/are-mothers-more-likely-to-get-child-custody-during-divorce/
[206] https://www.complexfamilylaw.com/featured-articles/gender-bias-where-are-we/

responsibility leads to a structural imbalance. Studies and field reports indicate that this orientation of the system systematically disadvantages men.[207] Many men also do not know that they can also have claims for maintenance, or do not want to be a burden on the woman.[208]

# 3. Societal expectations

In addition to the legal aspects, social expectations also have an effect. Fathers who actively strive for an equal parental model or want to get more involved in childcare often encounter prejudice and criticism. These expectations not only inhibit individual development, but also reinforce the image that men are less capable in the family context – which in turn promotes discrimination in custody and maintenance issues.

# 4. Spouse splitting

**What is that?** In the case of joint assessment of spouses, the income is added, halved and then taxed (splitting rate). This favors couples with unequal incomes (e.g., one main earner + one low-income partner).

## 4.1 Criticisms of spousal splitting[209]

**Gender inequality:**

Studies by the Leibniz Institute for Economic Research (RWI) show that splitting promotes traditional role models in which women usually take a back seat in their careers in favor of childcare. Abolishing it could increase women's participation in the labor market and increase gross domestic product by up to 1.5%.

---

[207] https://www.linkedin.com/pulse/bias-against-men-child-custody-cases-nbqxe/

[208] https://www.micklinlawgroup.com/3-statistics-point-to-men-sabotaging-their-alimony-rights/

[209] https://www.deutschlandfunk.de/ehegattensplitting-abschaffen-nachteile-vorteile-100.html

### Shortage:

Economist Nicola Fuchs-Schündeln argues that qualified women are kept out of the labor market. More than 50% of university graduates are female – a potential that currently remains untapped.

### Lack of accuracy:

Splitting also has an effect on childless marriages and especially on high earners. The German Institute for Economic Research (DIW) shows that middle-income couples hardly benefit from splitting.

## 4.2 Proponents' arguments

### Family support:

Proponents argue that splitting allows one parent to devote more time to raising children. Critics, however, point out that about 33% of children in Germany grow up outside marriages and that the model therefore does not reach all families.

### Equal tax treatment:

Economists such as Stefan Homburg warn that an abolition without comprehensive tax reforms could disadvantage married couples with single earners.

### Maintenance compensation:

Splitting is often seen as compensation for the legal maintenance obligation between spouses. Alternatively, proposals such as a double basic tax allowance are being discussed.

**Ideology – it's also a culture war**

From a feminist perspective, spousal splitting is often criticized because it supports outdated role models and undermines women's independence. Ironically, the abolition of splitting leads to financial constraints being imposed on the family. As a result, those who usually earn less – i.e. mostly women – are forced to work more. Instead of empowering women in their decision whether to choose childcare or more intensive employment, such a reform shifts financial pressure and pushes towards employment. Therefore, other views emphasize that the abolition only means discrimination against the traditional family.

Briefly explained: Some critics believe that households in which both partners earn a similar amount are disadvantaged by spousal splitting. But let's just look at the basic tax-free allowance in a simplified way to understand exactly what actually happens.

**With spousal splitting:**

- Both earn the same > both allowances are actively used
- Single earners → both allowances are actively used

**Without spousal splitting:**

- Both earn the same > both allowances are actively used
- Single earner → Only one allowance is actively used

The question is why the allowance should not be allowed to be used, since both people live on the income.

# 5. Conclusion

The disadvantages in family law show that structural and social norms often lead to men being pushed into an unfavorable position. Custody disputes and alimony arrangements as well as the pressure of traditional role models hinder a balanced treatment of both parents. A fairer design of family law would therefore have to focus on all sides.

# IX. Gender-Care-Gap

| Care-Arbeit/Workload[210] | | | | | | | |
|---|---|---|---|---|---|---|---|
| | House-work | One-buy | Household welfare | external care | Phone, e-mail | Gainful employment | Community activities |
| Man in marriage | 1.81 | 0.62 | 0.60 | 0.15 | 0.08 mm | 4.48 mm | 0.25 mm |
| Woman in marriage | 2.73 | 0.79 | 0.92 mm | 0.22 | 0.15 | 3.10 | 0.31 |
| Husband | 1.16 | 0.46 | 0.15 | 0.15 | 0.18 | 3.84 mm | 0.16 |
| Wife | 1.92 | 0.73 mm | 0.33 mm | 0.17 | 0.24 | 2.86 mm | 0.25 mm |

**Care work (sum of the first five categories):**

---

[210] https://www.bls.gov/news.release/pdf/atus.pdf

- Man in marriage: **3.26** hours
- Women in marriage: **4.81** hours
- Man: **2.10** hours
- Woman: **3.39** hours

## Total Workload and Mental Load :

- Male in marriage: **7.99** hours
- Women in marriage: **8.22** hours
- Man: **6.10** hours
- Woman: **6.50** hours

## Increase in care work in marriage (marriage vs. single):

- Men: **+1.16** hours (from 2.10 to 3.26)
- Women: **+1.42** hours (from 3.39 to 4.81)

## Increase in workload in marriage (marriage vs. single):

- Men: **+1.89** hours (from 6.10 to 7.99)
- Women: **+1.72** hours (from 6.50 to 8.22)

## Differences between women and men:

- Care work: **Women** work **1.55** hours **more** than men in **marriage**
- And **1.29** hours more than men when **single**.
- Workload: **Women** work a total of **0.23** hours **more** than men in marriage
- And **0.40** hours more than men when **single**.

## Care work and workload – between preference, pragmatism and partnership

The analysis of the data on care work and overall workload in different life situations reveals complex dynamics that need to be viewed in a more differentiated way. If you look at the differences between single and married people, an interesting pattern emerges: Single women have a higher workload surplus than in marriage. This suggests that individual preferences and entrenched patterns of socialization play a central role – even regardless of relationship status. Marriage seems to weaken this effect slightly.

Nevertheless, the **burden on women** in the area of care work in marriage is increasing – from an average of **3.39 hours** for single people to **4.81 hours**. This increase is most likely due to the assumption of **childcare** and expanded household tasks. At the same time, however, the total workload for men in marriage increases more than for women (**+1.89 hours** vs. **+1.72 hours**), but the difference remains marginal at **0.17 hours** per day. This minimal discrepancy relativizes the often blanket assumption that men live in partnerships "at the expense" of women.

**Feminist narratives**

The frequently circulated feminist narrative that men are per se a "main burden" for women in relationships cannot be derived from these figures. Although women do **1.55 hours more care work** than men in marriage, the total workload – i.e. the sum of gainful employment, care work and community activities – is almost balanced (**8.22 hours** for women vs. **7.99 hours** for men). This raises whether the demand for "more care work for men" is actually always fair – especially if it is formulated primarily from a **preference perspective.**

One could argue, for example, that this demand is intrusive because what women do more here is done out of their own preference and not out of necessity. But this is where the dilemma begins: What exactly defines "necessity" in the household? (One could also ask, who decides that? Who is soft power dominant here?)

## The riddle of "objective necessity"

If "necessity" is measured by what is done minimally in single households – such as rough cleaning, occasional cooking – the question arises whether the additional **1.29 hours** that women invest every day are actually indispensable or an expression of a **higher demand** on housekeeping. This could be due to internalized expectations ("A woman *must* have a clean home!") or to a greater sensitivity to hygiene and order. So the recommendation that can be made here is that women become aware of their socialization and perhaps do a little less, even the total workload of single women is **0.4 hours** more.

At the same time, there is a partial balance in marriage: Men take on **0.17 hours more total workload** than women – a small but symbolically important step that illustrates that partnerships certainly offer room for compromise. From a **fairness perspective,** however, it could make sense for men to take on additional tasks that go beyond classic "male domains" such as waste disposal – about **14 minutes a day** for planning activities (writing shopping lists, coordinating appointments). Because in marriage, women still do 0.23 hours (14 minutes) more work every day – and both partners benefit from it.

This applies to the USA, but it is the other way around for Germany. The total workload for all men aged 18 and over is 44:30 h and for women 45:53 h for the entire week, giving women an increase of 1:23 h.[211] For fathers, on the other hand, we have a workload of 59:01 h and for mothers 58:42, i.e. an additional workload of 19 minutes for fathers.[212] This means that men have a total increase in stress that is 1 hour and 42 minutes higher than women as a result of parenthood. And the subdivisions of the German tables here are a bit impractical. In "All" there are fathers in it, so the difference is rather greater. As already said, to demand that men do more care work under these conditions is simply

---

[211] https://tinyurl.com/5yj2ycww
[212] https://tinyurl.com/3jw45p8m

intrusive, you can swap yes, but to increase the overall workload even further while they are already more burdened is more than questionable.

In general, care work shows that if men earn as much as their wives, they could more often swap work for care work. But for this to happen, you would also have to know again what the preferences of women and men are here, otherwise we send women into full-time work and, as studies have shown, this tends to make mothers unhappy.[213] [214] Care work seems to enjoy too little recognition, full-time is too stressful.

## Long-term consequences and systemic gaps

The unequal distribution of care work has real consequences: women are more often affected by **poverty in old age** because they reduce or interrupt gainful employment in favor of care work. In Germany, this is partly compensated for by pension points for child-raising periods – although, in my opinion, insufficiently. The current regulation (three years per first child, one year per additional child) ignores the fact that many parents are forced to take longer out of work due to a lack of daycare places. Reforms are urgently needed here that give greater financial and social recognition to child-rearing.

## Pragmatic reasons and choice of partner

A central driver of this structure is the **gender pay gap**: Since men earn more on average, it seems rational for them to stay in their jobs longer while women take on care tasks.

In addition, so-called *hypergamy comes* into play: many women prefer partners with higher incomes, which further consolidates the traditional division of labor. This raises the question of **individual responsibility**: If women consciously decide against patriarchal

---

[213] https://www.apa.org/news/press/releases/2011/12/working-moms
[214] https://tinyurl.com/3rew9sn8

patterns in their choice of partner, i.e. against *hypergamy*, they could undermine existing power structures.

## Conclusion: Personal responsibility in a systemic context

It is undeniable that women can play an active role in breaking socialization patterns – whether through confident salary negotiations, choosing equal partners, or delegating mental load. But this personal responsibility must not be misunderstood as a panacea. As long as systemic factors such as a lack of daycare places or cultural stigmas against "househusbands" exist, freedom of choice remains limited.

## The solution lies in a dual strategy:

- **Individual empowerment** through reflection and conscious life decisions.
- **Structural reforms:** The pursuit of equal parental leave or the expansion of social infrastructure.

## Mental Load

Mental load is a part of soft power and women aren't the first to have trouble giving up power or control. The *phenomenon is called* maternal gatekeeping.[215] [216] [217]

(The figures are based on the "American Time Use Survey" of 2023. However, the category "single" does not only include singles, but also includes couples living together. A comparison between childless people living alone and childless couples (whether in a relationship or marriage) would have been optimal. However, since only about a quarter of the sample falls under the category of "cohabiting couples," I suspect that the bias is not too great and that my basic statements are not significantly changed.)

---

[215] https://www.mother.ly/parenting/maternal-gatekeeping-why-moms-end-up-doing-it-all/
[216] https://pmc.ncbi.nlm.nih.gov/articles/PMC9977166/#S17
[217] https://scholarsarchive.byu.edu/facpub/4214/

# X. Media Representation and Empathy

The way in which media portray gender roles has a significant impact on societal prejudices.

## 1. Stereotyping[218]

Men are less likely than women to seek psychological help, even though they have a higher risk of suicide. This is partly due to the fact that they often do not recognize when they need help, use unhealthy coping strategies and avoid therapy. The main reason: traditional male gender norms prohibit emotional behavior, promote self-control and independence. Emotional vulnerability is often stigmatized in men and interpreted as weakness.

To counteract this, society should encourage men to question old role models. Regular conversations about feelings and mental health can help break the taboo on mental illness and normalize help. By encouraging emotional openness in a supportive environment, we enable men to communicate without shame or fear. In this way, a healthier way of dealing with emotions can be established in the long term.

## 2. Gender-Empathy-Bias

Another aspect is that male victims often experience less sympathy than female victims in the public perception. As a result, the needs of male victims of violence receive less attention, although they too can suffer significantly from the consequences of violence.[219]

This media portrayal contributes significantly to the fact that male victims remain invisible in society, while at the same time stereotypical gender roles are reproduced. This not only entrenches the image of men

---

[218] https://www.mybestself101.org/blog/encouraging-men-to-open-up
[219] https://www.sciencedirect.com/science/article/pii/S175606162300071X

as predominantly violent, but also reduces the public's willingness to seriously support male victims.

# XI. Health

April 7 is World Health Day – and the article published by ZDF on the subject looks as if it came from the archive of 1980: "Women are disadvantaged in medicine because research was primarily conducted on men."[220] Right, that was (hopefully) the state of affairs back then. But what about today?

A look at the Federal Ministry of Education and Research (BMBF) shows that predominantly male animals and cell cultures are still predominantly used in preclinical research, and women are often underrepresented in clinical studies as well. The result is a so-called gender data gap – i.e. a data gap that leads to a lack of knowledge about gender-specific disease progression. The BMBF explains that it has recognized this problem and wants to specifically promote gender-sensitive research.[221] But I can't find any concrete figures on the current situation.

The National Institutes of Health (NIH) in the USA – the world's largest source of funding for medical research – is different. It says: Around half of all study participants are women today.[222] A separate budget of over five billion dollars is available for women's studies for 2025 (forecast).[223] For men? No specific information.

---

[220] https://www.instagram.com/p/DIJCBP7tryr/
[221] https://tinyurl.com/37rv632h
[222] https://orwh.od.nih.gov/sex-as-biological-variable
[223] https://report.nih.gov/funding/categorical-spending#/

# 1. Historical background

Traditionally, research has been conducted primarily on male animals and male subjects to reduce cost and complexity. The female cycle requires additional adjustments, making research more expensive and time-consuming. In addition, more data is needed. For this reason, basic research is still mostly carried out with male animals, and experiments are usually carried out with men as well.

## NIH Inclusion Policy 1986

In 1986, the *National Institutes of Health* (*NIH*) first introduced a binding guideline that requires all *NIH-funded* clinical trials to include women and ethnic minorities, unless there is a medical-scientific exemption. This requirement was enshrined in law in the [224]NIH Revitalization Act *in 1993* to ensure consistent implementation.

In the years that followed, the proportion of women in approval studies increased significantly: an analysis of 36 New Drug Applications (1998–2000) showed that 52% of the subjects were female, which proves the success of the reform.[225]

## Stable representation over the last 25 years

Several meta-analyses show that the proportion of women in clinical trials has levelled off between 40% and 50% since the end of the 1990s. For example, the total proportion of female participants across 274 RCTs was 40% with 57,544 participants. Among them were 12 male-specific and 30 women-specific studies.[226] For the years 2016 to 2019, the figure is 41.2%.[227]

---

[224] https://orwh.od.nih.gov/including-women-and-minorities-in-clinical-research-background
[225] https://tinyurl.com/s9j2zwa2
[226] https://pmc.ncbi.nlm.nih.gov/articles/PMC10062729/
[227] https://www.sciencedirect.com/science/article/abs/pii/S1551714422000441

## Representation in the EU

A 2017 analysis of 300 EU RCTs found a median female rate of 41%.[228]

## Reasons why parity was not achieved[229]

The involvement of women in studies is complex for various reasons – for three central reasons in particular:

- "hormonal differences before and after menopause"
- "hormonal differences due to cycle and contraceptives"
- "Pregnancies"

Hormonal fluctuations in women can mean that study results are not directly comparable. To do justice to this, test subjects would have to be examined in subgroups with the same hormone status. However, this would require a significantly higher number of participants to prove efficacy and safety – a very complex and costly undertaking.

The debate about the gender data gap is often mistakenly equated with a women's quota in clinical trials, as if it were always about a 50:50 ratio of female and male participants. In fact, however, it is not scientifically expedient to aim for exactly the same gender proportions for every disease study, especially if the prevalence of the disease is strongly gender-differentiated. Rather, the gender distribution in study protocols should reflect the real sex distribution of the respective disease in order to achieve meaningful and relevant results. For example, it makes no sense to include men in breast cancer studies to the same extent as women or, conversely, in prostate cancer.

---

[228] https://trialsjournal.biomedcentral.com/articles/10.1186/s13063-022-07004-2
[229] https://www.quarks.de/gesundheit/medizin/gender-health-gap/

# 2. Life expectancy[230]

**Gender gap**

In the EU, women's life expectancy in 2023 was on average 5.3 years higher than that of men (women: 84.0 years vs. men: 78.7 years).

**Development and variation**

- Compared to the previous year, the average EU life expectancy increased from 80.6 to 81.4 years in 2023, but the gender gap remains.
- The differences vary in individual countries: in Latvia the gap was 10.1 years, in the Netherlands only 3 years.

**Main causes of death among men in the EU < 65[231]**

- **Ischemic heart disease:** 27.1 deaths per 100,000
- **Accidents:** 21.4 per 100,000
- **Lung cancer:** 18.0 per 100,000
- **Chronic liver disease:** 14.5 per 100,000
- **Suicide:** 13.8 per 100,000

**Women in comparison:**

- **Breast cancer** (12.0)
- **Lung cancer** (9.9)
- **Ischemic heart disease** (6,2)
- **Accidents** (5.1)
- **Krebs Colorectal** (5.1)

If we add up the top 5, this results in 94.8 for men and 38.3 for women.

---

[230] https://ec.europa.eu/eurostat/en/web/products-eurostat-news/w/ddn-20250314-3
[231] https://tinyurl.com/78cya9t9

**Risk factors**

- **Occupational hazards:** Men are more likely to work in high-risk sectors (construction, industry) and account for 96% of all fatal accidents at work, influenced by longer working hours and the use of machinery.[232]
- **Car accidents**
- **Risk behavior:** Higher prevalence of smoking, alcohol abuse and risky driving leads to more cardiovascular diseases and accidents.
- **Suicidal tendencies:** Men are less likely to seek psychological help, which multiplies the suicide rate – 10.2 per 100,000 – compared to women (3.7×).[233]
- **Health care:** Reduced participation in preventive examinations and mental health care increases delays in diagnostics and therapy.
- **Biology**

# 3. Research

- In the UK, 282 **male-only studies were submitted in the approval process** from 2019 to 2023, but only **169** female-specific studies.[234]
- **Women's Health Research:** NIH allocates approximately $5 billion explicitly to Women's Health Research for FY 2025 (10% of the NIH budget).[235]
- **Men's health at the NIH:** No independent funding program or designated budget. Men are financed through general studies, without a special funding line.
- **Women-oriented research:** In programs such as the "Gender Data Gap" funding call, the BMBF emphasises the urgency of continuing to close gender-specific data gaps – concrete means for

---

[232] https://ec.europa.eu/eurostat/web/products-eurostat-news/-/edn-20210428-1
[233] https://tinyurl.com/ya9cavj3
[234] https://tinyurl.com/mr26nrnm
[235] https://www.ncbi.nlm.nih.gov/books/NBK612400/

women are mentioned, for example in framework programs for gender-sensitive medicine.[236]

# 4. Body image, sport and pressure to perform

Society's ideas of masculinity are strongly linked to body ideals and pressure to perform. Especially through the media and social networks, specific expectations of the male appearance are reinforced.

**Ideal image and advertising**

In advertising, films and social media, the image of an extremely muscular, athletic and well-trained body often dominates as an ideal for men. This portrayal puts many men under pressure, as it suggests that attractiveness and social recognition depend on physical strength.

**Psychological pressure**

Striving for this ideal can have negative effects on mental health. Men are more likely to develop body dysmorphia (e.g., muscle dysmorphia, also known as "bigorexia"), eating disorders, or excessive fitness behavior in order to meet societal standards.

**Comparison with images of women**

While diversity in representation has been increasingly propagated for women in recent years (e.g. through plus-size models or body positivity campaigns), male body ideals often remain rigid. This discrepancy can lead to men perceiving their own body perception as inadequate and suffering even more from social expectations.

Overall, it can be seen that the pressure to perform conveyed by the media and society does not only affect women, but can also put a

---

[236] https://tinyurl.com/28xmc6kn

considerable strain on men – with sometimes serious psychological and health consequences.

# 5. *Toxic masculinity*:

The concept of *toxic masculinity* has become a central – and polarising – buzzword in the gender debate. While feminist currents use it as a tool to criticize harmful behavior patterns, it is rejected by many men. This defensive attitude is not merely an expression of sensitivity, but a structural problem of the discourse itself.

The term is not originally aimed at men as individuals, but at socially shaped norms that promote harmful behavior:

- Emotional oppression ("A man doesn't cry")
- Violence as conflict resolution
- Dominance as a status symbol

But in the public debate, this differentiation is often blurred. Instead of criticizing *"toxic behavior patterns,"* the impression arises that *"masculinity in itself is toxic."* This generalization triggers reactance – a psychological defense mechanism in which people react with defiance to accusations that are perceived as unjust.

## 5.1 The reproachful character

The way the topic is communicated often undermines its own goals:

- Language as a barrier: Terms such as "perpetrator group" or "patriarchal privileges" portray men as oppressors across the board
- Lack of empathy: Appeals such as "Men must change"
- The feminist bias: If the fight against toxic masculinity is primarily framed as a "women's issue", men do not feel part of the solution, but rather opponents

**Psychological dynamics:**

The self-affirmation theory explains why blanket criticism is counterproductive: People need a positive self-image. If their identity is labeled as a "problem" across the board, they react with defensiveness – for example, by identifying with extreme counter-models (e.g. "alpha male" influencers).

## 5.2 Alternatives

In order to integrate men constructively, a paradigm shift is needed:

**Precise language instead of blanket judgments**

Instead of talking about "toxic masculinity", the focus could be on "toxic expectations". The "Man Box" study[237] shows that men themselves are under pressure to meet certain norms:

- Guys should be strong, even if they feel anxious or nervous inside. 50 % (18-30); 55 % (31-45)
- A man who always talks about his worries, fears and problems should not really get respect. 30 % (18-30); 35 % (31-45)

By naming concrete patterns of behavior (instead of "masculinity"), you avoid defensive attitudes.

Make men visible as those affected, because toxic norms also harm men:

- Men commit suicide almost 3 times more often than women.[238]
- Over 90% of the prison population is male – often the result of violent socialization.[239]

---

[237] https://cdn.iss.org.au/wp-content/uploads/2024/02/05144735/The-Man-Box-2024-7.1-LR.pdf
[238] https://tinyurl.com/42kdsemy
[239] https://tinyurl.com/2uxsktub

## 5.3 Is masculinity only harmful?

First, I would like to point out that this does not constitute psychological counseling, nor that I would be qualified to do such a thing. The studies that I present do not have to present everything on the subject, nor have I checked whether they have not been refuted in the meantime. It is only intended to inform and if you feel addressed by it, I always advise you to talk to a specialist about what this could mean for you. What I am referring to can be seen in the linked video[240] and I will go into a bit of the data in the studies mentioned.

**Sex differences in the pathways to major depression: a study of opposite-sex twin pairs[241]**

Kendler and Gardner's study uses a twin design (opposite-sex dizygotic twin pairs) to analyze the different risk pathways that lead to the development of major depressive disorder. 20 development-related risk factors were examined. The results show that there are significant sex differences in about 60% of the pathways studied. Specifically, 11 of the 20 risk factors had a different influence on the likelihood of developing depression. Five factors (such as parental warmth, neuroticism, divorce, social support, and marital satisfaction) had a greater impact on women, while six factors—including childhood abuse (sexual abuse), behavioral disorders, substance abuse, a history of depression, and certain stress-related life events (especially financial, professional, and legal)—had a greater impact on men.

The conclusion of the study is that personality traits and problems in interpersonal relationships play a central role in the development of depression in women. In men, on the other hand, external behavioral problems and specific "instrumental" stressors (i.e. those related to the failure of life goals) are more prevalent. These results support the idea

---

[240] https://youtu.be/XBov_16F1GU?si=ymXjMzQI_PAjEsnr
[241] https://pubmed.ncbi.nlm.nih.gov/24525762/

that there are two different types of depression that vary from gender to gender.

## Meta-Analyses of the Relationship Between Conformity to Masculine Norms and Mental Health-Related Outcomes

The meta-analysis by Wong et al. (2017) examined the association between conformity to 11 traditional masculinity norms and mental health or help-seeking behavior. Effect sizes were classified as small, medium, or not significant.

### The 11 norms of masculinity and their effects

### Winning

- Negative mental health: Small effect (e.g. stress due to pressure to perform).
- Help-seeking behavior: Medium negative effect (lower willingness to undergo therapy).

### Emotional Control (suppressing emotions)

- Negative mental health: Small effect (e.g., inner conflicts).
- Positive mental health: Negative small effect (lower life satisfaction).
- Help-seeking behavior: Medium negative effect (strong avoidance of help).

### Risk-Taking

- Negative mental health: Small effect (e.g., increased risk of addiction).
- Positive mental health: Small effect (paradoxical self-efficacy experiences).

## Violence

- Negative mental health: Small effect (e.g., tendency to aggression).
- Help-seeking behavior: Small negative effect (stigmatization of therapies).

## Dominance

Negative mental health: Small effect (e.g., relationship conflicts).

## Playboy (Promiscuity)

- Negative mental health: Small to medium effect (e.g., loneliness).
- Help-seeking behavior: No significant effect.

## Self-Reliance

- Negative mental health: Small to medium effect (e.g., social isolation).
- Positive mental health: Negative medium effect (low social connectedness).
- Help-seeking behavior: Medium negative effect (rejection of support).

## Primacy of Work

No significant effect on mental health or seeking help.

## Power Over Women

- Negative mental health: Small effect (e.g., relationship stress).
- Help-seeking behavior: Medium negative effect (low therapy acceptance).

## Disdain for Homosexuals

Help-seeking behavior: Medium negative effect (avoidance of "weak" behaviors).

## Pursuit of Status

No significant effect on mental health.

If I understood correctly, this is only about internalizing the norm. Living out the norm is not taken into account here. In the following video, other things are also addressed.[242] It would also be interesting to compare it with data from patriarchal societies to see whether these characteristics have a different effect in a less hostile society.

# 5.4 Conclusion

However, one open question remains: If men stop sacrificing themselves socially for deadly, dangerous, physically demanding or harmful work – who will take over these tasks? The construction industry, the skilled trades or rescue services, in other countries the extraction of resources still plays an important role, are often based on this traditional role. If the concept of male self-sacrifice were to disappear, we could face a fundamental social challenge: Who will do the jobs in the future that no one wants to do?

# 6. Therapy

Men's mental health suffers from specific societal expectations:

## Therapy offers

- Many therapeutic concepts and counselling services are primarily aimed at women, so that men often find less suitable support.[243]

---

[242] https://youtu.be/XBov_16F1GU?si=p84lXAviHpYaZ_VY
[243] https://www.continuingedcourses.net/active/courses/course040.php

**Emotional openness**

- Traditional role models prescribe men to always be strong and reserved. This expectation often prevents them from seeking help in time for mental health problems.[244] [245]

These factors lead to men being disadvantaged in their handling of psychological stress and in the use of therapy services.

# 7. The treatment-prevalence paradox[246] [247] [248]

## 7.1 Prevalence does not appear to have decreased

### Increase in false positives

- Normal stress or sadness is now more commonly diagnosed as depression.
- As a result, the number of cases is rising "artificially".

### Actual increase in new cases (incidence)

- There are more initial diagnoses today, e.g. due to social stress, loneliness, pressure to perform, etc.
- This increase could "overshadow" the effect of better therapies.

These two explanations find little empirical support: There is no strong evidence that either misdiagnoses or actual incidences have increased significantly.

---

[244] https://introspectioncounseling.com/what-are-mens-issues-in-therapy/
[245] https://tinyurl.com/4cafuejs
[246] https://pubmed.ncbi.nlm.nih.gov/34959153/
[247] https://pubmed.ncbi.nlm.nih.gov/37755928/
[248] https://pubmed.ncbi.nlm.nih.gov/38996078/

## 7.2 The treatments don't work as well as you might think:

### Overestimated effectiveness (publication bias, methodological weaknesses)

- Studies exaggerate the effect sizes (especially through selective publication, weak comparison groups).
- Short-term effects are better documented than long-term relapse prevention.

### Lower effectiveness in everyday life (reality of care)

What works in clinical trials often doesn't work in "real life":

- Less experienced therapists
- Crashes
- Lack of resources
- Inadequate diagnostics

### Non-targeted expansion of treatment

Many treatments mainly reach mild or one-off cases, not the chronically recurrent patients, who strongly influence the statistics.

### Insufficient relapse prevention

- Even if acute treatments work, relapses remain frequent.
- Relapse prevention is often less effective and under-implemented.

**Iatrogenic (treatment-related) damage:**

Treatments themselves can have negative effects, such as dependence on antidepressants, emotional blunting, or deterioration from incorrect interventions.

The authors argue that most of the explanatory power for the paradox lies in the following points:

- Effective therapies exist, but they do not systematically reach the most important patient groups (e.g. with chronic recurrent depression),
- they are not implemented in practice with the same quality as in studies,
- and the effect sizes in studies are exaggerated.

In addition, it is emphasized that a real decrease in depression in the population cannot be achieved through therapy alone, but through:

- better prevention
- Early intervention
- Structural promotion of mental health
- and, if necessary, the use of lay therapists or digital services to improve care.


# XII. Violence

Bernhard Bogerts reports in the SWR report that 98% of the population basically lives violence-free – which is proven by numerous studies involving tens of thousands of participants, as he explains in his book "Where does violence come from?". According to the study, only about 2% of people show a tendency to commit acts of violence. If, on the other hand, we look exclusively at people with mental illness, the proportion of those who are prone to violence is around 4%. Although 96% of the mentally ill also live without violence, the risk of committing acts of violence among them is twice as high as in the general population. A study by the University of Helsinki in Sweden even points to a three to four times increased risk among mentally ill people.[249]

Peter Döge gives an alternative figure: According to this, around 70% of men and women live violence-free. It is important to emphasize that violence does not play a role in the vast majority of the population, so that only just under a third of people are classified as violent.[250]

Note: I think the discrepancy between the numbers comes from the fact that Bogerts speaks of a psychological inclination, while Döge means actual violence.

# 1. Violence against men[251]

Coxell et al. (1996) described sexualized violence against men as a comparatively young field of research – not because this form of violence is actually rare, but because the assumption that reports by male victims are not credible (especially in the case of female perpetrators) has long hampered research. Accordingly, there is still a lack of reliable studies (Coxell et al. 1996, pp. 380–381). This criticism is often repeated to this day. However, a mere keyword search in specialist databases shows that there is quite a lot of research on sexualized violence in the English-speaking world – but less than 5% of it is dedicated to male victims. In German-speaking countries, the proportion is even lower: studies on men account for less than 0.1% of all papers. A closer look also reveals fragmentation and selectivity: In the English-speaking world, for example, there are numerous studies on rape of male victims as well as on myths, prejudices and the perception of male rape victims.

---

[249] https://tinyurl.com/yp4xkddd
[250] https://www.vaeter-zeit.de/vaeter-maenner/maennergewalt-gewalt-gegen-jungen.php
[251] https://tinyurl.com/mrxnynau

# 2. Murder and manslaughter[252]

| Sacrifice | Men | Women |
|-----------|-----|-------|
| completed | 337 | 339 |
| attempted | 1.595 | 587 |

| Offender | Men | Women |
|----------|-----|-------|
| from 21 | 1943 | 293 |

This means that women make up 50.15% of the victims in completed cases. Attempted homicides, on the other hand, are disproportionately experienced by men at 73.09%. On the offender side, women represent 13.09% of suspects aged 21 and over.

### Infanticide[253]

Infanticide is the only homicide in which women are disproportionately often the perpetrators. The proportion of perpetrators by mothers is between 65 and 100%, depending on the age of the child.

The specialist literature distinguishes:

- **Neoaticides**: Killing on the first day of life (almost always by the mother)
- **Infanticides**: Killed in the first year of life (≈ 80% by the mother)

---

[252] https://tinyurl.com/3br8z5ey
[253] https://tinyurl.com/4ft6ucss

- **Filizide**: Killed between the ages of 2 and 14 ($\approx$ 65–75%)

**Neoaticides** are usually committed by very young, overwhelmed mothers who became pregnant unintentionally and suppressed the pregnancy or kept it secret. The birth occurs secretly, often at home, and the newborn is then suffocated, drowned or disposed of (e.g. in garbage cans). In some cases, mothers keep the baby corpses in their environment (e.g. in the freezer or in flower pots). In extreme cases, several bodies are found.

**Data for 2020 (Germany):**

- A total of 152 infanticides
- Of which 30 neonaticides
- Human rights organization Terre des Hommes speaks of 20–30 neonaticides per year[254]

**Psychological problems (filizides)[255]**

Mothers were significantly more likely than fathers to have a history of mental disorders (66% vs. 27%) and were more likely to suffer from symptoms (53% vs. 23%) at the time of the crime, mostly affective disorders. Schizophrenia or delusional disorders were present in 17% of the mothers; a total of 8% had a schizophrenia diagnosis. At the time of the crime, 37% of the mothers were mentally ill. 20% had already been treated before, 12% within the last year before the crime.

**Infanticide in the USA**

**Filicide in the U.S. (1976–2007):[256]**

- 500 cases every year

---

[254] https://tinyurl.com/4n5nhp6c
[255] https://pubmed.ncbi.nlm.nih.gov/23593128/
[256] https://www.sciencedaily.com/releases/2014/02/140225122423.htm

- Almost three-quarters (72%) of the children killed were six years old or younger.
- One third of the victims were infants (under one year of age).
- Only about 10% of the children killed were between 7 and 18 years old.
- The rest of the victims were adult descendants.
- Boys were 58.3% more likely to be victims than girls.
- About 11% of the children killed were stepchildren (compared to 10-20% of all U.S. children living with a stepparent). In fact, the proportion is disproportionate – contrary to the claim in the source. If 10 to 20 percent of all children live with a stepparent, that means that only about 5 to 10 percent of parents are stepparents, as children usually live with two parents if they have stepparents. Comparing this proportion with the 11 percent of victims who were stepchildren reveals an overrepresentation. To put it simply: If 100 percent of all children lived with a stepparent and only stepparents killed their children, no one would seriously claim that this was evenly distributed.
- Father was accused in 57.4 % of the cases

## Underestimation of Infant Abuse Mortality in the United States[257]

From 1985 to 1996, it was estimated that 9,467 homicides of U.S. children under the age of 11 were due to abuse – instead of the reported 2,973 cases.

## Underascertainment of Child Maltreatment (1990–1998)[258]

Only half of the children who died as a result of abuse had the cause of death coded as abuse on the death certificate.

---

[257] https://jamanetwork.com/journals/jama/fullarticle/190980
[258] https://tinyurl.com/59rv9sfb

- 81 neonaticides in 10 years → about 8 per year
- 2,851 infanticides → approx. 285 per year
- Exact distributions of perpetrators are not mentioned, but in general the text is very political: after the first day of life, infanticide can occur in connection with young parenthood, frustration of the caregiver, maternal mental illness, the elimination of an unwanted child or abuse or neglect; depending on the context, the murder can be committed by the mother, the mother's male partner, or the infant's biological father.
- The death of an infant can be misclassified on the death certificate or go undetected, leading to possible under- or over-reporting of infanticides. The lack of precise pathological markers for live births or for determining the cause of death can lead to errors in the coding of the mode of death.

Neonaticides are 8 per year, while in Germany we have 20–30 with only a quarter of the population. Maybe they end up in infanticides because of some definitions.

## 3. Sexual offenses

Sexual violence is one of the pillars to which feminism shows structural violence against women. The narrative of 97, 98 or 99% male perpetrators in the area of sexual violence is also supported by German BKA statistics. Suspects in Germany for 2023 (rape, sexual assault and sexual assault): 7,648 men and 118 women make up 98.4% of male suspects.[261] On the victim side, we have 680 men and 11,617 women. Makes a proportion of 5.5% male victims.

---

[259] https://journals.sagepub.com/doi/abs/10.1177/19253621221077870
[260] https://www.cdc.gov/mmwr/volumes/69/wr/mm6939a1.htm/
[261] https://tinyurl.com/9xdekffu

Sexual offenses are often perceived as typically male crimes. However, the police data is not always representative of the real situation. Men are less likely to report when they become victims, or female perpetrators are (almost) excluded by definition. In Germany, it is a bit different from, for example, in the USA and UK, where you need a penis to be able to rape.

*The Tin Men* has taken a closer look at the figures for the US for rape.[262] While the initial situation spoke of 98.5% male perpetrators in rape, 65.6% to 69.7% male perpetrators in forced sex are found when evaluating the CDC report.

This seems a bit unusual, so the CDC's figures are looked at more closely: (last 12 months)[263]

## Rape

- Women 2,857,000 victims
  - ➢ Male offenders 97.7% → 2,791,289
  - ➢ Female offenders: 2.3% → 65,711
- Men: 340,000 victims
  - ➢ Male offenders 71.9 % → 244,460
  - ➢ Female offenders: 28.1% → 95,540

## Made to penetrate

- Men: 1,562,000 victims
  - ➢ Female offenders: 83.8 % → 1,308,956
  - ➢ Male offenders 16.2% → 253,044

So we have 4,759,000 victims or cases and 1,470,207 female perpetrators, making a share of 30.89%. That doesn't fit exactly, but comes close to his cause. His estimate is probably better, because I

---

[262] https://www.instagram.com/p/DJWXygbIt_K/?img_index=1
[263] https://www.cdc.gov/nisvs/documentation/nisvsReportonSexualViolence.pdf

completely ignored the fact that there is a category for both sexes as perpetrators, for which no information has been provided.

In Germany, according to § 177 para. 6, penis does not seem to be a necessary condition, but penetration is an "in particular": "in particular if they are associated with penetration into the body (rape)". Here, too, the passive form, i.e. the female equivalent, seems to be missing. However, I didn't study law, I can't explain what that means exactly.

## Sexual assault according to the CDC report (last 12 months)

### Female victims

- Male offenders 96.4% → 4,471,000
- Female offenders 3.6% → 167,000

(This is not entirely true, a small proportion of the 3.6% could also have both sexes as perpetrators, but this is not specified.)

### Male victims

- Male offenders 13.6% → 311,000
- Female offenders 83.6% → 1,908,000
- Both 2.8% → 64,000

### Altogether

- Male perpetrators 4,846,000
- Female perpetrators 2,139,000

The female proportion of perpetrators here is 30.6%.

## Unwanted sexual contact (last 12 months)

### Female victims

- Male offenders 92.6% → 6,076,000

- Female offenders 7.4% → 486,000

## Male victims

- Male offenders 26.1 % → 932,000
- Female offenders 70.5 % → 2,519,000
- Both 3.4% → 121,000

## Altogether

- Male perpetrators 7,129,000
- Female perpetrators 3,126,000

The female proportion of perpetrators here is 30.6%.

When it comes to the question of why men do this more often, there is again a dispute between socialization and biology. The biological perspective refers, among other things, to the sex drive as a factor. A meta-analysis from 2022 looked at 211 studies on this and says men have a stronger sex drive at the effect size 0.69, which is medium to strong.[264] Another point is again the *greater-male variability*. Studies have shown that 35.7% of perpetrators of sexual offenses have an IQ below 75 and what is true for the upper range of IQs is also true for the lower range due to the normal distribution. An IQ of 75, in combination with variability, would therefore lead to a similar distribution of 2 to 1 as can be observed in our figures. However, the 35.7% suggests that the average IQ is closer to 80. However, this does not change the fact that the largest discrepancy in quantity between male and female perpetrators can be explained biologically here.[265] If we mirror the 35.7%, then it is heading towards 71.4%, which could be explained approximately , but there are numerous restrictions to consider here. What this means purely hypothetically is that if the IQ variance were

---

[264] https://pubmed.ncbi.nlm.nih.gov/36227317/
[265] https://www.tandfonline.com/doi/pdf/10.3402/vgi.v3i0.14834

purely socialization-related and could be completely reduced, then the ratio of perpetrators could drop to as low as 54.8% men vs. 45.2% women. This corresponds roughly to the ratio we observe in the case of physically violence against children that is relevant under criminal law.

In addition, the source also points out the linguistic problems of the perpetrators and that a lack of education is not very helpful. Reducing the school drop-out rate and **reading support programs,** especially for boys, **could** therefore be helpful **here**.

It is also interesting that one in four has an IQ below 70 and if language problems, reduced social skills and or school/professional problems are added, then we can speak of "people with an intellectual impairment", which is a medical and legal disability.

Other sources speak of 19.1% that meet the conditions.[266] On the other hand, they are also more likely to be victims.[267]

## Barriers and Facilitators for Sexual Trauma Disclosure in Boys and Men: A Systematic Review[268]

### Gender-specific socialization and barriers to disclosure

Sexual abuse/rape is often associated with strong feelings of shame in boys and men, in part because these acts violate traditional male norms of physical strength, dominance, stoicism, autonomy, agency, and heterosexuality, as such experiences inevitably involve feelings of fear, powerlessness, and loss of control. This illustrates why direct questioning can be particularly difficult for men.

---

[266] https://tinyurl.com/mreyzzsh
[267] https://en.wikipedia.org/wiki/Sexual_abuse_and_intellectual_disability
[268] https://journals.sagepub.com/doi/10.1177/1524838025132521 0?int.sj-abstract.similar-articles.8

## Myths about male rape

The text mentions: Established myths about male rape include beliefs such as: boys and men cannot experience rape, only gay boys and men experience rape, boys and men are unaffected by rape, and physiological arousal necessarily indicates consent to sexual acts. These myths contribute to underreporting and necessitate sensitive survey approaches.

## Low disclosure rates and delays

Compared to girls and women, boys and men are more inclined not to turn to their social environment, the police or health care professionals. Estimates suggest that boys and men reveal their experiences with an average delay of 15–20 years. This further underlines how difficult it is to get men to disclose directly.

## Lack of appropriate support services and expertise among professionals

These factors are exacerbated by the lack of adequate support services and a lack of expertise among professionals. This implies that existing support systems are often not sufficiently geared to absorb revelations from men and therefore require more indirect or specially tailored approaches.

## What do German dark field studies say?

The SKiD 2020[269] says in essence: In the case of assault and sexual offences, the gender of the perpetrators is usually known. The majority of these offences are committed by men: 91.1% of bodily injuries and 95.2% of sexual offences. Women are much less likely to be suspected of these offences – their share is 8.1% and 3.0% respectively.

---

[269] https://tinyurl.com/25w7jubb

3% vs. 30% is of course a significant difference. But where does it come from? However, cultural factors alone do not seem to fully explain this significant difference, even if women in the U.S. have about 5% higher rates of criminally relevant intimate partner violence, for example, but this could also be due to a broader definition of what falls under intimate partner violence.

I have basically already hinted at another possibility here in advance.

- The recording of victim experiences through general trauma questionnaires is less successful than through questionnaires specially adapted for sexual violence.[270]
- It is probably not easy for anyone to talk about their victim experience, but men find it particularly difficult.[271]
- Questions in SkiD 2020 do not seem to be particularly sensitized, because as I understand it, one should not ask about "**victims of sexual** violence" or rape. However, the questions in the SKiD looked something like this:
  i.   *"I was sexually harassed or the victim of a sexual assault."*[272]
  ii.  *"Someone sexually abused or raped me."*

- The CDC NISVS under *Limitation*, on the other hand, states in essence: Secondly, there are differences in the methodology between the NISVS and other surveys, for example in the sample design, the language and terminology used, and the context in which respondents are asked the questions about victimization. NISVS uses various techniques to increase participants' well-being and encourage openness to share their experiences, such as a tiered, comprehensive consent process, a safety plan, and the use of interviewers who are specifically trained to conduct interviews on

---

[270] https://pmc.ncbi.nlm.nih.gov/articles/PMC10732194/
[271] https://pubmed.ncbi.nlm.nih.gov/26934546/
[272] https://tinyurl.com/yc7njjjy

sensitive topics. These measures are explained in more detail in the Summary Report 2010.

Whether the CDC's measures really make such a difference that they explain a difference of 3% vs. 30% for female offenders, of course, cannot be said without testing.

**Violence in the family and in the close social environment[273]**

In Austria, another study comes to 45 per 1000 female offenders vs. 122 per 1000 male offenders, which results in a share of about 26.9%. The questions looked something like this:

- "Someone touched or caressed me intimately, even though I said or showed that I didn't want to."
- "Someone entered my body against my will with a penis or something else."

The 27% is not representative of Austria, there is no offsetting on demographics, etc. I just wanted to see in which direction it goes.

# 4. Intimate partner violence (IPA)

Intimate partner violence is a central issue on which feminism shows structural violence against women.

Every year, the new figures on intimate partner violence are published, which report about 80% female victims.[274]

## 4.1 Dynamics of violence in partnerships

But let's also take a closer look at the dynamics of violence in partnerships, for example through "Differences in Frequency of Violence

---

[273] https://uscholar.univie.ac.at/detail/o:1162297
[274] https://www.hilfetelefon.de/aktuelles/weiter-steigende-zahlen-im-bereich-haeusliche-gewalt/

and Reported Injury Between Relationships With Reciprocal and Nonreciprocal Intimate Partner Violence".[275] The study comes from the USA and was done in 2007, so it is no longer relevant, but it gives an insight into the dynamics of intimate partner violence, which is hardly communicated in the media or by feminism.

Important findings from the study on the frequency of mutual (reciprocal) and one-sided (non-reciprocal) partner violence:

- Prevalence of violence in relationships: Violence occurred in almost 24% of the relationships studied.
- Distribution of reciprocal and non-reciprocal violence: Of the violent relationships, **49.7% were characterized by mutual violence.**
- Gender-specific distribution of perpetrators in non-reciprocal violence: In cases of unilateral violence, **more than 70% of the assaults were committed by women.**

**Initiation of violence:**

- Several studies suggest that both men and women initiate violence.
- For example, 66% of adolescents surveyed in violent relationships reported that both partners started violence at least once, and in the National Family Violence Survey, each partner initiated the violence at least 40% of the time.

**Relationship between reciprocity and frequency of violence:**

- Among women, mutual violence was associated with a higher frequency of assaults.
- In men, there was no significant correlation between mutual violence and the frequency of assaults.

**Injury:**

---

[275] https://pmc.ncbi.nlm.nih.gov/articles/PMC1854883/

- Men caused injuries more often than women.
- Mutual violence was generally associated with a higher risk of injury than one-sided violence, regardless of the gender of the perpetrator.

In addition, the study of community samples showed that only a relatively small percentage of women reported self-defense as the primary motive for violence. These findings suggest that self-defense cannot fully explain the phenomenon of reciprocal violence.

Implications for prevention strategies: The type of violence (mutual vs. one-sided) is a strong predictor of the occurrence of injuries. Prevention approaches should therefore address the escalation of partner violence, especially in cases of mutual violence.

Other studies, such as that of Michael P. Johnson (2008), suggest that power as a motive for intimate partner violence – i.e. the effort to control and dominate the partner – occurs in both men and women, with men dominating it.[276] But we'll go into that in more detail in a moment, because he doesn't agree with his colleague (that men dominate it).

According to these figures, it can also be estimated that 76.7% of female victims of intimate partner violence are also perpetrators.

Invoice:

- Perpetrators and victims: 49.7%
- Only perpetrators: 50.3 % - women 70 % and men 30 %
- 49.7% / ([50.3% x 30%] + 49.7% = 76.7%
- 49.7 % / ([50.3 % x 70 %] + 49.7 %) = 58.5 %

Among male victims, on the other hand, the figure is 58.5%. These figures show that most victims are also perpetrators and that our simplified apportionment of blame does not quite do justice to the reality of life. In addition, it also shows that ignoring male victims and setting

---

[276] https://tinyurl.com/2bhf6v9e

up shelters is not doing women any favors either, because it obstructs the possibility that men can step out of the toxic spiral of violence when they have reached their limit.

A German study also found a high overlap. 54% of men have been victims, 55% have been perpetrators.[277]

Other sources: The source is an overview of the current state of research from 2024. The results are not very different from what I have shown here. 52.8 % on both sides. In 31.4% of cases, violence is perpetrated by women and in 16.9% by men. The 2012 summary, with which we compare here, also came to similar conclusions.[278]

Perhaps someone knows of other sources that speak of 30% to 40% male victims. For example, the source linked under No. 8 even speaks of 43%.[279] Aren't the findings contradictory? Not really. These studies tend to look at criminally relevant violence, while the one shown is based on a broader definition of violence. An example would be the next chapter.

Just to put this into context again, these research results have been available for over 40 years, albeit rarely, because the focus is more on male perpetrators and for 40 years the federal government has not managed to provide places for male victims. For 40 years, we have had an increasingly good idea of what the dark field of intimate partner violence looks like and that men do not necessarily have to be portrayed as the primary perpetrators. Nevertheless, every year we get the crime statistics with about 80% male perpetrators presented without comment. This is also criticized from time to time in the press, as here in 2010 in Der Spiegel.[280]

---

[277] https://www.maennergewaltschutz.de/neuigkeiten/kfn-studie-maenner-partnerschaftsgewalt/
[278] https://tinyurl.com/55d5rcbx
[279] https://tinyurl.com/wfmy9hfr
[280] https://tinyurl.com/ym6pv3n4

## 4.2 Discourse Battle & Meta-Analyses Crossover

Many studies in the field of intimate partner violence use the Conflict Tactics Scales (CTS), but they have been criticized for not adequately capturing the context, motivation, and severity of the violence. Critics argue that CTS does not take into account important aspects such as control behavior and sexual violence, so let's take a closer look at other aspects.

### 4.2.1 Langhinrichsen-Rolling 2009[281]

Actually, it's primarily about the next 3 studies, but let's still take a look at how the abstract summarizes the study:

- Diversity of IPV types: There is clearly more than one type of intimate partner violence.
- Central role of gender and male perpetration in controlling violence: The "feminists are right" – gender is of central importance for the analysis of intimate partner violence.
- Adaptation of models to IPV types: The different types of intimate partner violence have different causes, development paths and consequences. Therefore, different models are also needed to understand them.
- Need for qualitative research: More qualitative research is needed, especially on the least understood forms of intimate partner violence: violent resistance and situational couple violence.

### 4.2.2 RE: Langhinrichsen-Rolling 2010

It is an answer in the sense of a correction by Michael Johnson. Johnson argues that understanding control is crucial to distinguish the different forms of violence and to develop effective intervention strategies.

---

[281] https://psycnet.apa.org/record/2010-06192-009

Here are the key points for control:

## Coercive control as the core of the concept of "domestic violence"

- Johnson emphasizes that most people understand "domestic violence" to be coercive, controlling violence.
- This form of violence, which feminist theorists and activists have long denounced, is primarily perpetrated by men against their female partners, according to his analysis.

## Johnson's Control-Based Typology of IPV

Johnson distinguishes three main types of intimate partner violence, with the role of control being the defining characteristic:

- So-called "intimate terrorism" is a form of intimate partner violence in which the perpetrator deliberately combines physical violence with different, systematic control and power techniques in order to gain control over the partner. In heterosexual relationships, this type is mainly perpetrated by men. This form of violence is ongoing, systematic and more likely to lead victims to seek help or suffer injuries.
- Violent Resistance: This is the violence perpetrated by the women (and a few men) who are trapped in a relationship with an "Intimate Terrorist". It is a reaction to the partner's compulsive attempt to control.
- Situational Couple Violence: These are disputes that escalate into verbal and possibly physical aggression. It does not include a general pattern of compulsive control. The escalation can have various causes, such as anger management problems, communication difficulties or substance abuse. Surveys often show a gender-symmetrical distribution of perpetrator roles in this form of violence.

## Discrepancy between sample types and the role of control

144

- **Agency samples** : Studies using data from authorities (police, courts, hospitals, women's shelters) show that IPV in heterosexual relationships is largely perpetrated by men. This is because "intimate terrorism" (the controlling form of violence) leads to seeking help, injuries, and official attention.
- **General** Samples: Studies based on general population surveys often show that IPV is roughly gender-symmetrical in terms of perpetration. Johnson argues that this is a bias, as "intimate terrorists" and their partners do not participate in such surveys for fear of consequences or revenge. These surveys therefore mainly cover "Situational Couple Violence", for which there is no systematic control.

### Criticism of the "gender symmetry" debate

- Johnson criticizes that advocates of gender symmetry in IPV ignore the data from "Agency Samples" and the distinction between "Intimate Terrorism" and "Situational Couple Violence".
- He emphasizes that even in studies that find gender symmetry in terms of the frequency of acts of violence, men's violence tends to cause more physical injuries, negative psychological consequences, and more anxiety among victims. The mere counting of acts of violence without taking into account the context of control and the effects is misleading.

### Importance of Control-Based Typologies

Johnson reaffirms the validity of his and other typologies based on control. He argues that these distinctions are essential to advance analyses and develop **effective interventions**, as different forms of violence have different causes, dynamics, and consequences.

In summary, the text emphasizes the central importance of "coercive control" in understanding the complexity of intimate partner violence. He argues that the most serious and well-understood form of domestic violence – "intimate terrorism" – is mainly perpetrated by men and is characterized by systematic control. Other forms of violence that appear to be gender-symmetrical in general surveys are mostly "situational couple violence", which lacks such a control pattern.

## 4.2.3 Langhinrichsen-Rohling 2012[282] (Motives for IPV)

Langhinrichsen-Rohling's text is a comprehensive overview of motivations for the practice of intimate partner violence (IPV) in men and women. The concept of "control" plays a central role as one of the motivation categories examined.

Here are the main points that the text emphasizes regarding "control":

### "Power/control" as a central motivational category

- In their review, the authors summarized empirical data from 74 articles (75 samples) and coded the motives into seven broad categories. "Power/Control" is one of them.
- It was one of the most commonly measured motivations in the studies examined (76% of the samples dealt with it).
- Theoretically, it is believed that aggressors could use violence with the expectation of gaining an advantage, such as "regaining a sense of power or control".

### Discussion about gender differences in motive for control:

- An important and controversial question was whether the motives for exercising physical IPV differ between men and women.
- **Traditional assumption:** It is often assumed that men's violence serves to subjugate women and keep them in a position of vulnerability and powerlessness (i.e., to exert control). Accordingly, women would commit violence mainly in self-defense.

---

[282] https://tinyurl.com/299tkseu

**Results of the review**

- Only 18 of the 75 studies examined (24%) contained data that allowed a direct gender comparison of the stated motivations.
- Among these studies, very few gender-specific motives for the perpetration of violence were identified, although the authors urge caution, as methodological and measurement challenges as well as significant heterogeneity of the studies make direct comparisons difficult.
- Criticism of previous reviews: They criticize previous reviews (e.g., Malloy et al., 2003; Swan et al., 2008), who, despite limited studies, concluded that men mainly use IPV to control their partners and women for self-defense. The present, more comprehensive review suggests that these earlier conclusions may have been premature or not sufficiently supported by the data.

**Heterogeneity of motives in both sexes:**

- The review expected and found that there may be **multiple motivations** for exercising physical violence among both men and women , not just "power/control" or "self-defense." These include the expression of negative emotions (anger), communication difficulties, retaliation or jealousy.
- This supports the idea that there is **heterogeneity** among perpetrators, suggesting that different types of interventions may be needed that address psychological issues and relationship-specific concerns, rather than relying solely on gender-specific approaches.

In summary, Langhinrichsen-Rohling et al. identify "power/control" as a common and important motive for exercising IPA. However, their comprehensive review challenges the common assumption that "power/control" is a predominantly male motive and "self-defense" is a predominantly female motive. They find little empirical support for pronounced gender differences in motives for acts of violence and emphasize the need to recognize the diversity of motivations in both sexes in order to develop more effective interventions.

## 4.2.4 Langhinrichsen blank 2012[283] (bidirectional IPA)

This review compared 48 studies (from 1990 onwards) and an earlier meta-analysis to find out how often violence in relationships is seriously bidirectional (both partners are involved) versus unidirectional (male → female or female → male only). The most important points:

Bidirectional violence is common: in all types of samples (from large population surveys to court data), it is normal for both partners to use violence.

### Different patterns by context

- **Everyday community samples:** Often more female lone perpetrators (e.g. out of frustration or communication explosion).
- **Crime statistics:** More often that men dominate the violence, because only cases reported by the police end up here.
- **Couples from minority backgrounds:** Bisexual, lesbian and gay couples had similar rates of unidirectional and bidirectional violence as heterosexual couples – no "male dominance" trend was seen here.
- **Race/ethnicity:** According to some studies, African-American couples had higher rates of bidirectional violence, but this is strongly correlated with socioeconomic stress.

### Power/Control Dynamics in Comparison

If one examines these studies according to *coercive control,* then strong power patterns are more likely to emerge in cases where the use of force was one-sided. At most, about 5–10% of the couples showed real "mutual violent control" (both partners systematically try to

---

[283] https://psycnet.apa.org/record/2012-19696-004

dominate the other with power). The vast majority of bidirectional violence is situational: that is, both argue, one then calls back violently, both escalate, and there are fisticuffs from both sides – but not because both want to exercise power at all costs.

### Man vs. Woman – Overall, Most Data Shows

- Women are not "automatic victims", but also strike back in conflicts – especially in situations where they feel overwhelmed or emotionally pressured.
- Systematic exercise of power by men (e.g. physical or psychological control over longer periods of time) is mainly found in cases that are being dealt with legally.
- However, surveys of the general population show that women develop similar aggressive impulses as men under comparable stress – and that both sexes often fall into reactive escalation patterns.

## 4.2.5 Review of Risk Factors for IPV 2012[284]

This review (over 228 studies) specifically collected risk factors for intimate partner violence (IPV).

### Risk factors that affect men and women differently:

- **Demographic/social factors:** low income, unemployment, low level of education. Men with such backgrounds are more likely to commit physical IPV acts; Women in a similar situation are more likely to have higher rates of psychological violence.
- **Developmental/behavioral factors:** Youth violence, aggressive peer groups → has a stronger effect on later IPV propensity in men; in women, violence experienced at an early age, poor parent-child bonding and psychological problems often play a greater role.

---

[284] https://pmc.ncbi.nlm.nih.gov/articles/PMC3384540/

- **Relationship influences:** Stressful partnerships, role conflicts, poor communication, → contribute to IPV in both sexes, but men are more likely to escalate these conflicts with physical violence, while women tend to react first with withdrawal or emotional violence.

- **Measurement:** Most studies (62%) use the Conflict Tactics Scale (CTS) to measure IPV. While many studies used to look only at men versus women, significantly more bidirectional data has been collected since 2005.

- **Developmental direction:** Since most studies (61% adults, 55% adolescents) are cross-sectional data, it is only possible to say to a limited extent whether the risk (e.g. depression, antisocial behavior) was there first or a consequence of violence. However, it is often assumed that severe emotional problems precede IPV incidents – especially in men.

## 4.2.6 Risk Factors Review 2018[285]

This overview has brought together 22 meta-analyses, each of which evaluated a wide variety of risk factors for violence (not only IPV, but violence as a whole). Key points:

- **Neuropsychiatric causes at the top:** Mental disorders were most strongly associated with acts of violence – especially addictions (such as alcohol/drug abuse) and antisocial personality disorder. In the case of substance problems, the proportion of violence in the population is roughly 14.8% (PAF – Population Attributable Fraction).

- **Experiences of violence in childhood:** Experiencing or observing violence as a child has a similar weight (PAF 12.2%). These early traumas have a strong impact on the potential for violence later on.

---

[285] https://pmc.ncbi.nlm.nih.gov/articles/PMC6157722/

- Although control and dominance behavior is discussed as a relevant predictor in the context of intimate partner violence, it does not appear among the five risk factors with the highest population relevance (PAF) in this umbrella review. Instead, substance abuse and childhood violence are at the top of the list, followed by schizophrenia, antisocial personality disorder and poor parental bonding. Control behavior was recorded in the underlying meta-analyses, but did not reach the prevalence or effect size of the factors mentioned to make it into the top 5. Thus, it remains a significant, but numerically less influential risk factor compared to the neuropsychiatric and biographical main drivers of violence.

## 4.2.7 Meta-analysis of intervention programs in 2019[286]

This meta-analysis looked at how well programs to treat male IPV offenders work.

- **Decrease in violence within participants:** Men who participated in the perpetrator intervention programs showed on average d ≈ –0.85 (almost a standard deviation) less violence after completion compared to baseline.
- **Substance and trauma modules:** Intervention programs that also included addiction or trauma processing achieved greater effects (substance modules: d ≈ –2.14; Trauma modules: d ≈ –1.47).
- **Gender-role-oriented approaches:** Delivered weak results – sometimes moderately effective, sometimes without significant difference.
- **Control group comparison**: Only three of the 13 studies worked with a minimal control group (e.g. pure information sheets). In these direct comparisons, the differences were partly significant, partly non-significant. This means that the control groups themselves showed a certain decrease in violence through the

---

[286] https://tinyurl.com/dcs35hrr

observation effect or minimal measures alone, which reduced the net benefit of the intervention.

This means that perpetrator programs that specifically address problems such as substance abuse or trauma are more effective in relative terms than those that only teach general aggression control. The gender-role-oriented approach does not work so well without control groups.

## 4.2.8 Coercive Control and Mental Health Meta-Analysis 2023[287]

This analysis (68 studies, 45 in the meta-analysis) looked at how *coercive control (controlling, manipulative form of psychological violence) in relationships is linked to PTSD and depression. The most important results:*

- Strong association of coercive control and PTSD: mean correlation coefficient r≈0.32. So those who are constantly monitored, isolated or emotionally blackmailed in the relationship have a significantly higher risk of post-traumatic stress disorder.
- Moderate association with depression: r≈0.27 – so here, too, controlling violence is a significant risk factor for depressive symptoms.
- Similar strengths to broader psychological violence: If you only look at "normal" psychological violence (verbal abuse, belittling), r≈0.34 for PTSD and r≈0.33 for depression. Coercive Control is thus on an equal footing.

## 4.2.9 Emotional violence in IPV 2024[288]

The study examines how emotional violence in partnerships (e.g. humiliation, intimidation, blame – without physical violence) is related to

---

[287] https://pmc.ncbi.nlm.nih.gov/articles/PMC10666508/
[288] https://pubmed.ncbi.nlm.nih.gov/38506141/

other forms of violence, both on the perpetrator and on the victim side. To this end, it analyzes many previous studies together (a total of 188 studies with 382 individual values).

## What was found out?

If someone is a victim of emotional violence, there is a strong correlation with:

- Controlling behavior by the partner (e.g., monitoring cell phones, forbidding contacts)
- Physical violence by the partner
- Own use of physical violence
- Sexual violence by the partner
- Stalking by the partner
- Own use of sexual violence

Those who are victims of emotional violence often also experience other forms of violence – especially control and physical violence. However, many of these people also commit violence themselves.

When someone engages in emotional violence, there is a strong correlation with:

- Stalking behavior
- Physical violence
- Inflicting injuries
- Being self-controlled (victim of control)
- Sexual violence
- To have been physically injured himself
- Self-controlling behavior
- To have been a victim of sexual violence

Those who emotionally abuse others were often victims and/or perpetrators in other forms of violence themselves. There is an intertwining of perpetrator and victim roles.

**Gender differences:**

- The study found only minor differences between men and women.
- A possible (not entirely significant) difference: Women who experience physical violence are slightly more likely to also commit emotional violence.

# 5. Domestic violence in England[289]

For the year to March 2024, using the new definitions of domestic violence, it is estimated that about 2.3 million women and 1.5 million men have experienced domestic violence in the past year.[290] The definition has been expanded to recognize more than violence. Anyone who still has the studies on intimate partner violence in mind should have an idea of what this means. Whereas in the past there was talk of "one in three men", it is now almost 40%.

# 6. Femicide

Femicide is probably another pillar where feminism shows structural violence against women.

## 6.1. Definition and introduction

"The term femicide refers to the targeted killing of women because of their gender. Not every (intentional) killing of a woman is necessarily femicide. Femicide are those homicides in which women are killed because of their position as women in society, not by chance or due to individual circumstances. For example, women are disproportionately often victims of killings in existing or former partnerships. Often the acts are preceded by intimate partner violence."[291]

---

[289] https://www.instagram.com/p/DIyLYafIQ-P/
[290] https://tinyurl.com/yc7cwtf2
[291] https://tinyurl.com/y6jy33ed

➤ "Femicide – the deliberate killing of women because of their gender or because of 'violations' of the traditional social and patriarchal roles attributed to women – is not only the most extreme form of gender-based violence against women, it is also an extreme expression of their discrimination and gender inequality."

**– EU-Projekt FEM-United –**

"The designation as femicide or femicide helps to make the acts more visible and to make it clear that this form of violence is deeply rooted in society and structure: feticides are not isolated cases, but the result of patriarchal, structurally anchored power relations and social unequal treatment between the sexes."

**– Frauenhauskoordinierung e.V. –**

I saw an interesting addition in an SWR article: "The term refers to violence for what it is: the killing of a woman or a girl by a man."[292] I also think that the term is used that way.

## 6.2 Analysis methods

Since the groundbreaking publications of 1992, the scientific examination of femicide has produced a variety of approaches. Wikipedia[293] lists five basic methods of analysis, of which two should be singled out: the feminist and the sociological approach. Both shed light on different dimensions of the phenomenon and contribute to a deeper understanding of how systematic violence against women arises and can be combated.

---

[292] https://www.swr.de/swraktuell/baden-wuerttemberg/suedbaden/kommentar-femizide-in-suedbaden-100.html
[293] https://de.wikipedia.org/wiki/Femizid

The **feminist approach** interprets femicide as a direct consequence of patriarchal power structures in which men dominate and violence against women is culturally legitimized. Feminist researchers such as Diana Russell and Roberta Harmes define femicide as "*the killing of women by men because they are women*". This perspective emphasizes that sexism and structural inequality – for example in employment relationships, wage gaps or social roles – promote violence and even murder. Russell explicitly distinguishes killings by women in order to focus on male perpetration and systematic oppression.

However, critics complain that this approach neglects differences between women (e.g. class, ethnicity) and presents all women as potential victims. This makes it difficult to carry out a differentiated analysis, which would be necessary to develop targeted countermeasures or to precisely grasp the extent of the problem. Studies on intimate partner violence also seem to be already questioning the one-sided exercise of control by men.

The **sociological approach,** on the other hand, examines femicide empirically and contextually. In 1998, Jacquelyn Campbell and Carol Runyan expanded the definition to include "*all killings of women, regardless of motive or perpetrator status*". The focus here is on circumstances such as relationship conflicts, family violence or socio-economic factors. By analyzing case types, perpetrator profiles and regional patterns, the aim is to find out under which conditions women are particularly at risk – for example in partnerships, where they are statistically more likely to be victims than men. This approach emphasizes that gender relations are central, but must not be considered in isolation; rather, they interact with other social dynamics. The aim is to develop prevention strategies that address specific risk factors, for example through protection programs for those affected by domestic violence.

## 6.3 Statistics

### Why femicide numbers seem to be rising

Just two years ago, there was talk of about 130 femicide per year in Germany – i.e. one femicide every three days. Today, on the other hand, there is talk of 360 femicide a year, which corresponds to almost one daily case. This apparent increase is not due to the fact that the number of crimes has tripled, but to a change in definition:

- The previous figure (130/year) referred exclusively to killings by (ex-)partners and is now around 155 cases.
- The current figure (360/year), on the other hand, includes all women and girls killed – regardless of the perpetrator context, but excluding robbery-murders.[294]

The reason for the discrepancy is therefore not an increase in violence, but an extension of the underlying concept of femicide from partnership murders to all female victims of homicide.

## 6.4 Hate crimes

### 6.4.1 Definitions – Hate Crime

Refers to crimes motivated by prejudice or hatred against a particular group, such as those based on:

- Ethnicity, religion, gender, sexual orientation,
- Disability, political affiliation or social status. Examples: bodily harm, damage to property, insult with a racist or homophobic background.

---

[294] https://tinyurl.com/y3e3esn8

### 6.4.2 Definitions – Hate Murder

A murder in which the victim is specifically selected based on belonging to one of the above groups. Example: The anti-Semitic attack in Halle (2019), in which two people were killed.

## 6.4.3 Current debates and challenges

### Underreporting

Studies by the EU Agency for Fundamental Rights (FRA) show that up to 90% of all hate crimes in the EU are not reported to the police and are therefore missing from official statistics.[295] Victims often state that they believe that a complaint would "change nothing" or do not trust the authorities, which further inflates the number of unreported cases.

### Political demands

Human rights NGOs such as Amnesty International have been calling for years for an independent hate crime law in the EU based on the US model.[296] Such a law is intended to enshrine clearly defined motives for the crime (e.g. race, religion, sexual orientation) as aggravating penalties and to strengthen victim protection.[297]

### USA: "Hate Crime Laws"

In the USA, there have been stricter regulations against hate crimes at the federal level since 1968: Section 245 of the Civil Rights Act of 1968 makes it a criminal offense to use violence or threats of violence

---

[295] https://tinyurl.com/csyu773h
[296] https://tinyurl.com/35unrjru
[297] https://tinyurl.com/yn728wtb

against persons because they belong to a certain race, religion, skin color or nationality or engage in a federally protected activity.[298]

## EU: Directive 2012/29/EU

At EU level, Directive 2012/29/EU (Victims' Rights Directive) obliges Member States to provide special protection for victims of hate crime and to ensure adequate access to counselling, victim protection services and legal assistance. It sets minimum standards, but does not explicitly deal with the tightening of penalties for hate motives – that remains the task of national legislators.[299]

# 6.5 Criticism

### Global Homicide

Femicide draw attention to violence against women, while boys and men are over 4 times more likely to be victims of homicides worldwide.[300] Across Europe, almost always 3 times more common.

### Criticism in Der Spiegel[301]

Thomas Fischer criticizes the term "femicide" from a criminal law perspective and considers it legally useless. He argues that criminal law distinguishes according to the wrongfulness of an act – such as murder characteristics such as malice or low motives – and not according to ideological or sociological categories. Although killings out of gender-based hatred could certainly fall under existing murder paragraphs, this is a case-by-case examination, not a blanket categorization. The existing criminal offenses such as murder and

---

[298] https://www.justice.gov/crt/hate-crime-laws
[299] https://eur-lex.europa.eu/eli/dir/2012/29/oj/eng
[300] https://www.unodc.org/documents/data-and-analysis/gsh/2023/GSH23_Special_Points.pdf
[301] https://tinyurl.com/kvmm6zcj

manslaughter are sufficient to adequately assess killings regardless of the gender of the victim.

Fischer warns against instrumentalizing the originally criminological term, which is aimed at concrete gender-specific phenomena of violence, for political purposes beyond its analytical function. An excessive spread of the term "femicide" leads to a mixture of scientific analysis and activist ideology. He also criticizes the tendency to automatically consider every killing of a woman as gender-specific motivated, while killings of men or other groups are not given similar terms to "androcide". This selective conceptual logic is unsystematic and undercomplex, as it ignores the variety of possible motives for the crime.

Finally, he questions the media and activist rhetoric that often uses the term without legal differentiation. Such blanket attributions blur the criminal law assessment of individual cases and create distortions in public perception. For Fischer, the central task of criminal law remains to evaluate individual guilt and concrete circumstances of the crime – but not to translate socio-political narratives into laws.

## Criticism in the context of the Left Party motion "Investigate, name and prevent femicide in Germany"[302]

In the context of the application, there were critical voices that questioned both the necessity and the conceptual precision of the project. Prof. Dr. Thomas Fischer, former judge at the Federal Court of Justice, rejected the creation of a separate category "femicide". He argued that this would not lead to better analysis or clarification, but on the contrary could even be counterproductive. Fischer emphasized that there are already extensive research results and data on gender-based violence, so that an additional monitoring center is neither necessary nor useful.

---

[302] https://www.bundestag.de/dokumente/textarchiv/2021/kw09-pa-familie-femizide-822324

The ethnologist Prof. Dr. Susanne Schröter (Goethe University Frankfurt) also criticized, especially the term "femicide". In her view, the term is too imprecise: On the one hand, it is too broadly defined, for example when hate crimes against women are described as femicide – as in the case of Marc Lépine, who murdered 14 women in Canada in 1989 out of misogyny. However, such acts have little in common with the contexts mentioned in the Left Party motion (e.g. intimate partner violence). On the other hand, Schröter criticizes that the term is too narrow, as it excludes male victims of gender-based violence as well as non-lethal forms of violence. This leads to an incomplete presentation of the problem.

There was also approval, which can be viewed at the source mentioned.

## Feminist critique

Differentiated voices within feminism, above all Christina Hoff Sommers and Camille Paglia, warn against narrowing or generalizing the concept of femicide too much.

## Reduction of complex dynamics of violence

Christina Hoff Sommers argues in Who Stole Feminism? (1994) that the exclusive focus on gender as a motive for murderous violence ignores essential factors such as socio-economic backgrounds or individual mental disorders. She criticizes the fact that some feminist debates politicize statistics and, for example, exaggerate domestic violence or rape figures in order to underpin a narrative of systemic women's oppression.[303]

---

[303] https://en.wikipedia.org/w/index.php?title=Who_Stole_Feminism%3F

### Criticism of the attribution of victims

Camille Paglia describes the current femicide discourse as tending to be philistine and debilitating, because it stylizes women as passive victims of patriarchal structures. She reminds us that men are also often victims of intimate partner violence and general crime, and often sees violence more as an expression of general human aggression patterns than solely as a misogynistic phenomenon.[304]

## 6.6. Quote from Federal Minister of the Interior Nancy Faeser

"If women are killed because they are women – then these are femicide. These must be named and punished in this way: with life imprisonment."[305]

## 6.7 Homicide in England[306] incl. Partnership Murders

The report examines deadly violence in relationships or families and shows:

- Women mostly die at the hands of (ex-)partners: 76% of female victims were killed by current or former partners. Often there was already violence, threats or control behavior before.
- Men are less likely to die in partnerships: they are more likely to be killed by family members (e.g., sons) or roommates. For men, mental illnesses or conflicts over care/inheritance often play a role.

Why does this happen?

---

[304] https://en.wikipedia.org/wiki/Rape_culture
[305] https://tinyurl.com/y3e3esn8
[306] https://tinyurl.com/3ns5nd52

**Mental crises**

- In 64% of the perpetrators, there were psychological problems (depression, delusions) and in 76% of the cases, if victims are included
- Substance abuse (alcohol/drugs) exacerbated conflicts in over 64% of cases.

**Other Sources of Mental Disorder**[307]

- **Mental disorder** diagnosed in the course of life (without substance): approx. 33% of all perpetrators (Intimate Partner Femicide + Male-to-Male Homicide)
- **Substance-related disorders:**
  - Intimate Partner Femicide perpetrators: 15 %
  - Male-to-Male Homicide perpetrators: 37 %
- **Severe mental disorder (lifetime + time of crime):** 11% of all perpetrators (intimate partner femicide + male-to-male homicide)
- **Homicide-Suicide (perpetrator commits suicide after crime):** 20% of all intimate partners Femicide perpetrators

This study does not necessarily have to contradict the one from England. Once in England, something like this has to be recorded immediately after the crime. Furthermore, what they capture is more broadly defined.

**Other Sources Literature Analysis**[308]

- **Substance use disorders**: Significantly more common feature in intimate partner femicide offenders than other mental health diagnoses.
- **Major Mental Disorders** (psychosis, severe affective disorders, personality disorders): Mixed evidence, sometimes strong

---

[307] https://tinyurl.com/2mhy32bw
[308] https://pmc.ncbi.nlm.nih.gov/articles/PMC8977448/

association, sometimes no risk factor (depending on the study and country).

- **Prevention**: Early risk detection, especially suicidality, may be important, as intimate partner femicide offenders are more likely to realize homicide-suicide constellations.
- **Comparison Intimate Partner Femicide:** Intimate Partner Femicide Perpetrators tend to be in the middle of the psychopathological continuum; Perpetrators of non-intimate or fleeting relationships sometimes have higher rates of mental disorders

## Spirals of violence

- Mutual violence was found in 18% of the couple relationships.
- Many perpetrators had a history of violence (e.g. previous relationships, stalking).

## Authorities overlook risks

- In 73% of cases, victims showed signs of abuse before – but no one acted.

## Men as victims are invisible

- When men experience violence, they are less likely to report it. The police and doctors also take them less seriously ("Can't a man answer for himself?").

## Lack of suicides: The overlooked problem

The report does not mention how many suicides are due to domestic violence! The report criticizes this.

- Example: A woman/man kills herself after being humiliated by her partner for years. Such cases do not count as murder, although the violence led to death.
- Why this is important: Suicides are often the "last escape" from hopeless violence. They show how deadly psychological abuse can be.

# 6.8 Conclusion

### Femicide and the problem of generalization

Femicide – i.e. the killing of women because of their gender – can theoretically be interpreted as hate crimes. The dilemma here is that such a classification generally assumes a hate motive or equivalent. This implies that every killing of a woman is automatically motivated by misogyny – a generalization that does not do justice to reality or the judiciary.

### Danger of two-class justice

Murder is an emotionally charged topic, and no one wants to defend murderers. But if the generalization of femicide as hate murders becomes the norm, there is a danger that all violence will be handled in this way. The result would be a legal two-class society.

### The lack of equivalences and I digress

There is no term that classifies the killing of a man by a woman as "hate murder" – rightly so, because such a generalization would also be absurd. Even if at the same time slogans like "men kill" are increasing at demonstrations. Is this a false generalization or a request[309] like "Kill All

---

[309] https://de.wikipedia.org/wiki/Imperativ_%28Modus%29#Infinitiv

Men" – as it was mentioned in a Welt article[310] – or is the person simply a fan of the book?[311]

In the context of Bielefeld graffiti ("men kill", "toxic masculinity kills", "abolish men"), what is meant may become a little clearer: it is both. Because in addition to the bold statement "Men kill", there is also criticism of toxic masculinity, but also the radical demand "Abolish men".

Apparently, such false generalizations can be tolerated and left standing when it comes to men. This ignores the fact that these messages can also be understood as a request or can confirm existing bias and socialization.[312]

# 7. Violence against children

### Interview with Peter Döge[313]

Acts of violence against boys are twice as high as against girls.

Victims of violence tend to commit acts of violence later on, as around 80% of perpetrators have previously experienced violence themselves – a correlation that is similarly pronounced across genders.

10% of women practice parenting violence and 8% of men.

### Other sources

The risk for children to experience violence is two to three times higher than for adults.[314]

---

[310] https://tinyurl.com/v4d6m46h
[311] https://www.dtv.de/buch/maenner-toeten-14922
[312] https://tinyurl.com/4undsnc8
[313] https://www.vaeter-zeit.de/vaeter-maenner/maennergewalt-gewalt-gegen-jungen.php
[314] https://www.gewaltinfo.at/fachwissen/gewalt-an-kindern-und-jugendlichen-durch-erwachsene.html

Sexual abuse is committed by men and male adolescents in about 80 to 90% of cases, while women and female adolescents are responsible for about 10 to 20% of cases. A central motive of the perpetrators is often the striving for power and the need to experience a feeling of superiority through the act. In some cases, however, also the so-called pedosexuality.[315]

A nationwide study from 2004, according to a dissertation published in 2009, found that between 10% and 20% of boys are sexually abused in some form, with about 33% of the perpetrators being female.[316]

In the area of child abuse, 53.6% of suspects were men, while women accounted for 46.4%.[317]

# 8. Bullying among children[318]

- **31.2% of students** have been "beaten up or bullied" at least once recently.
- **37%** state that they have been the perpetrator of bullying themselves.
- **10%** report at least one incident of physical violence on the way to school or on school grounds.
- Boys and girls are affected **about equally often** – both as perpetrators and as victims.
- Relational aggression, **such as deprivation of friendship or targeted gossip, is particularly important for girls – forms that are particularly often exercised by and against girls.** [319]

---

[315] https://tinyurl.com/4bxrnd3y
[316] https://en.wikipedia.org/wiki/Rape_in_Germany#cite_note-16
[317] https://www.aktion-tu-was.de/fileadmin/dokumente/infotext-kindesmisshandlung-p.pdf
[318] https://www.leuphana.de/news/meldungen/titelstories/mobbingstudie.htm
[319] https://tinyurl.com/39wxejp5

**Health consequences of bullying**

- **14% of the victims of bullying** regularly complain of physical complaints (e.g. headaches, abdominal pain, back pain, sleep disorders).
- For non-affected students, this figure is only 4%.
- Victims of bullying are more likely to feel dissatisfied with their appearance and are more socially isolated.

# 10. Women's fear, rational or irrational

The fear of violence is a central topic of social debates, especially when it comes to women. But how much of this fear is actually justified, and how much results from media coverage, social narratives or feminist enlightenment? Is irrational fear now more present than rational fear?

As early as 1996, the literature review *Fear of Crime: A Review of the Literature* provides us with an interesting perspective. It reads in essence:

"Proponents of this view argue that the focus should be on fighting crime – with the aim of reducing anxiety. However, while this approach fits well with traditional policing, research clearly shows that the actual risk of becoming a victim is not the only relevant factor in the level of anxiety. In fact, it is now hardly disputed that it may not even be the main factor."[320]

"Fear seems to be only weakly related to one's own victim experiences. However, indirect information about crimes – for example from word of mouth or the media – when it relates to events in the local neighborhood that affect people to whom the recipient feels a certain affinity, can have an impact."[321] (One could criticize the fact that outdated research results are used here. In the next chapter, however, I

---

[320] https://journals.sagepub.com/doi/10.1177/026975809600400201
[321] https://tinyurl.com/y2cjdf3c

show more recent findings from a 2022 study in the introduction, which Hale (1996) cites six times. This current work does not contradict this statement, but complements it: It has been proven that victim experiences are one of the factors through which the media increase fear.)

In other words, fear of crime is not only a reaction to real threats, but is shaped by other influences – including social discourse and the media.

# 11. Fear of crime vs. reality

## 11.1 Introduction[322]

Sociodemographic characteristics such as gender, age, ethnicity and socioeconomic status are associated with the fear of crime. People may feel particularly at risk of becoming victims because they are more likely to be targeted by criminals, because the impact of crime would be particularly severe, and because they are unable to control whether crimes happen or not. Women often report higher anxiety due to perceived physical vulnerability and internalization of societal messages about female fragility. Social vulnerability, influenced by social networks, financial situation and access to resources, contributes to higher anxiety among disadvantaged minorities. Psychological factors, including emotional states and personality traits, also play a role in fear of crime. Women are more likely to worry about themselves and their social group due to a feeling of being less able to defend themselves, a lower sense of self-efficacy, a higher perceived negative impact and a higher perceived likelihood of victimization. Perceived risk and restricted behavior generally predict fear of crime. Individuals may feel endangered by crime, even if they are not objectively vulnerable. Women are often more afraid than men, although they are less likely to become victims. Dispositional fear of crime, which results from a long-term development influenced by personal conditions and experiences, influences situational

---

[322] https://journals.sagepub.com/doi/10.1177/07340168221088570

fear of crime. The consistent finding of higher anxiety among women despite lower victimization rates in many crimes suggests a "gender paradox" that needs further investigation. Social and psychological factors seem to play an important role here. This paradox suggests that fear of crime is not based solely on objective risk, but is also influenced by social constructs, perceived vulnerability, and possibly different socialization. The role of socioeconomic status and ethnicity in shaping anxiety highlights the social inequalities related to crime and security. Marginalized groups often experience higher levels of anxiety due to increased vulnerability. This link suggests that fear of crime can exacerbate existing social inequalities, leading to further marginalization and a reduced quality of life for vulnerable populations. The concept of dispositional anxiety suggests that some individuals are inherently more susceptible to the fear of crime because of their personality and life experiences. This could moderate the influence of external factors such as media. Understanding dispositional anxiety is important to explain why individuals might react differently to the same crime-related information or media content.

Media consumption and fear of crime are not necessarily correlate, certain factors are needed:

- **Sensationalism:** Dramatic, exaggerated depiction of crimes ("news framing") that reinforces negative images and charges them emotionally.
- **Realism perception:** The conviction that media content is "real" reinforces its influence on the perception of fear.
- **Credibility perception of the source:** The more credible a source is assessed, the stronger its reporting has a positive effect on feelings of insecurity.
- **Identification with victims:** Common characteristics (e.g. the same social group or nationality) can trigger emotions more intensely.

- **Proximity/proximity of the reported event:** The closer a crime is spatially or socially to one's own environment, the greater the fear can increase.
- **Location of the crime:** Reports on local crime have a stronger anxiety-provoking effect; Reports about distant places can even have a calming effect.
- **Type and intensity of media use:** Frequent consumption (especially long TV consumption) can lead to viewers perceiving the world as more dangerous (cultivation).
- **Lack of direct alternative sources of information:** If personal experience or trustworthy informants are missing, media images are more likely to be used as the only source of information (substitution).
- **Consistency with one's own experiences:** If media representations correspond to one's own experiences, this intensifies fear (resonance).
- **Previous experiences and vicarian victimization:** Direct or indirect victim experiences (e.g. stories from the environment) increase susceptibility to anxiety-inducing media content.
- Personal attitudes, social networks and dominant patterns of interpretation shape how media reports are interpreted and evaluated.
- **Spreading misinformation / fake news:** If false, distorted or out-of-context reports are deliberately or unconsciously disseminated, this can deliberately stir up fears and increase distrust of real sources of information. Fake news mechanisms therefore play their own role in how media consumption increases the fear of crime. (One can argue about whether the official statistics, which only depict what has been recorded under criminal law, are really representative, especially since the results of dark field research, which better reflect the actual reality of life, sometimes differ considerably and thus show a clear distortion.)

In many of these points, public broadcasters and feminist violence education score points.

## 11.2 Irrational Anxiety

There are clear indications that the subjective fear of violence does not always correspond to the real threat situation:

- *Fear of Crime: A Review of the Literature* also shows that women continue to have high anxiety scores despite falling crime rates.
- The topic is also taken up in cabaret. For example, Christoph Sieber made the remark that a headline like "A burglary every six minutes" statistically means that someone visits you every 283 years.[323]
- Social psychologist and director of the Center for Criminological Research Saxony, Frank Asbrock, talks in an interview with MDR AKTUELL about the discrepancy between perceived and actual security. While crime statistics show a decline in registered crimes over decades, many citizens perceive Germany as increasingly unsafe. According to Asbrock, factors such as individual threat perception and media coverage play a decisive role. Dark field studies also confirm that crime has fallen overall.[324]
- *Mean world syndrome:*[325] As early as the 70s, George Gerbner researched this psychological phenomenon of increasing anxiety through the media. Our studies have shown that growing up from early childhood with this unprecedented dose of violence has three consequences, which in combination I call the "Mean World Syndrome". This means that if you grow up in a household where you watch TV for more than about three hours a day, you live in a crueler world – practically speaking – and behave accordingly than the neighbor next door who lives in the same world but watches less TV. The television content reinforces people's worst fears, fears and paranoid ideas.

This discrepancy is particularly evident in the perception of risks: women are more likely to fear attacks by strangers on the street,

---

[323] https://www.instagram.com/p/DH0H1ZsPPru/
[324] https://tinyurl.com/336tun5e
[325] https://en.wikipedia.org/wiki/Mean_world_syndrome

although crime statistics show that most assaults come from acquaintances or partners. At the same time, men are more likely to be victims of violent crime, which is hardly discussed in the public debate.

## 11.3 Influence of media and social networks

A decisive factor for the perception of fear is media coverage:

**Social Media, Fear of Crime, and Social Trust[326]**

The study shows several key findings:

- **Social media and trust** – The consumption of crime content on social media is associated with reduced trust (e.g., lower community orientation and inclusive trust, increased distrust).
- **Mediation factors** – Fear of crime mediates the link between social media exposure and mistrust.
- **Avoidance behaviors** – People who consume crime content tend to be more avoidanced, which in turn reduces their willingness to trust.
- **Risk perception** – The subjective assessment of becoming a victim further increases mistrust.

**Crime and its fear in Social Media[327]**

The study examines whether real-time information contained in social media posts can be used to identify trends in crime and the fear of crime. For this purpose, numerous tweets from the 18 largest Spanish-speaking countries in Latin America were collected over a period of 70 days. These tweets were then classified according to their relationship to crime – additional information such as the nature of the crime and, where possible, geographic location data (city level) was extracted.

---

[326] https://digitalcommons.pace.edu/dissertations/AAI30249838/
[327] https://www.nature.com/articles/s41599-020-0430-7

Key findings include:

- **Frequency of criminal content:** About 15 out of 1000 tweets contain text references to crime or the fear of crime.
- **Comparison with real crime data:** The frequency of tweets that address criminal content was compared with the number of murders, the murder rate, and the fear levels determined in surveys.
- **Media bias:** Like traditional mass media (e.g., newspapers), social media platforms have a strong bias in favor of reporting on violent and sexual crimes.
- **Limited significance** for crime: Social media posts correlate only weakly with actual crime rates. Instead, they rather reflect the extent of the fear of crime.

## Media and Social Media's Impact on Citizens' Perception of the Frequency of Crime Occurrence in the United States[328]

The study examines how media – both traditional (such as television, radio, newspapers) and social media – influence perceptions of crime rates in the US. For this purpose, 370 US citizens were surveyed via online survey. Participants indicated how often they watch the news, how often they see posts about crime on social networks, and whether they believe these sources influence their perception of crime.

### Experimental set-up and methodology:

- **Sample:** 370 U.S. citizens, mostly under 45 years of age, mostly female and with at least a college education.
- **Questions:** The survey included questions about the frequency of news consumption, the viewing of social media posts about crime, and one's own assessment of whether media or social media influence the perception of crime.

---

[328] https://www.aijssnet.com/journals/Vol_6_No_3_September_2017/11.pdf

**Findings and causes of perception:**

- **Media influence:** Overall, many participants believe that both social media (69.5%) and traditional media (73.0%) influence their perception of the crime rate.
- **Quantification by frequency of exposure:** The analysis shows that the more often participants see posts about crimes on social networks, the more likely social media is perceived as the dominant influencer – and less so the traditional news channel.
- **Causes of irrational fear:** The study suggests that the media portrayal of crime, which often relies disproportionately on violence and sensationalism, creates a distorted picture. This overrepresentation leads people to believe that crime is more common than it is in reality, contributing to an irrational fear of crime.

# 11.4 Radio Contribution[329]

Over 90% of young women say they feel great to very great fear at night when encountering unknown men. 0% are not afraid. 89% have already had bad, cross-border experiences with men, it says at the bottom of the post. I suppose that's supposed to explain the fear. Why don't we explain here what science knows about the development of fear of crime? No, instead you come up with an extremely high number for cross-border experiences.

**What are cross-border experiences?**

You have cross-border experiences where others exceed your subjectively set boundaries, as the term itself actually explains. This can be too close, touch on the shoulder, be ignored in conversation, etc. 89% percent do not really describe how many have experienced it, because when you are among people for a certain time, you experience

---

[329] https://www.instagram.com/p/DJOVsJSCBxj/?img_index=1

something like this, but rather clarify how far you set your limits and how actively you make sure that they are crossed.

## 11.5 Feminist Enlightenment

**Feminist education about violence against women has its merits:**

- It has contributed to the fact that domestic violence and sexual assault are taken more seriously in society.
- Women are better informed about their rights and protections.
- Legal improvements, such as the prohibition of marital rape, were driven by feminist movements.

**But it also has problematic sides:**

- It can create an exaggerated threat perception when violence against women is portrayed as an omnipresent problem.
- In some currents, it is suggested that all men are potential perpetrators, which can increase mistrust and fears in everyday situations.
- Crime statistics are often presented in a one-sided way: the fact that men and children are more likely to be victims of violence overall is rarely discussed. Provocatively, one could even point out that women already have the fewest experiences of victimhood.

# 12. Violence prevention

Violence prevention is carried out internationally with widely varying budgets: In the USA, the Crime Victims Fund (VOCA) had USD 4.3 billion at its disposal in January 2025.[330] Child Protection (CAPTA) received only $91.6 million in 2022, despite the fact that the Nurse-Family Partnership model demonstrates a 48% reduction in child abuse and

---

[330] https://ovc.ojp.gov/about/crime-victims-fund

intergenerational effects.[331] [332] Cure Violence programs reduced shootings by 63% in New York City.[333]

In Germany, EUR 243.8 million will be made available for violence prevention in the Children and Youth Plan for 2025.[334] The Action Plan on Violence against Women funds 350+ women's shelters and records 52,650 counselling contacts in 2022;[335] There are municipal projects such as BIG Berlin,[336] StoP Hamburg, (it works, but there is no data again) [337] while "Live Democracy!" also promotes the prevention of men and extremism with 182 million euros.[338]

Globally, the WHO recommends standardizing data and checking programs for success. It also recommends programs that address different types of violence.[339] Compared to 2000, 16% fewer homicides were recorded in 2012.[340] With the help of social workers in Sweden, corporal punishment dropped from 90% of all children in their 60s to just 10% in 2010.[341]

[331] https://www.nursefamilypartnership.org/about/proven-results/prevent-child-abuse-neglect/
[332] https://oig.hhs.gov/reports-and-publications/workplan/summary/wp-summary-0000782.asp
[333] https://cvg.org/impact/
[334] https://national-policies.eacea.ec.europa.eu/youthwiki/chapters/germany/17-funding-youth-policy
[335] https://tinyurl.com/h2tnkn85
[336] https://tinyurl.com/yhyzys2s
[337] https://stop-partnergewalt.org/stop-wirkt-erfolgsgeschichten/
[338] https://www.demokratie-leben.de/dl/foerderung/wen-wir-foerdern
[339] https://www.who.int/publications/i/item/9789241564793
[340] https://pubmed.ncbi.nlm.nih.gov/26689979/
[341] https://en.wikipedia.org/wiki/Child_discipline

# 13. Security and Crime in Germany[342]

## 13.1 Dark Field Study SKiD 2020

### Prevalence and incidence rates – brief explanation

- **Prevalence rate** indicates the proportion of a defined group (e.g. men or women) who have been affected by a crime at least once in a given period.
- **Incidence rate** describes how many individual offense events per 1,000 people in this group were registered in the same period. So while prevalence counts how many people were victims, incidence counts how often crimes took place in total (including multiple victims).

### Summary of crime risks by gender

### Bodily injury

### Prevalence:

- men: 2.8%
- Women: 1.3%
- Female-Gender-Gap: - 53,6
- Male-Gender-Gap: 115

### Incidence:

- Men: 55.1
- Women: 29.8
- Female-Gender-Gap: - 45,9

---

[342] https://tinyurl.com/25w7jubb

- Male-Gender-Gap: 84,9

**Cases per capita:**

- Men: 1.97
- Women: 2.29
- Female-Gender-Gap: 16,3

**Verbal violence on the Internet**

**Prevalence:**

- Men 5.2%
- Women 4.6 %
- Female-Gender-Gap: - 11,5
- Male-Gender-Gap: 13

**Incidence:**

- Men 671.1
- Women 352.0
- Female-Gender-Gap: - 47,5
- Male-Gender-Gap: 90,7

**Cases per capita:**

- Men: 12.9
- Women: 7.7
- Female-Gender-Gap: - 40,3
- Male-Gender-Gap: 67,5

The female gender gap represents a disadvantage for women, basically in the same format as we know it from the gender pay gap. Male-Gender-Gap the discrimination of men in the same format.

## 13.2 Gender-based violence according to SKiD 2020

According to current data, prejudice-based bodily injury is significantly more common among men than among women. The prevalence rate is about 1.40% in men, while it is only about 0.66% in women.

When looking at individual groups of characteristics – such as social status, origin, religion, political views, gender or gender identity, skin color or sexual orientation – the gender differences are statistically significant. In almost all categories, men have higher rates of prejudice-based attacks. The only exception is the characteristic "gender or gender identity", in which women are affected somewhat more often.

**Prevalence rates of prejudiced assault (12 months)**

Man | Woman | Female-Gender-Gap | Male-Gender-Gap

- Total                              1.40 | 0.66 | - 53.0 | 112
- Social status              **0,55** | 0.11 | - 80.0 | 400
- Immigrant:                  **0,59** | 0.06 | - 89.8 | **883**
- Religion:                     **0,43** | 0.08 | - 81.4 | 438
- Political views:          **0,42** | 0.04 | - 90.5 | **950**
- Gender/ closed Identity:  0.04 | 0.35 | —————
- Age:                            0.22 | 0.14 | - 36.4 | 57
- Skin color:                 0.25 | 0.03 | - 88.0 | **733**
- Disability:                  0.10 | 0.09 | - 10.0 | 11
- sexual orientation:     0.08 | 0.02 | - 75.0 | 300
- other group:              0.03 | 0.01 | - 66.7 | 200

## Incidence rate of prejudiced assault (12 months)

Man | Woman | Female-Gender-Gap | Male-Gender-Gap

- Social status  11.05 | 1.22 | − 89.0 |   805,7
- Immigrant  **21,61** | 0.81 | − 96.3 |**2 567,9**
- Religion  10,90 | 1,60 |− 85,3 |   581,2
- Political attitude  **24,46** | 8.06 | − 67.0|   203,5
- Gender  0.25  | 5.46 |  —————————
- Age  1.85 | 1.43 | − 22.7 |    29,4
- Skin color  7.77 | 0.64 | − 91.8 |**1 114,1**
- Disability  10.71 | 0.40 | − 96.3 |**2 577,5**
- Sexual orientation  4.76 | 0.63 | − 86.8 |   655,6
- Other group  0.23 | 0.14 | − 39.1 |  64,3

## Average number of incidents per person affected by prejudiced bodily injury

Man | Woman | Female-Gender-Gap | Male-Gender-Gap

- Social status  20.1 |  11.1 |   − 44.8 | 81.1
- Origin  36.6 |  13.5 |   − 63.1 | **171,1**
- Religion  25:3 |  20.0 |   − 20.9 | 26.5
- Political attitude  58.2 |**201,5** |   **246,0** | −
- Gender  6.2  |  15.6 |  ————————
- Age  8.4  |  10.2 |  + 21.5 | −
- Skin color  31.1|  21.3 |   − 31.5 | 46.0
- Disability  **107,1** |  4.4  |  − 95.9  | **2 334,1**
- Sexual orientation  59.5 |  31.5 |   − 47.1 | 88.9
- Other group  7.7 |  14.0 |  + 81.8 | −

In intersectional feminism, the synergy effect (in feminism rather called "multiplicative", "additive" or "super-additive" experience of discrimination) refers to the fact that two (or more) forms of discrimination do not simply add up, but interact and thus create an intensified, qualitatively different disadvantage. E.g.: Gender + Ethnic Origin.[343]

Although gender-based violence against men is often denied, the intersectional analysis shows that men from certain groups are particularly affected by the combination of gender with other discrimination criteria (e.g. origin or religion). First, if anyone wonders why the gender / closed Identity line was not offset because gender-based violence cannot have a synergy effect with itself. By mentioning them several times in the questionnaire, it would have been possible to show where people subjectively suspect gender-based violence, but this is not the question I would like to answer, but where gender-specific deviations in the increase or accumulation of violence can be found.

Let's start with the proportion of men who have such experiences: In the areas of social status, origin, political attitudes and religion, a particularly large number of men are affected. The gender difference is most pronounced in terms of origin and political attitudes – in these categories, men experience such incidents about ten times more often than women.

When looking at the total violence a group experiences, men most often experience violence because of their origin or political views. In the groups of origin and disability, the gender-specific difference is almost 27 times higher than for women. I.e. purely quantitatively, for one blow that a woman experiences, there are 27 that a man experiences, always considered within the group.

Looking at the average number of incidents per person affected, it can be seen that women have over 200 incidents per capita because of their political views, while men with disabilities still have more than 100 incidents per capita. However, these high case numbers relate to relatively small groups (0.04 ‰ for women due to political attitudes and

---

[343] https://de.wikipedia.org/wiki/Intersektionalit%C3%A4t

0.10 ‰ for men with disabilities). The four largest categories mentioned at the beginning still add up to 20 to 60 incidents per capita. In terms of gender, it is striking that male victims with disabilities experience an average of about 24 times as many incidents as female victims with disabilities, female victims about 3.5 times as often as male victims due to their political views, and male victims are almost 3 times more likely to experience violence because of their origin than female victims.

In conclusion, it can be stated that subjective experience reports provide important indications of intersectional disadvantage.[344] However, in order to check whether, for example, men in certain groups (e.g. with a migration background or low education) are actually disproportionately affected, I would have liked to see an additional objective view – for example by means of a difference model within the data collected. You look for statistical deviations of the group from the whole, and then you have to adjust relevant characteristics, such as age, wealth. What remains could be real prejudice-driven violence.

And while the three tables open up different perspectives on prejudice-motivated experiences of violence – the first shows the individual risk of becoming a victim, the second the full extent of violence against certain groups, and the third the average burden per affected individual – one important dimension is missing: the intensity of the violence experienced. A gender-specific comparison is difficult here, as men in particular tend to downplay the severity of their own experiences. Nevertheless, the perceived intensity of violence could at least be compared to the overall group.

## 14. Double standards briefly shown

Trans women (MtF) were more than 6 times more likely to be convicted of a crime than the comparison group of cisgender women – and even 18 times more likely to be convicted of a violent crime.[345]

---

[344] https://de.wikipedia.org/wiki/Standpunkt-Theorie
[345] https://committees.parliament.uk/writtenevidence/18973/pdf/

Gender-diverse offenders with a history of sexual offenses (SOH) accounted for 37% (n = 57) of the total of 155 gender-diverse offenders recorded in the study period (December 2017 to September 2021); 86% were trans women, 0% were trans men, and 14% identified as "other" gender-diverse offenders.[346]

Trans women exhibit violent behavior that resembles men. While mainstream feminism rightly criticizes the generalizations and treatment of trans women by some TERFs, it overlooks the fact that it follows the same principle with men. If TERFs are anti-queer, then feminists are likely to be hostile to men by their own standards.

It's just as double standards *to say Not All Men* and criticize the generalization of men, only to generalize against trans women in the next moment.

Of course, it can be mentioned that trans women are also more often victims of violence. Violence creates trauma and is not conducive to mental health. But mental illnesses explain at most a 3 to 4 times higher potential for violence, not 18.[347] However, if you have thought this way for a moment, you may develop empathy for the chapters of violence against children, partner violence or hatred of men.

## 15. Conclusion

Any kind of violence is bad and should be reduced from a societal point of view.

Primary problems in sexual violence seem to be intelligence and education, in partner violence their mutual dynamics, traumas and addiction problems, and in cases of partner murder there are often problems with the psyche and alcohol / drugs. And that's already simplified to what seems to be the biggest cause I found in my short

---

[346] https://tinyurl.com/4cuum9sa
[347] https://tinyurl.com/yp4xkddd

research. Feminism refers to patriarchal oppression, power and control behavior. Although such behavior is actually often found within the criminally relevant cases and is therefore quite a justified point, in the totality of intimate partner violence, this behavior is fortunately rather rare and by no means gender-specific, but is also practiced by women.[348] [349] Denise Hines says something similar in the following source and brings here other sources and data that are interesting:[350] In the Canadian General Social Survey (GSS) of 2004, for example, 40% of all male victims of domestic violence were victims of "terrorist violence" (i.e. controlling, ongoing violence). In addition, 36.8% of the total 583,800 victims of terrorist violence were men – a finding that was similarly noted in the 1999 GSS (Laroche, 2005). The meta-studies and reviews even spoke of a balanced picture.

In the chapter on intimate partner violence, I have already pointed out that most conflicts involve mutual violence. If more places for men's shelters were financed, then men would also have the chance to break out of this toxic spiral of violence and prevent an escalation.[351] In the chapter on sexual violence, on the other hand, that the source points out that the perpetrators often have problems with communication and education. What about nationwide reading promotion for problem cases?

Men are perpetrators and women are victims, women need help and men can cope on their own, are patriarchal biases and stereotypes that can influence behavior and are certainly also confirmed and promoted by feminism. But it's not quite that simple and I hope I was able to convey a more differentiated picture here.

---

[348] https://pmc.ncbi.nlm.nih.gov/articles/PMC3154094/
[349] https://familyconflict.eu/wp-content/uploads/BatesFrankfurt-DEU.pdf
[350] https://ijfrp.journals.yorku.ca/index.php/ijfrp/article/view/39581
[351] https://pmc.ncbi.nlm.nih.gov/articles/PMC3154094/

# XIII. Social media

Social media such as Twitter, TikTok and Instagram have significantly influenced the gender debate. While on the one hand they provide space for feminist and masculist movements, on the other hand they also reinforce polarizing narratives. Algorithms, viral trends and the dynamics of "cancel culture" play a decisive role in this.

## Psychological phenomena & disambiguation

### 1.1 Demonization – The Art of Demonization[352]

Demonization describes how individuals, groups, or ideologies are systematically portrayed as fundamentally evil in order to delegitimize them morally, politically, or culturally. Originally rooted in religious contexts, where, for example, "pagans" or "witches" were considered tools of the devil, this technique has developed over the course of history into a central instrument in political and ideological conflicts. The aim is not only to criticize the opponent, but to portray him as an existential threat that seems to exist beyond any human morality. An essential component of this strategy is dehumanization: Through the use of dehumanizing language – such as animal comparisons such as "rats" or "vermin" as well as disease metaphors such as "social cancer" – it becomes possible to prevent empathy and justify violence. During the Cold War, for example, communists in the West were defamed as "godless subhumans", while in the Eastern Bloc "decadent capitalism" was portrayed as the spawn of evil.

Demonization fulfills three central functions. On the one hand, it mobilizes the emotions of the population by using hate propaganda to create clear enemy images that can then be used to justify violence – as in the case of the "war on terror". On the other hand, the constant portrayal of the opponent as the epitome of evil leads to a moral

---

[352] https://de.wikipedia.org/wiki/D%C3%A4monisierung

self-enhancement of one's own position. Finally, this technique simplifies complex political, economic, and social conflicts by transforming them into a binary struggle between "light and darkness." Scholars such as Castro Varela and Mecheril point out that this form of delegitimization contributes significantly to stabilizing social power relations, for example by demonizing migrants in Europe as criminal or misogynistic in order to justify restrictive asylum policies and secure the privileges of the majority society.

Historically, demonization can be traced back to the times of witch hunts, the Crusades, and anti-Jewish propaganda. During the colonial era, Indigenous peoples were dehumanized as "savages" or "cannibals" to justify conquest and enslavement. In the 20th century, these techniques were used, among other examples, in Nazi propaganda, where Jews were depicted as "subhumans" and "parasites," and during the McCarthy era in the US, when Communists were branded as "traitors to freedom." More recently—after the events of September 11 or in the portrayal of political figures like Putin—one can see that demonization remains a powerful tool to this day.

The techniques used are diverse. Opponents are often devalued by dehumanizing language by describing them with negative animal images or disease metaphors. Another method is personalization: complex conflicts are reduced to individual, charismatic leaders, whereby the entire conflict is presented as a fight against the personified evil. Likewise, moral absolutes and conspiracy narratives are used to ascribe a purely malicious agenda to the opponent.

A decisive side effect of demonization is the formation of cultural taboos that make any constructive dialogue with the other defined as evil almost impossible. In the GDR, for example, Western media were considered "enemy broadcasters" whose consumption was punishable by law, and today the idea is often propagated that one cannot negotiate with right-wing extremist parties, even if they are democratically elected.

Numerous examples from the past and present illustrate these dynamics: In Nazi Germany, Jews were staged as "world conspirators" in propaganda materials such as "Der Stürmer", while in US war propaganda in Iraq, Saddam Hussein was portrayed as the "Butcher of Baghdad". . Modern media also use demonizing strategies, such as in the current coverage in Russia, which brands Ukraine as a "Nazi state," while we claim the same about Russia.

Nevertheless, demonization is not without controversy. Critics complain that it escalates conflicts, as it makes compromise almost impossible and can prolong wars – as can be observed in the Middle East conflict. It also leads to a loss of differentiation, as internal differences within the demonized groups are ignored, leading to blanket hostility. After all, technology is often cynically instrumentalized to distract from one's own grievances.

In summary, it can be seen that demonization is by no means a relic of past times, but continues to exist as a central tool of modern power politics. Anyone who recognizes and sees through this strategy can better understand that the supposedly monolithic "evil" is often merely an expression of unresolved social, economic or psychological tensions. A de-demonized debate is therefore a decisive step towards a differentiated, de-escalating conflict culture.

## 1.2 Mean World Syndrome[353]

The Mean World Syndrome describes a cognitive bias in which people perceive the world as more dangerous than it actually is. This effect is caused by long-lasting, moderate to intensive exposure to violence-related content in the mass media. Originally, this phenomenon was studied in the context of television consumption, with communication professor George Gerbner coining the term in the 1970s. He showed that intense exposure to violent television content can lead

---

[353] https://en.wikipedia.org/wiki/Mean_world_syndrome

to increased anxiety, pessimism, and a constantly vigilant state of face to potential threats.

Gerbner's Cultivation Theory shows that the continuous portrayal of violence on television has a lasting impact on the perception of reality. Research has shown that people who spend a lot of time in front of the TV often develop a distorted view of the world, in which they assume that violence is omnipresent. This media imprint directly influences attitudes, beliefs and opinions about the real world and leads to increased fear, increased mistrust and the need for more safety precautions.

Although the original studies focused on television consumption, media consumption has changed significantly in recent decades. Nowadays, social media plays an equally important role in the spread of Mean World Syndrome. Platforms such as Facebook, Twitter and Instagram – despite possibly having a lower visual intensity than television – create a similar effect through the constant presence of negative news, controversial discussions and viral content. Users who regularly lose themselves in online debates or so-called "troll wars" and consume violence-related content incessantly – often as part of phenomena such as "doomscrolling" during the COVID-19 pandemic – increasingly perceive their environment as more threatening. This permanent confrontation with negative content reinforces the feeling of fear, insecurity and leads to an overall distorted view of the world.

Overall, the Mean World Syndrome impressively shows how strongly mass media can influence our perception of reality. While early research focused on the influence of television consumption, the current development underlines that social media also make a significant contribution to people perceiving the world as more dangerous and hostile than it actually is. This finding illustrates the responsibility that the media – in whatever form – bear in the portrayal of violence and negative events.

# 1.3 Cognitive dissonance[354]

Cognitive dissonance describes the psychological state in which people carry conflicting thoughts, feelings, beliefs, or actions within themselves at the same time. This inner discomfort arises when new information or experiences contradict existing beliefs and thus trigger a conflict in thinking. Leon Festinger, the founder of cognitive dissonance theory, postulated as early as the 1950s that we strive to maintain a consistent inner world – any break in this consistency triggers discomfort that we try to reduce through various strategies. These strategies include, among other things, the adaptation of attitudes or behaviors, the selective perception of information or the conscious rejection of contradictory facts.

A striking example of cognitive dissonance emerged in conversations with some "bear voters" on Instagram. When asked how violence in the U.S. has evolved over the past 30 years, I received almost the same answer: "It's gotten worse" or "We're in the worst state ever." But the crime statistics prove something completely different: violent crime has fallen drastically in the last three decades - from 79 to 23 cases per 1,000 people, and sexual offenses have also decreased significantly. Nevertheless, many people cling to the idea of living in an increasingly dangerous world. This discrepancy between objective facts and subjective perception is a classic example of cognitive dissonance. The discrepancy between the internalized, negative ideas and the contradictory empirical data causes psychological stress, which those affected try to alleviate. This is often done by ignoring alternative information, defaming the facts, or reducing discourse in online debates to emotional, simplified categories. In some cases, attempts are even made to protect one's own point of view through aggressive reactions, such as blocking or deleting comments.

The mechanism of cognitive dissonance plays a central role in the way we process information and how we maintain our self-image and

---

[354] https://en.wikipedia.org/wiki/Cognitive_dissonance

beliefs. When our actions or attitudes are at odds with new experiences, we feel discomfort. To reduce this, we rationalize our behavior, for example, by only taking in information that confirms our view – a phenomenon that is closely linked to the so-called confirmation bias. In this way, an inner consistency is established, even if this comes at the expense of an objective confrontation with reality.

The dynamics that arise from cognitive dissonance have far-reaching societal consequences. They explain why people cling to outdated or distorted worldviews despite overwhelming evidence to the contrary and why collective fears and prejudices can intensify. Especially in today's digitally connected world, where information is available in abundance and where social media serves as a filter for perception, cognitive dissonance is becoming a powerful engine of political and social divisions. By selectively absorbing only information that confirms their existing beliefs, individuals and groups contribute to the suppression of alternative views and the manifestation of a one-sided, often pessimistic view of the world.

In conclusion, cognitive dissonance is not only a fascinating psychological mechanism, but also contributes significantly to how we perceive our world and how we respond to challenges. The example of the "bear voters" impressively shows how, despite clear statistical evidence, a subjective perception of a more dangerous world can be maintained – a state that not only causes personal stress, but also shifts the social climate towards fear and hostility. Understanding these processes is therefore crucial to promote constructive dialogues and overcome the distorted perceptions that can ultimately lead to social division.

## 1.4 Indoctrination

Indoctrination is a process of targeted influence that aims to impose a certain ideology, thought pattern, or worldview on people. In doing so, alternative perspectives are deliberately suppressed and critical examinations of the content conveyed are prevented. In contrast to open education, which promotes reflection and discussion, indoctrination is characterized by a one-sided, often manipulative transfer of information.

A central feature of indoctrination is the use of propaganda to present a desired opinion as having no alternative. This is done by selectively presenting information, censoring or defaming contradictory or critical content. In authoritarian systems, indoctrination is a common means of securing power by trimming the population to an ideological line from an early age. But indoctrinating tendencies are also recognizable in democratic societies, be it in political education, advertising or in certain religious contexts.

Historically, the term indoctrination has not been clearly distinguished from education for a long time. Especially in the Middle Ages, when education took place primarily in religious institutions, the imparting of knowledge was inseparably linked to dogmatic guidelines. It was not until the Enlightenment that the idea arose that upbringing and education should be based on critical reflection and independent thinking. The term "indoctrination" did not become common in the German language until the 1960s, often with a view to ideological training under National Socialism or the reeducation programs of the Allies after World War II.

In modern pedagogy, indoctrination is usually viewed negatively, yet the boundary to legitimate education remains fluid. While education aims to shape people into mature, self-thinking individuals, it always carries the risk of becoming a form of indoctrination. Some scholars argue that indoctrination is an inevitable part of any pedagogy, since every form of education is linked to certain values and norms. Others, on the other hand, insist that education and indoctrination must be clearly distinguished from each other, especially by the methods and intentions behind the transmission of knowledge.

The debate about indoctrination is also so relevant because it is emerging in various areas of society. In political systems, in religions, in the media and even in advertising, there are mechanisms that aim to consolidate certain opinions and hide divergent points of view. Especially in today's world, in which information via digital media is disseminated faster and more purposefully than ever before, it is crucial to critically examine the sources and intentions behind the content conveyed.

Ultimately, indoctrination remains a fine line between influencing and manipulation, between legitimate education and ideological appropriation. The ability to critically reflect and form independent judgments is therefore a central prerequisite for recognizing indoctrination and counteracting it.

# 1.5 Critical Social Justice[355]

Social justice refers to justice with regard to the distribution of wealth, opportunities and privileges within a society in which the rights of individuals are recognized and protected. In Western and Asian cultures, the concept of social justice often referred to the process of ensuring that individuals fulfill their social roles and receive from society what they are entitled to.[356]

The Critical Social Justice (CSJ) movement has gained increasing influence in recent years and is shaping numerous social debates. Its roots lie in critical theory and postmodern philosophy, especially in the writings of thinkers such as Michel Foucault, Jacques Derrida, and Judith Butler. CSJ interprets social realities through a lens of power structures anchored in language, institutions, and cultural norms. This perspective has far-reaching implications for the way societal problems are perceived and addressed.

---

[355] https://merionwest.com/2021/09/02/the-psychology-of-critical-social-justice/
[356] https://en.wikipedia.org/wiki/Social_justice

A central feature of CSJ is the conviction that social inequalities are not merely due to individual differences or economic conditions, but to deep-rooted power relations that manifest themselves in discourses and social structures. The movement argues that these power structures are often invisible or normalized and therefore need to be deliberately deconstructed. Language plays a central role here: certain terms and expressions are seen as instruments of power that maintain social hierarchies.

Psychologically, CSJ is based on several assumptions about human behavior and social interactions. A central thesis is that identity politics is a primary determinant of an individual's self-image and social position. This means that people are not primarily seen as autonomous individuals, but as members of socially constructed groups who either benefit from privilege or are oppressed. This collectivist approach contrasts with classical liberal ideas, which regard the individual as a central unit of action.

The movement tends to take a strong moral perspective on social issues. It divides society into perpetrators and victims, with the victim narrative having a particularly strong emotional appeal. Psychological mechanisms such as cognitive dissonance and groupthink play a crucial role in the spread and stabilization of CSJ ideology. People who are confronted with CSJ narratives often find themselves in a situation where they either signal approval or are labeled as immoral or ignorant. This can lead to a climate of conformity and self-censorship.

Another psychological element is the concept of "awakening" or "being woke". This state describes an increased awareness of social injustices and one's own position within these structures. The process of awakening often follows a certain pattern: First, the person experiences a cognitive restructuring in which he or she questions previous assumptions about society, identity and power. This leads to a new self-definition in which one's own actions are increasingly determined by the principles of the CSJ ideology. This dynamic is similar to religious conversion experiences and can have a high emotional intensity.

The impact of CSJ is felt in many areas of society, especially in educational institutions, media and companies. Critics argue that the movement leads to a restriction of open discourse, as dissenting opinions are often portrayed as morally reprehensible. This can lead to an atmosphere of fear and self-censorship, where freedom of expression is restricted. Proponents, on the other hand, see CSJ as a necessary correction of historical injustices and an opportunity to empower marginalized groups.

In conclusion, Critical Social Justice is deeply rooted in philosophical and psychological concepts. Its influence on social debates is enormous, and it shapes the way people think about power, identity and justice. Whether it will lead to a fairer society in the long term or create new forms of social division remains an open question.

## Review by James Lindsay[357]

Who is James Lindsay?

James Stephen Lindsay, known as James A. Lindsay, is an American author. He became known for the so-called *Grievance Studies affair*, in which he, together with Peter Boghossian and Helen Pluckrose, submitted fictitious articles to scientific journals in 2017 and 2018 to test academic quality and rigor in various subject areas. Lindsay has authored several books, including *Cynical Theories* (2020), which he co-authored with Pluckrose. He has also spread right-wing conspiracy theories, such as those of "cultural Marxism" and the "LGBT grooming" conspiracy.[358]

He describes himself on newdiscourses as a professional troublemaker and leading Critical Race Theory expert that led to rejection of it.

---

[357] https://newdiscourses.com/2020/02/naming-enemy-critical-social-justice/
[358] https://en.wikipedia.org/wiki/James_A._Lindsay

In 2017, James Lindsay and Peter Boghossian published a fictitious scientific paper entitled The Conceptual Penis as a Social Construct, in which they presented the penis as a social construct in terms of performative toxic masculinity. The work was intended to imitate the style of poststructuralist gender theories. After initially being rejected, it finally appeared in the journal Cogent Social Sciences.

As of August 2017, Lindsay, Boghossian and Helen Pluckrose wrote a total of 20 such fake articles, which they submitted to trade journals under pseudonyms and the name of an acquaintance. The aim was to test the scientific integrity of certain fields in the humanities and social sciences. The project ended prematurely after a particularly absurd article in the feminist journal Gender, Place & Culture aroused suspicion and was uncovered by a journalist.

The action was later made public through a YouTube video[359] and a Wall Street Journal report. At that time, 7 of the 20 articles had been adopted, 7 were still under review and 6 had been rejected. One of the accepted texts contains passages from Hitler's Mein Kampf, which have been rewritten into feminist language.

Remarkably, some of these hoax articles have been positively evaluated by peer reviewers and praised as innovative and relevant to feminist and social science discourses.

## 2. The influence of Twitter, TikTok and Co.

Platforms such as Twitter, TikTok and Instagram have become central places where gender roles are discussed and often radicalized.

- **Twitter:** Heated debates about equality, toxic masculinity and feminist concerns dominate here. Through its brevity, the platform promotes pointed, often emotionally charged statements that polarize the debate. Men's rights activists and feminists often face

---

[359] https://www.youtube.com/watch?v=kVk9a5Jcd1k&ab_channel=MichaelNayna

each other in confrontational discussions, which makes factual discussions more difficult.

- **TikTok:** The video platform reinforces certain gender roles through viral trends. While fitness influencers often promote the ideal of the muscular, successful man, beauty and dating trends reinforce stereotypical expectations of women.
- **Instagram:** Influencer culture and beauty ideals often create unrealistic ideas about bodies and relationships. Women often receive encouragement for body positivity in feminist circles, while men continue to face pressure to perform in terms of fitness and success.

# 3. Algorithmic bias

Social media algorithms determine what content becomes visible. This creates distortions that favor certain narratives, the phenomenon is called the filter bubble:

- Polarizing content often gets more engagement because outrage, anger, and controversy generate high clicks. Extreme feminist or masculist content therefore often has a wider reach than differentiated debates.
- Men's rights issues such as custody, domestic violence against men or discrimination in criminal law receive less media attention than feminist concerns, as they often do not coincide with the main social narratives.
- Certain terms or opinions may be classified as "problematic" by platforms and algorithmically suppressed, while others may be preferred. This can lead to certain perspectives being less heard in the gender debate.

# 4. "Cancel Culture" and Censorship

Another phenomenon that shapes the debate about gender roles is the so-called "cancel culture".

## 4.1 Men as the main target of "cancel culture"

Men in public positions are particularly often affected by public shitstorms when they are considered "problematic". Accusations of sexism, misconduct or inappropriate comments can quickly lead to professional and social ostracism. This raises the question of the extent to which accusations are always justified or whether social media sometimes condemn prematurely.[360]

A tragic example would be Alexander Rogers. The media report that after sexual contact with a student, she felt uncomfortable - a statement she only shared in the confidential circle of her friends. It is not clear from the reports that there was criminally relevant misconduct, but rather that this subjective feeling led to his friends sharply condemning him and socially ostracizing him. This informal reaction, described as part of a *cancel culture,* changed the image of a previously popular and promising young man so drastically that he ended his life in deep despair.[361] [362] [363] There are similar incidents at the university.[364]

## 4.2 Manipulative representations and block tactics

Posts are increasingly circulating on social media that deliberately portray men as "creeps" – for example, through staged scenes in gyms, in which even a *quick glance* in the direction of a content creator is interpreted as "intrusive staring". Such representations create a climate

---

[360] https://nycmuseumgallery.org/1196/entertainment/how-has-social-media-affected-cancel-culture/
[361] https://tinyurl.com/mv7u7rh8
[362] https://tinyurl.com/3muc2azm
[363] https://www.bbc.com/news/articles/cdd0gvjlqyvo
[364] https://freespeechunion.org/i-lived-in-fear-of-being-cancelled-as-an-oxbridge-student-we-all-did/

of general suspicion in which even harmless interactions are considered a threat. The real implications are evident in cases such as a blind man who, despite his cane, was thrown out of a gym because he was accused of "conspicuous staring" – an accusation that is obviously absurd due to his disability.[365]

## 4.3 Blocking and controlling narratives

Content creators use block features strategically to suppress critical voices:

- Example: A creator claimed in a reel that *"violence and sexualized assault are a purely male phenomenon"*. When I objected with a Justin Bieber video, I was blocked by the creator.[366]
- As a result, all my comments disappeared from her posts – the comment column now resembles an "echo chamber" in which only agreeing opinions are visible.
- Others, on the other hand, leave a few negative comments, but they clearly do not come from the brightest minds. Since I was blocked here myself, I think that this is less of an echo chamber and more of an environment where feminism acts as the voice of reason, while the men seem like "angry gorillas".
- Someone else seems to handle their settings in such a way that every comment has to be approved first – or it is simply deleted if it doesn't fit into the picture.

## 4.4 Pinning posts

Another strategy seems to be pinning posts: Either particularly ill-considered comments are pinned to the top to demonstrate one's superiority, or interesting, irrefutable posts are pinned so that the community can pounce on them. The latter may seem a bit unfair, but it at least promotes a culture of debate.

---

[365] https://www.kosmo.at/frau-angestarrt-blinder-mann-aus-fitnessstudio-geworfen/
[366] https://youtu.be/o84rnYTuunQ?si=TtnvKGYobl-szpmY

## 4.5 Blocking by other users: sabotage of debate

Users also use blocks to manipulate debates:

- Tactics: Someone replies to a comment and blocks immediately afterwards. The blocked person can then no longer react, or does not even know that they have been replied to, while the blocking person gives the impression that he has "the last word" and is therefore right, because both comments are still visible to everyone else.
- Observation: This method is often used when argumentative weaknesses become apparent. Instead of countering in terms of content, the dialogue is broken off – to outsiders it looks as if the person blocking has "won".
- Men report more content when women talk about finance or other male-dominated areas.[367] I have heard similar statements from Pro Male Content Creators, that sometimes even trivial statements are deleted from them. However, the interest of research here seems to be more focused on the female side, which is why I have to say that I have not found a source for these claims.

## 4.6 Consequences for the discourse

- **Distorted perception of reality:** One-sided representations characterize the picture
- **Erosion of dialogue**: Critical perspectives are filtered out, debates degenerate into pure self-portrayal shows
- **Loss of trust:** Critical users doubt the authenticity of discussions if only striking polemics remain instead of exchange
- **Custodians of the Internet:** The majority of users want their Twitter feed, Facebook page, and YouTube comments to remain free of harassment and pornographic content. Whether it's "fake news" or live-streamed violence, content moderators who censor or

---

[367] https://tinyurl.com/yf7hudcp

highlight user-generated posts are now in unprecedented importance. This is especially true since the tools used by social media to curb trolling, stop hate speech, and censor pornography can also silence **the very voices that should be heard.**[368]

- **Restriction of freedom of expression:** When debates are stifled by strategic blocking, "cancel culture" or one-sided censorship, the open exchange of ideas is undermined. This contradicts the ideal of a pluralistic democracy, in which controversial points of view must be discussed – even if they are uncomfortable.
- **Amplification of polarization:** Echo chambers and targeted narratives lead to **social division**. Users are unlearning how to deal with differences, and extreme positions are gaining power (e.g., red pill vs. radical feminism).

## 4.7 Conclusion

Blocking should actually serve to protect against harassment – and in many cases it will. However, our examples show that this measure can also be misused to gain control over narratives. Whether by creators or users – the goal is the same: to stifle criticism and maintain the appearance of moral superiority. As long as platforms reward such tactics, real exchange will fall by the wayside – in favor of a culture of division and performative "being right".

I suspect that this behavior is less common among men. However, I lack the clear expertise for this. It is possible that many are less sensitive to it or simply do not care more often. Addendum – I've changed my mind: If men do this, it's as if they've played through Instagram. In my case, the person in charge seems to activate all comments manually. He also approves your initial comment and then admits people who agree with him. Your answers, on the other hand, are apparently never unlocked, but simply deleted.

---

[368] https://www.degruyter.com/document/doi/10.12987/9780300235029/html

# 5. Bear-vs.-Man

## 5.1 Introduction

Reels are spreading on social media that draw the comparison between a bear and a man. They are intended to make it clear that men can pose a greater threat to women than wild animals. This is an attempt to illustrate women's deep fear of men – for example, that they are not believed when reports of violence are reported, or that some women would even rather die than take the risk of rape. The question is: Does this drastic format justify the purpose?

These representations reveal two central aspects: generalization and demonization. The conclusion that men are worse than bears is a form of demonization. This is not just an individual transgression, but the demonization of an entire group by millions of women, which is tantamount to a systematic construction of an image of the enemy – the fundamental function of demonization. While individuals can judge men irrationally, this way of thinking becomes hate propaganda as soon as it is spread in the media.[369] The comment columns on the reels look accordingly.

## 5.2 Objection undesirable

Anyone who criticizes such reels as a man, because the general suspicion is a form of discrimination and the demonization also triggers many, is often labeled as "part of the problem". The chain of argumentation follows a manipulative pattern:

- Why do you question the content instead of showing "solidarity"?
- Those who defend themselves have something to hide.
- Those who reject the comparison want to trivialize violence against women.

---

[369] https://de.wikipedia.org/wiki/D%C3%A4monisierung

- If you don't agree, you're probably a perpetrator

This rhetoric is a classic example of psychological manipulation: it makes criticism impossible by making men collectively responsible for acts they did not commit. This is a form of psychological violence that goes largely uncriticized.

## 5.3 Double standards

Collective responsibility of men is demanded. Women, on the other hand, are rarely held collectively accountable for crimes that are statistically more likely to be committed by them:

- **Intimate partner violence**: About half of the violence is bilateral, one-sided violence often comes from women[370] [371]
- **Neonaticides, infanticides and filicides** (infanticides up to 14 years of age)[372]
- **Violence against children:** 10% of women practice parenting violence and 8% of men[373]

It's ironic: If you talk about neonaticide and infanticide, for example, you often hear immediately: "Yes, but the perpetrators are mentally ill!" That may be true, but what does it change in the situation? Strictly speaking, nothing at all. A study from England, for example, showed that 64% of the perpetrators of partner murders were mentally ill. While the focus used to be strongly on male perpetration and female perpetrators received little attention, reference is now made to mental illnesses, which are rejected as differentiation in men or even criticized as an attempt to trivialize the crime.

Here you can see how collective responsibility suddenly no longer plays a role, and you fall into exactly the pattern that previously

---

[370] https://pmc.ncbi.nlm.nih.gov/articles/PMC1854883/
[371] https://tinyurl.com/55d5rcbx
[372] https://tinyurl.com/msv32ehv
[373] https://www.vaeter-zeit.de/vaeter-maenner/maennergewalt-gewalt-gegen-jungen.php

criticized men. This behavior does not seem to me to be patriarchal misogyny, but rather human reactance.

One could now say: "But mentally ill is a really valid explanation!" – Absolutely, it is a circumstance that should always be considered.

Where exactly does this principle of collective responsibility come in? I am of the opinion that collective responsibility is a task for society as a whole that should not be projected onto a specific group. Otherwise, the whole thing comes across as a reproach, which in turn leads to reactance. The result is then only the typical demonization, which is probably also partly intentional.

## 5.4 "Mean World Syndrome"[374] and Irrational Fear

Another topic that is often ignored is that comparisons such as the bear-vs. man comparison not only show fear of actual violence by men, but also the problem of irrational fear caused by media distortions – a point I have already addressed in the chapter on violence. Another explanation for this would be the Mean World Syndrome. This psychological theory describes how excessive consumption of violence-centered media can lead to an exaggerated fear of violence.

Women spend an average of 2.52 hours a day on social media.[375] Anyone who is interested in the topic of "violence against women" there will be flooded with increasingly drastic content by algorithms. The problem with this is that it is not reality that determines the perception of danger, but the frequency and drama of the content shown. Here you could use the example we already had in Cognitive Dissonance again. Violence is decreasing: from 79 to 23 cases per 1,000 people.[376] Even

---

[374] https://en.wikipedia.org/wiki/Mean_world_syndrome
[375] https://www.presseportal.de/pm/64713/5540659
[376] https://bjs.ojp.gov/press-release/criminal-victimization-2022

sexual offenses.[377] But not fear: "It got worse" or "We have the worst state ever."

This distorted perception is not without consequences. It can intensify collective fears and contribute to the formation of social enemy images – in this case towards men as a group. In a society in which fear increasingly serves as political capital, the central question arises: Who benefits if women believe that they live in a more dangerous world today than ever before? One could assume: feminism. After all, who do women turn to when they are afraid and looking for understanding?

But even if some feminists consciously use this dynamic, the real problem lies deeper. The topic is often avoided for fear that the experiences of female victims of violence could be relativized. But if we put the emotional level aside for a moment and look at it soberly, what has it done in the last 20 years to primarily take hurt feelings into account? Are women better off today – or are we not rather experiencing a significant increase in anxiety disorders, especially among young women who have a strong presence on social media?

This reveals a real dilemma between mental health and emotional consideration. By the way, there is a video by Varnan that is worth seeing, which sheds more light on this connection.[378]

## 5.5 Where is the media literacy?

In view of the negative effects of scaremongering on mental health and e.g. In the *bear vs. man* debate, the question arises: Where is media literacy in the feminist discourse? Instead of empowering women by learning to see through manipulative fear rhetoric, such narratives are often reinforced. It would be equally important to educate content creators about their responsibility for the emotional impact of their messages.

---

[377] https://www.statista.com/statistics/251923/usa-reported-forcible-rape-cases-by-gender/
[378] https://youtu.be/6w_96Hnz8JM?si=sMGvMQw9lzedSWCA

**There is simply a lack of clarification on 3 fronts:**

- How does fear of crime arise?
- What do content creators have to pay attention to
- And what media consumers are looking for

# 5.6 Speaking of media literacy

In *quer*[379] (BR), the man is portrayed as an emotionally sensitive idiot who is presented with a standard explanation of violence against women – without any reflection on generalization, demonization or hate propaganda. Not a word about the real core problem: irrational fear and a lack of media education in public discourse.

- In the *Parship* video,[380] a participant says after the choice of the "bear":
- "... There are too many stories that you have heard."

When asked what would have to change for her to vote for the man, she answers:

- "... The general picture would have to change..."
- And "... That men also understand what it's like to be a woman ...".

The participant suggests that men can acquire women's fears through **imagination.** But this approach is naïve:

**Experiences of violence are not transferable:**

A man who has never experienced sexualized violence cannot "empathize" with the omnipresent fear of catcalling, rape or femicide – just as a woman cannot understand what it is like to be laughed at as a

---

[379] https://youtu.be/lxeEI_tnKkw?si=CWyzllF_Jgacd21X
[380] https://youtu.be/KwLNSAn1AAo?si=t1VYsc_myNMOHXxJ

man as a victim of domestic violence. Ok, maybe the example is too clichéd.

Let's take me as an example: I was beaten, robbed, beaten and robbed, and there was an incident where, while holding me down, they argued about where to dispose of my body. I was grabbed by the butt at least 2 times by women, and at least once by a man who harassed me in the crowd at the same club for several weeks – I had to tell him twice to stop before he finally stopped. Once I was kicked so hard that I had acoustic hallucinations for three months. Another time there was an argument at a party, only insults, nothing physical. We decided to leave the party. On the way home, we were followed by a car the whole time. This psycho, who was the main protagonist of the conflict, became one of my best colleagues years later.

I don't expect anyone to understand that. I probably can't explain it either. These experiences simply have no weight, it's like waiting at a bus stop for a delayed bus. Shit happens. A few years later we talked about it and he apologized.

I don't think that's anything special; that's how it goes for middle-class men in a small town. You just don't tell us anything new. The only thing I can't relate to is the fear, even though the incident in which they planned to dispose of my body had traumatized me for two months and it was uncomfortable to go out. But the trauma healed on its own. What we don't need is another generation of boys to whom we **only** tell them not to beat girls.

**Asymmetry of the perception of violence:**

- Women are more likely to experience sexualized violence.
- Men experience physical violence in public more often (e.g. fights, robberies) and, above all, quantitatively more violence.
- Both are traumatic – but the social reaction differs massively: While violence against women is scandalized as a "system failure",

violence against men is often considered a "normal" part of masculinity.

## On the empathy problem

Men often fail to understand women's everyday fears – not out of malice, but because both sexes go through different socializations. Vera Birkenbihl provided an example in her lecture "*Men and Women*":[381] In a survey, men were asked to rate how women rate rape on a scale of 1 ("harmless") to 7 ("murder"). The result: While women rated rape at an average of 6.5, the men's estimate was 3.5, and it should be noted that they estimated the opinion of the women.

This gap is also reflected in the statement of the Parship participant, who implicitly serves a sexist cliché: "Men are per se lacking in empathy, women per se innocent." But the problem lies deeper – in social structures that actively prevent empathy. Men learn from childhood to hide pain ("An Indian knows no pain!"), while women are stigmatized as "weak".

The participant's demand ("Men must understand what it's like to be a woman") is not a call for dialogue, but a symptom of our failed gender discourse. As long as we understand empathy as a one-way street – women as victims, men as perpetrators – nothing will change.

In '*Bosetti wants to talk!*'[382] I briefly had the impression that it would be a constructive contribution. She explained that the general suspicion was fundamentally wrong for the time being, always! – A correct approach. But then she gets her act together again by asking whether we really want to put the general suspicion under general suspicion? And this opens the door to blanket discrimination against men. In men, this is considered normal – they are considered strong and are expected to cope with it on their own. But if social pressure or psychological

---

[381] https://youtu.be/ZuAaD33vW5k?si=Hg-YOgRiWV9S1P31
[382] https://tinyurl.com/4y3dbf4y available until 14.05.2026

violence, which we all too often do not recognize as such, ends in killing, violence or suicide, then suddenly we only speak of individual guilt.

Back to the topic – yes, we want to put the general suspicion under general suspicion – because that is the exception that proves the rule. It also claims that the general suspicion is fact-based. But she apparently never did any research on the facts about fear of crime. But let's see what she might mean when she says that the general suspicion is fact-based.

What is a general suspicion anyway? It describes a suspicion that is expressed to an entire group without concrete evidence.[383] Isn't fact-based general suspicion by definition already a contradiction? I rather understand it to mean that she speaks of a generalization in the sense of a generalization.

Colloquially, we like to generalize – for example, when someone says: "Women can't drive a car." If you look at the accident statistics, you can see that men are more often involved in accidents. But that's not what this statement is about. Rather, it is about the fact that women on average have poorer hand-eye coordination and limited spatial capacity. This does not mean that these characteristics apply to all women, but only to a majority. The key point is that it is about the majority of a group – and here you can discuss whether such a generalization is okay.

However, it is important to distinguish between generalization to the entire population group from the majority of this group or the majority within a special event. Because there is no data to prove that over 50% of all men would be sex offenders, let alone that over 50% lurk in the forest on weekends to attack lonely joggers. A generalization with less than half of the cases is more of an exaggeration or a cliché and not a logically meaningful statement. So, for example, 80% of all 5-star quivers would be men, which makes the statement "Men are 5-star chefs" still not tenable.

---

[383] https://de.wikipedia.org/wiki/Generalverdacht

In view of the fact that media reports make a significant contribution to the intensification of fear of crime – a phenomenon that is intensively researched in media psychology – one could ask whether such reporting is not itself part of the problem.

And there are plenty of such examples, even in newspapers.[384] [385] [386] [387] The TU Dresden has even classified the demonization of men under Fun (Women's Environment Network).[388] (No criticism, but ironic in a slightly macabre way.)

- Their fact checks refer to a WHO report that says that every 3 women have experienced violence in their partnership.
- The White Ring, on the other hand, speaks of every second man.[389] (different locations, different definitions of violence, it's not comparable, but we've already looked at what intimate partner violence looks like.)
- Then they go into all the deaths by bears again, but overlook, so that they can compare the danger, they have to calculate it down to one encounter.
- The insights they take away from the topic are that the topic is not taken seriously.
- I would rather suspect that the answer they want to hear is only a fragment of the whole.
- Lack of self-reflection and empathy.
- Yes, but on both sides.
- And that men react to psychological violence with psychological violence. (They didn't put it that way)
- And that I am currently participating in misogyny.

---

[384] https://www.wienerzeitung.at/a/mann-oder-baer
[385] https://www.glamour.de/artikel/mann-oder-baer-auf-tiktok-kommentar
[386] https://tinyurl.com/34y28k3c
[387] https://tinyurl.com/46z9kbhv
[388] https://tinyurl.com/4bdmtfwx
[389] https://weisser-ring.de/gewalt_gegen_maenner

➢ Such accusations are perhaps also one of the reasons why no one wants to address the causes of fear of crime in this context and why the core problem is ignored instead of tinkering with solutions.

You should be aware: Each of these posts was written, produced and approved by someone. Somewhere in this process, someone could have questioned whether sexist narratives are being served here.

In addition, when writing the incel chapter, I noticed that this "bear-vs-man" narrative has strong parallels to the incel shitstorm: From a victim's perspective, demonization is done. A social problem for which one is not responsible is pointed out so radically that psychological violence becomes the means of communication of choice – for women often in the form of manipulative tactics, for men more through direct threats. Both sides are convinced that they are morally right and believe that the end justifies the means. They seek validation and show no empathy for the "enemy".

## 6. Conclusion

Social media has radically changed the gender debate. While they provide platforms for exchange and awareness-raising, they often also reinforce polarizing narratives and algorithmic biases. *Cancel culture* particularly affects men in public positions, while women who are critical of feminist issues can also be attacked. This shows that the gender debate on social media brings not only progress, but also new challenges.

## XIV. Misandry

"There is no hatred of men" – a claim that comes up again and again on social media, talk shows and even in academic debates. But if you go through the world with your eyes open, you will come across countless examples that prove the opposite. Hatred of men is not a figment of the

imagination of sensitive individuals. It is real, often tolerated by society –
and sometimes widely accepted.

# 1. Introduction[390]

**Definition:**

Misandry refers to a deep-rooted hatred or hostile attitude towards
men because of their gender. It is considered a form of sexism and can
occur in both women and men.

**Manifestations:**

- Open contempt or violence against men
- Subtle portrayals in the media (e.g., men as boobies or threats)
- Spreading stereotypes (e.g., men as violent or emotionally
  underdeveloped)
- Feminist discourses that portray men as oppressors across the
  board. This leads to a distorted view. In Spain, for example, 84% of
  men prefer an equal distribution of tasks, only 48% of them do
  so.[391] (largest difference of 6 countries studied)

**Historical and literary examples:**

- Radical feminist positions
- Pop culture statements (e.g. song "Men are pigs / Männer sind
  Schweine")
- Societal tendencies to stigmatize men as "problematic"

**Scientific perspectives:**

- (Rather) Feminist view: Misandry is often seen as an individual, not
  a structural problem.

---

[390] https://www.bionity.com/de/lexikon/Misandrie.html
[391] https://docs.iza.org/dp17493.pdf

- Sociological view: Some researchers see a cultural anchoring of misogyny, while others deny structural discrimination.
- (Rather) Feminism critical view: Critics accuse feminism of promoting misandry and demonizing men across the board. Sometimes also general, sometimes more differentiated.

Misandry is a controversial but increasingly discussed phenomenon. While some classify it as socially relevant, others dispute its structural importance. The debate shows a polarization between feminist and masculist positions.

## 2. Pop culture

Hatred of men is not a niche phenomenon. He shapes films, series, music and much more:

- Comedians like Daniel Sloss[392] or Hannah Gadsby[393] base their performances on generalizations such as "Men are dangerous" – and earn standing ovations for it.
- Series like *The Handmaid's Tale* portray men as oppressors.
- Music: Songs like *KETA AND KRAWALL* by Ikkimel normalize contempt.
- Or "Dead Men Don't Rape" by Delilah Bon.[394] [395] The quote "Dead men don't rape" is often attributed to Aileen Wuornos. However, there are indications that it originally came from feminist circles and was adopted by Wuornos. Regardless of the exact origin, it reflects Wuornos' attitude. As a former prostitute who killed seven men – according to her own statements in self-defense against rape attempts – she expressed strong hatred for men and society as a whole in interviews.

---

[392] https://youtu.be/0uZFHpEh5So?si=r3NI1qYl5FmLYZuT
[393] https://youtu.be/OEPsqFLhHBc?si=er6Yb1rVwS8jYCQG
[394] https://youtu.be/m9keJhpRG5o?si=gLHOieyzUGYuoH6J
[395] https://www.instagram.com/p/DITkT4qo-ze/

- Also, available as a T-shirt.[396]
- Book: "How to Piss Off Men: 109 Things to Say to Shatter the Male Ego"[397] – Basically, a guide on how to manipulate men or effectively inflict psychological violence against men. I understand that some people find it funny, my humor is not much better. But I also see that it is directed against insecure people who try to pretend. I also see that I wouldn't even find it funny if the insecure person was a woman. Which basically shows that I, too, have internalized social hatred of men.
- Book: "I hate men" by Pauline Harmange. "... Compulsory reading for all women. Pauline Harmange hates men – all but her husband. ..." says the book description on Amazon.[398]

Criticism of this is quickly  dismissed as "mimosa-like" – an indication of how deep the acceptance of such stereotypes is. I don't want to boost a reverse *cancel culture* now  . Media and artists only represent society – and while misogyny is criticized, men apparently "deserve" it.

German rap, on the other hand, has always been questionable in  this regard. But if those  who have criticized German rap as misogynistic now say, that's okay, or those who celebrated contempt for women suddenly complain that it's going too far, then this double standard has already made it halfway to empathy.

# 3. Social Media

## 3.1 Hashtags, agitation and double standards

A look at the search on Instagram is enough to guess the extent:

- **#killallmen** is used over **18,900 times** – disguised as a "provocative joke", but often with a serious background.

---

[396] https://www.amazon.co.uk/Aileen-Wuornos-Shirt-American-Serial/dp/B0CS3K54KC
[397] https://www.amazon.com/How-Piss-Off-Men-Shatter/dp/1728291925
[398] https://www.amazon.de/Ich-hasse-M%C3%A4nner-Pauline-Harmange/dp/3499006758

- **#menaretrash** is found **40,600 times** – a blanket condemnation that would be harshly criticized in the event of gender swapping.

For comparison:
- **#killallwomen**: around 500 mentions.
- **#womenaretrash**: about 1,000.

The discrepancy is no coincidence. While hatred against women is rightly scandalized, similar statements against men are considered "rebellion" or "satire". The supposed context – feminism as "resistance" – justifies for many what would be considered agitation if roles were reversed.

## 3.2 Live Action

Let's start the topic with a quote from the SKiD 2020: "Verbal violence on the Internet is also significantly more common against men (671.1) than against women (352.0)." (per 1000 per year)

When I see that something like this is discussed, it's usually against women.[399] But the dark field study shows that men experience almost twice as much verbal violence on the Internet. However, this takes on a completely different dimension if, like me, you actively follow many feminists or radical feminists.

- Hatred of men is a revolution, and it is important and right.[400]

---

[399] https://youtu.be/Lxpe5vYL5Ks?si=zQVJOKoxE0TJ5afB
[400] https://www.instagram.com/p/DKckannNxIe/

- The loneliness of men is not regretted – it is celebrated. It is the goal of men. Your own fault. And anyway – women are doing well.[401][402][403][404][405][406][407][408][409]
- *Paint loneliness* and felt truths that we've already taken a closer look at.[410]
- Male Loneliness is actually just a joke.[411][412][413]
- She thinks of the *Male Loneliness* as she does it. And in the comments, one thinks of the suicide rates of men.[414]
- As an alternative to combat the *Male Loneliness* AI robots as partners. There is a certain irony in the fact that digisexual-shaming is being carried out here by someone who himself belongs to a minority. He projects demonizing patriarchal clichés onto an old lonely man. Does he know him personally?[415]
- The men's problems? Made by men. Any problems? Men.[416][417]
- Men are the problem.[418] Even if they are absent.[419]
- I don't hate men.[420]
- There is no hatred of men.[421]
- Men are too fragile.[422]

---

[401] https://www.instagram.com/p/DIGotktOcbP

[402] https://www.instagram.com/p/DC9VLMEpsRX/

[403] https://www.instagram.com/p/DIHjhvFpqp7/

[404] https://www.instagram.com/p/DH855jfpw44/

[405] https://www.instagram.com/p/DH84GXMJ2Za/

[406] https://www.instagram.com/p/DI-5sM-uRby/

[407] https://www.instagram.com/p/DI3xcIMotWj/

[408] https://www.instagram.com/p/DJmtvogMqUG/

[409] https://www.instagram.com/reel/DJkIPg_yHlb/

[410] https://www.instagram.com/p/DI4gmH-pTmM/

[411] https://www.instagram.com/reel/DIpWrvDTmJY/

[412] https://www.instagram.com/p/DIAEF5Zhwsc

[413] https://www.instagram.com/p/DJuP1Duv1BD/

[414] https://www.instagram.com/p/DJUkv92sYD4/

[415] https://www.instagram.com/p/DI0w22esKuG/

[416] https://www.instagram.com/p/DH_ARIYgtJj/

[417] https://www.instagram.com/p/DH9Mx_upKUU/

[418] https://www.instagram.com/p/DJEGzDDO9QR/

[419] https://www.instagram.com/p/DJBst4-ItAR/

[420] https://www.instagram.com/reel/DJFZBXRvIfw/

[421] https://www.instagram.com/p/DI0EwKuRV9H/?img_index=2

[422] https://www.instagram.com/p/DJTZTRjgZBg/

- Femicide.[423]
- A reel from The Times about problems of men and boys.[424] The problem is not the reel, but a large part of the comments. No empathy, no proposed solutions, hardly any dialogue. Self-aggrandizement. Patriarchy is to blame, men are to blame. As a society, we ignore men's problems and if it gets out of hand, it's their own fault, so we can continue to ignore it.
- Feminist education on violence against men, with women as perpetrators? Oh, no. The death of a man is instrumentalized to further criticize men.[425] What she thinks about it.[426] What happened.[427]
- Many women cheat, but it's mostly the man's fault if they accidentally sleep with someone else.[428]
- Difference between feminist and conservative man. One sees women as private property, the other as public property.[429]
- "All men" at Death Note.[430] To explain: Death Note is an anime and everything you write in the Death Note dies.
- Without men, children would be safe.[431]
- His penis fell off because a woman wrote something on the Internet.[432]
- All men hate women, but no one wants to be hated.[433]
- I love men.[434] And more of her.[435] [436]
- Femosphere[437]

---

[423] https://www.instagram.com/reel/DJm1oP4owTj/
[424] https://www.instagram.com/p/DJog_JRv2cZ/
[425] https://www.instagram.com/p/DJb14APMjKH/
[426] https://www.instagram.com/p/DJUNVbGsLry/
[427] https://tinyurl.com/2w7tfant
[428] https://www.instagram.com/p/DJbKyizPhSY/
[429] https://www.instagram.com/p/DJTp2dAKn8X/
[430] https://www.instagram.com/p/DKZ3Pi9R4k7/
[431] https://www.instagram.com/p/DJT0n7bIayc/
[432] https://www.instagram.com/p/DJFSGk9z1LE/?img_index=1
[433] https://www.instagram.com/p/DJKU5ivyZ-O/?img_index=2
[434] https://www.instagram.com/p/DI4SLRJRXBi/
[435] https://www.instagram.com/p/DI-I0U_ozIk/
[436] https://www.instagram.com/p/DIuvxgooEzZ/
[437] https://www.instagram.com/p/DJKDl11KS7y/

- Ick list.[438] [439]
- The truth is: The Ick is Emotional Intelligence in Action.[440]
- Women are superior. (scientifically proven) What she's talking about is the Matilda effect, which says that men have passed off women's achievements as their own or generally undermine them. She commits a *non sequitur* ("it does not follow") to present her belief in female superiority as scientifically proven.[441] And of course also because of her clitoris.[442]
- I need children so that my line doesn't die out.[443]
- She can believe a pregnant virgin, but 3 wise men.[444]
- Childless single woman is the greatest danger to patriarchy. Be that danger.[445]
- And again and again selective demonization.[446] What she's talking about: 21 percent of partnerships break up when the woman suffers from cancer – compared to only 3 percent when the man was affected.[447] The reasons are that men feel overwhelmed by care.[448] There is also a study that looks at what happens when a partner wins the lottery. Divorce rate is twice as high if the woman wins, the divorce rate decreases by 40% if the man wins.[449] One is times 7, the other almost times 4, neither is so cool.
- Death to the patriarch, incels, rapists and billionaires.[450]
- God forbid a woman has a hobby.[451]
- God forbid a man has a hobby.[452]

---

[438] https://www.instagram.com/p/DI9pKBiouMd/
[439] https://www.instagram.com/p/DI4hJQ-InVq/
[440] https://www.instagram.com/p/DJALGe7TUIv/?img_index=1
[441] https://www.instagram.com/reel/DImITufRDuV/
[442] https://www.instagram.com/p/DJSvB18pHy_/
[443] https://www.instagram.com/p/DJKfFvCJ-km
[444] https://www.instagram.com/p/DJgx4MftBi6/
[445] https://www.instagram.com/p/DJMj3PcSYaA/
[446] https://www.instagram.com/reel/DJHuK-7pUGi/
[447] https://tinyurl.com/4mpdfjuz
[448] https://www.forum-gesundheitspolitik.de/artikel/artikel.pl?artikel=1669
[449] https://tinyurl.com/3t3dkx7c
[450] https://www.instagram.com/p/DJimxDASMeK/
[451] https://www.instagram.com/p/DJSuSAtJeLI/
[452] https://www.instagram.com/p/DJCH1FDh9VO/

- God forbid a man has rights.[453] How quickly you take patriarchal role models for granted if it benefits you. Alimony payments should be fair and appropriate and not based on outdated role models.
- All problems start with MEN. MENopause, MENstrual cramps, MENtal breakdown, MANipulation, GovernMENt.[454]
- Women get the kids ready for school and men sit on the toilet for 40 minutes and play with their cell phones.[455] Is there really a statistic for this, ask for a friend.
- Love is a woman. Never a man.[456]
- After mansplaining, now messed around.[457] Sexist ideas for neologisms.
- Pollen are male.[458] We are also to blame for the pollen allergy.
- Men control women with their penis or with cruelty. Anything that restricts their penis or cruelty scares them.[459]
- The demonization of all possibilities of rapprochement between the sexes. Here, a guitar is destroyed so that he can't play *Wonderwall*.[460]
- Men should have a curfew so that women can feel safe.[461] And the comments also say directly: "Put her in a cage."
- Respect as recognition of human dignity is philosophically "natural", biologically supported by empathy, but women owe you nothing.[462] The interpretation may be daring, but in the context of the other examples, I hope it makes sense.
- Women's paranoia – it's made by men.[463]

---

[453] https://www.instagram.com/reel/DI_exaBBDiz/
[454] https://www.instagram.com/p/DI8M4-LAR0H/
[455] https://www.instagram.com/p/DJBFXCeAsny/?img_index=1
[456] https://www.instagram.com/p/DH9KsxzJEza/
[457] https://www.instagram.com/p/DI1Tigvquyj/
[458] https://www.instagram.com/reel/DJCUT2YtRRF/
[459] https://www.instagram.com/p/DH59LT4IErl/
[460] https://www.instagram.com/reel/DI9X6pCTqb2/
[461] https://www.instagram.com/p/DJj0dIrS7-N/?img_index=1
[462] https://www.instagram.com/p/DJEHDpZu2hd/
[463] https://www.instagram.com/p/DHuMzWXtadQ/

- A world without men would be better.[464] [465]
- "I'm different," he says. – "Yes. Another disappointment." *Sliders* – full of psychological violence against men.[466] [467]
- Further humiliations[468] [469] [470]
- What men want is all women's happiness and other demonizations.[471]
- Incels don't deserve love. No pity. No compassion[472]
- Violence against men[473] [474] [475]
- She raises her daughter to violence against men.[476]
- Men have to be killed literarily in order to be repaired.[477]
- Double standard[478]
- It is impossible to cure men.[479] Almost every one of her posts is like that.
- Patriarchy keeps itself alive by pushing every woman into motherhood and then rejecting her.[480]
- Women are right – even if they are wrong. Because they do everything right. Because they are women.[481]
- Not all men - Not all snakes. Animal comparisons are dehumanizing.
- Explaining generalization on the basis of ticks or Covid – and because we can thoughtlessly discriminate here – shows that we

[464] https://www.instagram.com/p/DHrTHUBoW9W/
[465] https://www.instagram.com/p/DJEmiDTI8B2/
[466] https://www.instagram.com/p/DHlpeiJo3-m/
[467] https://www.instagram.com/p/DHHoYWapKLw/
[468] https://www.instagram.com/p/DHjPCDOpEKD/
[469] https://www.instagram.com/reel/DDIWYmqp1hs/
[470] https://www.instagram.com/reel/DIvRWcJR3G4/
[471] https://www.instagram.com/p/DJKN7oQMC09/
[472] https://www.instagram.com/reel/DIG8JZcp6rM/
[473] https://www.instagram.com/p/DHOdvx0pLTH/
[474] https://www.instagram.com/p/DGuAGW3IhzW/
[475] https://www.instagram.com/reel/C8ahOcLSnTl/
[476] https://www.instagram.com/p/DJPNJ_IIxle/
[477] https://www.instagram.com/p/DHMna1Vp3yL/
[478] https://www.instagram.com/p/DIoXrJtvQv0/?img_index=1
[479] https://www.instagram.com/p/DIExC9kstm9/?img_index=2
[480] https://www.instagram.com/p/DJbwLsmARbW/
[481] https://www.instagram.com/p/DHMIcMRp00T

can do the same with men. This is also dehumanizing again.[482] (Even if she doesn't mean any harm – and I certainly believe her – but: If I am beaten up by three North Koreans and conclude from this experience that all North Koreans are violent, then that is racist and discriminatory, until the day when really all North Koreans beat me up.)

- Cancel suicide education event for men.[483] Unfortunately, the video does not explain where or what the exact circumstances are. What I found is that there was such an incident in 2015 in York at the university. In the context of *International Men's Day*, the aim was to draw attention to suicides in particular, because it is the biggest killer for men under 45 and less than 24 hours earlier, a fellow student took his own life. There was a collection of signatures from 200 signatories who believe that this would undermine women's structural problems. As a result, the university canceled the event. Then there was a collection of signatures against the cancellation and it came to 1000 signatories, seems to have changed nothing in the decision.[484] [485] [486] [487]

- The first comment: "'Suicide Awareness' is not just any therapy session ... It's sad that his friends have died, but a suicide prevention rally won't give him any answers. The fact that he tries to relate the whole thing to himself, even though it's about suicide education, speaks volumes." – Empathy none.

- Another comment: "Every year on Remembrance Day, feminists post in my veteran groups, 'I miss it when men went to war and didn't come back.' I've lost friends to their demons – and for the feminists, it seems like it's a game."

- Men are lured, robbed and/or killed by women through dating app[488]

---

[482] https://www.instagram.com/reel/DIJxyEFpOy5/
[483] https://www.instagram.com/reel/DIKmhIFyEpM/
[484] https://tinyurl.com/5c74stux
[485] https://www.bbc.com/news/uk-england-york-north-yorkshire-34857143
[486] https://www.york.ac.uk/news-and-events/news/2015/events/mensday-gender-equality/
[487] https://tinyurl.com/yc8rktx4
[488] https://www.instagram.com/p/DIK4Gq_xFxy/

- Demonizing men is an insult to demons.[489]
- Criticism of the human interaction of women is a joke.[490]
- There is no single father, all other women in his life do that.[491]
- "Why are MORE AND MORE MEN SINGLE?"[492]
- "WOMEN DON'T NEED MEN ANYMORE!"[493]
- She is not interested in criticism that she hates men.[494]
- When will we finally abolish Men's Day?[495]
- I think many of the examples shown have the problem of understanding men as (equal) people at all – the result of internalized misandry. But finally, a positive example. Not everyone is like that.[496] And most of her comments agree. So it always depends on where you look and that the algorithm prefers toxic behavior or content is, I think, known.[497]

Of course, this is not a study, it is rather intended to convey what is presented to men as completely normal. It's maybe half of the misogynistic or contemptuous reels I see in a month. There is certainly something in the other direction as well.

## 3.3. Instagram Reel: Men suffer in silence[498]

I classify this as hatred of men, but it doesn't quite fit – but it fits more here than elsewhere. The creator of the reel is tired of reading daily comments claiming that men suffer in silence. Her answer to this is that she listens to the concerns and has even offered to fight patriarchy together.

---

[489] https://www.instagram.com/p/DJgqgeDict8/?img_index=2
[490] https://www.instagram.com/reel/DJ2wMU8JZrr/
[491] https://www.instagram.com/p/DJFMURoIygV/
[492] https://youtu.be/4kf8RcpX82U?si=li7dbj46jxocMnjz
[493] https://youtu.be/_ShWaIErHP4?si=mWEIY1K1CSvVlucL
[494] https://www.instagram.com/p/DJIQ1WIoZQ7/
[495] https://www.instagram.com/p/DKPKthbMQOw/?img_index=1
[496] https://www.instagram.com/p/DJJcuXRM8mv/
[497] https://www.iccl.ie/news/82-of-the-irish-public-wants-big-techs-toxic-algorithms-switched-off/
[498] https://www.instagram.com/p/DIJAMJqtqpw/

The question arises as to how this is supposed to help, e.g. to get a piece of the cake for victims of violence from the federal government's state aid, which are already predominantly in feminist hands. How is it supposed to prevent industrial jobs from being continuously reduced and thus long-term unemployment among men from rising?

Yes, she's probably talking about toxic masculinity. However, patriarchy has primarily led to men being considered the leaders of the group. Secondarily, it has directed existing toxic traits to support feudal structures. So if we think away the patriarchy, we are where men are beating each other's heads in because of quarrels or women and a large proportion do not reach the age of 30.

Of course, that's not what she meant; simplified: her rhetoric portrays patriarchy as the root of all evil, and if it falls away, everything will get better.

It goes on, they solve their problems themselves, and men have to solve their problems themselves. She seems to believe that these comments claim to solve our problems. I think that's a misunderstanding. For me, these comments rather signal that one should do sensible and differentiated educational work, e.g. not exclusively educate about violence against women, so that male victims remain invisible. Because this is how patriarchal role structures are consolidated, such as men are perpetrators and women are victims. Basically, it would be great if you would do what you claim to do. In addition, feminists in positions of power or as equal opportunity commissioners should do their job sensibly in the sense of real equality for all. I don't think that's too much to ask, at least in public places.

At the end of the reel, she recommends suffering in silence — although her last sentence remains unclear; maybe she meant that you should refill the dog's food bowl. Basically, what she expresses fits with many currents within feminism that are not about equal rights for men and thus equal rights for all. So if you had this idea, please stop asking, they feel annoyed by your requests.

**Pair of selective dialogues from the reel**

- ➤ **Statement**: "Imagine swapping the words "men" and "women", then look at the comments and think about how you would feel and how you would react to them. Time to unfollow"
- ➤ **Answer**: "Off to crying National Park."
- ➤ **Answer**: "Why don't you do it quietly! QUIET! JUST WALK AND KEEP YOUR MOUTH SHUT!"
- ➤ **Extended statement**: "let's briefly summarize the reactions: I am uneducated, emotionally unstable, not capable of criticism, "SHUT UP", a lot of sarcasm, etc. - Because I said imagine someone would treat women the way men are treated here. Are the people still realizing their own double standards? So really - anyone who acts like this has no interest in constructive change. This is just bashing, only hate and absolutely misanthropic."
- ➤ **Answer**: "Cry quietly."
- ➤ **Extended statement**: "I know, was already suggested in the reel. Completely normal and healthy way of dealing with people."

The selection is selective, of course, but nothing out of the ordinary. Some are a bit more constructive and there is a bit of dialogue, others explain why they think they are in moral superiority: because men kill and rape. Others declare "pro everyone" to be discriminatory.

- ➤ **Statement**: "I do not necessarily find this group-related devaluation of people to be constructive. Some activists don't even realize how much they resemble those they (rightly) fight."
- ➤ **Answer**: "You man, you.(Perhaps this is the worst insult imaginable to them.)
- ➤ **Answer**: "pssst, don't complain so much"
- ➤ **Answer**: "My ego is hurt because women don't always explicitly say that there are good men. That's why I prefer to invalidate their statements, which are underpinned by hundreds of actions and

situations caused by men, because my ego is more important than the daily experience of women." I translated that, you."

It doesn't get any better either. A dialogue cannot be conducted in this way, the collective suffering of the woman gives them the license to "Whatever this is". Here, injustice does indeed justify injustice. That, too, is feminism, but not everyone is like that.

The appeal, you don't want to hear any criticism. Where have we seen something like this before, oh yes, when feminism rightly criticizes something? The rejection of this criticism is interpreted as a defense of patriarchy, but when you compare it, it seems to be more normal human, albeit questionable, reactance. The defense of offenders who are released due to lack of evidence may also be based. That no one wants to be portrayed as a monster all the time. Feminists say it's ok to generalize, then men will defend all men out of reactance. Because this generalization also explained his judgment on our stamp.

The irony is: If the feminist appeal is that men should show more feelings and if they do, they should rather be quiet again.

I also took part in the discussion a bit. The opening comment was about her talking to a friend, and it was about the fact that there is less help for men who are victims of violence. She seems to counter this by saying that women have fought for their protection programs themselves. Then comes a counterattack, and he points to Erin Pizzey, that men have also fought for it (and still do) and to the *female empathy bias*. Then it gets a little more unobjective, and then I agree with him for the time being:

> ➢ Me: "When Erin Pizzey, in the course of her work at women's shelters, realized that men can also be victims of domestic violence, and dared to address this, she received death and bomb threats from her former colleagues. She had to leave the country, and her achievements were erased from feminist history. Let's look at Germany: The Ministry of Family Affairs has been in the hands of

women since 1982 (correction in 1985). Since 2000, nine women have held the office of Minister for Family Affairs – I think seven of them were feminists. The federal government's support for men's shelters is zero (three federal states, as far as I know, have their own programs). There are currently 49 places for men and about 7700 for women. The actual need for men is estimated at around 420 places. If one assumes that men would take advantage of these services to the same extent as women, it would be more like 1900 – and taking into account the number of unreported cases, even about 3800 places. In 2000, the then feminist family minister was asked whether she planned to financially support men's shelters. Their answer was something like this: As long as men (the victims) do not use violence, they do not need places of refuge. In January, the topic was up for debate again and was even planned, but was the first to be deleted in the negotiations with the CDU - together with the help for trans people. No one is asking you to solve our problems. What we want is for you to do your educational work sensibly and, if you are in positions of power, your job."

In between, someone claims that Erin had to go into exile, comes from anti-feminist forums and I refer to Wikipedia, there it is because it is in her book, (even in the description). She thanks him for the hint. (I say, not everyone is like that.)

➢ **Others**: "you already know that anyone can write on Wikipedia, including you!? Take care of the men here, you want us to do our job and are crying right now! Get active, take to the streets. Don't just write and discuss with us here and try to silence! As an example, I like to watch crime documentaries, who do you think gets killed the most? We were on the streets, our ancestors were on the streets. And you want to change the world for yourself from your armchair! Or say: Women do your job. How do you think we got the men to do their job? Just because of the above! Many private women's shelters have also been built! Let each other build, help each other. But don't always expect the women to do your shit! We have enough to do with ourselves! Just because there were a few men who demonstrated with us. Majority of men were still against it and still are today! We women are not done yet to deal with yet another topic! So don't just strain your fingers here, but become active! Nobody gave us anything! Nobody will either!"

> **Me**: "Subsidies for men's shelters are decided in the Ministry of Family Affairs. In January, a new reform was decided. Initially, men were in the program, but it was also the first to be rejected in the negotiations with the CDU, along with the help for trans people. Now the 7700 is being expanded somewhere towards 21000, while men still have 49 seats. When you say we should take care of it ourselves, you say that we should either keep the feminists out of the Ministry of Family Affairs or vote for the AfD. That's a bit anti-feminist what you're proposing."

> **Others**: "Fun fact on the side: EVERY change regarding human rights (e.g. women's suffrage, homosexuality is not a disease, rape within marriage, etc.) could only be enforced through massive pressure from outside - through protests & organizations. The reason why the topic of women's shelters is much more present for the Ministry of Family Affairs than men's shelters is simply because there are many organizations with influence that take care of it. For transgender people, this is just beginning to form - that's the only reason why it was on the agenda in the first place. The sad truth about men's shelters is unfortunately that there are too few organizations with a focus on them (there are also feminist organizations that are committed to this) & too few people talk about it, so politicians can afford to ignore it. That's not good, but unfortunately it's reality. So instead of sitting down and complaining about the evil feminists in the Ministry of Family Affairs, it would make more sense to take an example from feminists & feminist organizations (or queer organizations) and do what has proven itself for centuries if you want to bring a topic into the social focus:

spread information, mobilize people, found organizations & then get loud and annoying, until you can no longer be ignored."

> **Me**: "There are also organizations that are committed to men's shelters, the remaining 49 came from somewhere. However, such feminist-staffed authorities avoid working with organizations that advocate for men's rights contrary to the current regulation. E.g. here are the ADS with Manndat. https://manndat.de/jungen/antidiskriminierungsstelle-fuer-jungen-nicht-zustaendig.html We are going round in circles."

My next comment was AI generated. It was about whether the ministry (not ADS as above) can refuse cooperation, even if their criticism (criticism of their policy, seems to be one of the reasons to deny it), such as the lack of support for boys at school, is correct.

- **Others**: "We're not going around in circles, the basic problem has now been explained to you several times, in detail by several users, but you just want to rant against the evil feminists (and then with ChatGPT, how embarrassing is it going to be?). Ironically, you actually illustrate the basic problem very well. Bye "

I had already explained it in Chapter II.3.2 "Individual responsibility vs. socialization and structural limitations", but here is another example:

Not only is the structural problem that violence against men is largely ignored overlooked. The so-called *female empathy bias* – the tendency to show more compassion to women than men – is also not taken into account. Nor is it acknowledged that the fact that 22% of all women and 8% of all men describe themselves as feminists means that one in four (27%) feminists is male.[499] Even the recommendation that feminists in positions of power, according to Article 3 of the Basic Law – "Men and women have equal rights. The state promotes the actual implementation of equal rights for women and men and works towards the elimination of

---

[499] https://tinyurl.com/39wdvp38

existing disadvantages."[500] – is not recognized. Instead, reference is made to personal responsibility: Deal with your problems yourself.

Of course, I could have pointed to events such as the above-mentioned event on suicide prevention, which was cancelled because of feminists. But as she says, I only want to rail against "evil feminism" and any further example would rather strengthen her opinion based on experience – and I certainly understand where this thought comes from. I, too, find the constant emphasis on violence against women, in which the perpetrator is always male, to be a form of problematic rhetoric, which manifests itself in examples such as *man-vs. bear.*

However, there is a difference between the one-time factual and differentiated pointing out of disparities and inflationary, repetitive, demonizing rhetoric. This book also runs the risk of doing the latter, as it tries to illustrate the imbalance not only through studies and statistics. That's why I sometimes repeat myself – but **not all feminists are like that**. However, there is a radical fringe that holds this view. On the other hand, it is difficult to describe *man vs. bear* as a radical fringe phenomenon.

What she is right about is that men have to do more for their own equality, otherwise the current trend will continue.

## 4. Everyday life

But hatred of men is not only digital or media - it shows itself in daily life:

- **World of work**: Initiatives such as *"women-only spaces"* are celebrated, while men's groups are considered "backward-looking".
- **Education**: Boys are increasingly perceived as "disruptive factors" in schools .

---

[500] https://www.gesetze-im-internet.de/gg/art_3.html

- **Feminist leisure park** where you can beat up men's dolls.[501]

# 5. Social misandry in a self-test

Take 2 times 5 to 10 minutes and try to find the current number of infanticides by women. The best source I had found on this and had also linked here spoke of shares in the 3 subdivisions.[502] What I also found is the number of killings for 2021 and 2022 and Statista still has the number of murders until 2024, but no name how many of them women have as perpetrators.[503] Often you can also find that the perpetrator group is parents. In the first case, the risk factor of intimate partner violence is also mentioned, usually perpetrated by the male partner.[504] You write about infanticide and still manage to demonize men.

Maybe you find one or two sources, then you are more skilled at finding sources than I am. And now they are trying to do the same with how many partnership murders have been committed by men, or they are now called femicide.

I feel the same way all the time when writing the book, certain things are difficult to find, others very easy.

# 6. Male expendability

"There is no hatred of men," it is often said. But if you look closely, you can see a pattern: Men die earlier, work more dangerously, are mourned less often – and have been for thousands of years. In prehistoric mass graves such as Halberstadt, almost exclusively men lie, often with combat wounds, without ritual burial.[505] Ethnographies show that in tribal cultures, men were "burned out" for hunting and war, and

---

[501] https://youtu.be/OObJmnsjnsY?si=y4jYONe1bMoG0O5m
[502] https://tinyurl.com/38n8fwyd
[503] https://tinyurl.com/8a3v3d9p
[504] https://tinyurl.com/mswamx9c
[505] https://www.nature.com/articles/s41467-018-04773-w

230

their deaths were considered "natural". Women, on the other hand, are protected as a "reproductive resource".[506]

This functional logic was not hatred, but a survival strategy. But in patriarchy, it became an ideology. Suddenly it was said: "A man sacrifices himself – out of honor, not out of necessity." The conscription of the 19th century forced poor peasants into war, while elites bought their freedom. Today, corporations send men into mines or on oil platforms, while CEOs populate secure offices.

## Modern continuities

More than 80% of men still die in wars. But their victims are considered "normal" – see the UN statistics on the Gaza war: "70% of the dead are women and children".[507] The headline conceals the fact that almost 10,000 of the 34,000 victims were men – many of them civilians. Why do male deaths trigger less empathy? Because we assume that men are "always involved in some way".[508] This indifference is deeply rooted.

# 7. Between Fatherland and #MenAreTrash

"Better to meet a bear than a man!" – this social media trend shows how misandry works today: Men are stylized as a threat across the board, even if statistics say otherwise. Violence has been declining for 30 years, but algorithms flood us with violent videos – until women believe that the world is more dangerous than ever and that all men are potential perpetrators.

---

[506] https://en.wikipedia.org/wiki/Male_warrior_hypothesis
[507] https://tinyurl.com/3v3c2d8r
[508] https://tinyurl.com/m57z3n86

## Nationalism

"Honor", "fatherland", "protection of the nation" – these terms conceal a brutal business. Nationalism sells death to men as salvation: "Die for a line on the map that never belonged to you." The logic is always the same: men are expendable as long as they are given power – even if it is only the fantasy of control.

## Feminism

Radical currents of feminism serve this narrative. Series like The Handmaid's Tale reduce men to oppressors, hashtags like #MenAreTrash are trivialized as "satire". At the same time, politicians ignore male victims: In Germany, there are 49 shelters for men, but 7,700 for women. When Erin Pizzey pointed out domestic violence against men in 1971, she received bomb threats – from feminists.

## Bear vs. Man: Why Generalization Kills

The viral comparison "Better bear than man" is not a harmless joke. It dehumanizes men collectively – similar to how racism demonizes entire ethnic groups. 75% or 80% of infanticides are committed by mothers, 50% of intimate partner violence is mutual. But while we talk about "psychological distress" for women, the following applies to men: "perpetrators".

This way of thinking costs lives. When the University of York cancelled a suicide prevention event for men in 2015, it said: "Women's issues are more important." Suicides are the most common cause of death for men under 45. The message is clear: your pain, your life doesn't count.

# 8. Psychological phenomena

If misandric stereotypes are internalized, they can potentiate all common empathy and evaluation biases against men. The following phenomena show how this manifests itself in concrete terms.

## 8.1 Intergroup Empathy Bias[509]

- **Definition**: People automatically feel less empathy for people perceived as "outgroup". In internalized misandry, men become an outgroup, whose pain resonates less strongly.

## 8.2 Ambivalent Sexism / SDO-Korrelation[510]

- **Definition**: Those who internalize misandrial clichés achieve higher scores on Social Dominance Orientation (SDO) and in the Ambivalent Sexism Inventory (ASI) – and at the same time lower empathy scores for men.
- **Example:** Glick & Fiske (1996) developed the ASI and showed that people with high benevolent sexism scores (e.g., "women need to be protected") simultaneously have a stronger hierarchy preference (SDO) and less compassion for men.

## 8.3 Advantage in the domain of harm[511]

- **Definition:** Female victims are per se classified as more vulnerable and worthy of empathy, even if objective circumstances (e.g. severity of a violent crime) are the same.
- **Example:** In an American study, test subjects were asked to rate their willingness to help in fictitious victim scenarios. In all

---

[509] https://tinyurl.com/mpctps8j
[510] https://en.wikipedia.org/wiki/Susan_Fiske
[511] https://royalsocietypublishing.org/doi/10.1098/rsbl.2024.0381

cases, women received higher empathy and donation subsidies than men, even though the suffering was described identically.

## 8.4 Benevolent Sexism ("Protective Paternalism")

- **Definition:** A form of sexism in which women are "benevolently" protected, but at the same time declared less competent – at the expense of male equality.
- **Example:** Respondents in Glick & Fiske's studies strongly agreed that "women need to be protected," while rejecting that men are similarly vulnerable.

## 8.5 Moral Typecasting[512] [513]

- **Definition:** Women are classified as "moral patients" (sufferers), men as "moral agents" (perpetrators/responsible).
- **Example:** In newspaper reports about accidents or assaults, regardless of the gender of the person involved, the female victim was more often staged as worthy of protection, while male victims often seemed to be "to blame themselves".

## 8.6 Just-World Bias[514]

- **Definition:** The belief in a just world ("people deserve their fate") hits men hard: their suffering is more likely to be interpreted as "self-inflicted".
- Men have stronger Just World beliefs. Meta-analyses show that, on average, men achieve minimally higher values on just-world scales than women.[515] I mention this because it also works the other way around, e.g. the criticism of women's clothing style in

---

[512] https://pubmed.ncbi.nlm.nih.gov/19254100/
[513] https://www.sciencedirect.com/science/article/abs/pii/S0749597820303630
[514] https://tinyurl.com/3v7sf69z
[515] https://tinyurl.com/3s486cew

the context of catcalling or harassment can be explained by it. Why don't you wear a burqa, it wouldn't have happened with a burqa. The logic behind this is that catcalling is common sense, if you don't wear a burqa, but something that provokes such behavior, then you get what you ask for. The world is fair, you had a choice and you decided that way.

## 8.7 Court verdicts & sentencing

- **Definition:** Male defendants are punished more severely than women for identical facts – an effect that is further intensified by hostility towards men.

## 8.8 Child and family dynamics

- **Definition:** In custody or abuse cases, mothers tend to be given more empathy and care than fathers – misanthropic attitudes increase this imbalance.

## 8.9 Male Expendability[516]

- **Definition:** The assumption that men are biologically and socially expendable – e.g. in wars or dangerous professions.
- **Example:** Anthropological studies show that men are more often pushed into dangerous activities in hunting cultures because their reproductivity is considered less limiting.

# 9. Structural hatred

Following what feminism says about structural misogyny, what are the conditions for structural hatred?

---

[516] https://www.artofmanliness.com/character/behavior/male-expendability/

Structural misogyny does not simply mean that individuals hate women, but that social structures — i.e., rules, norms, institutions, traditions, etc. — are such that women are systematically disadvantaged, devalued, or treated worse.

It is about social structures that enable or even promote misogyny or discrimination – regardless of whether someone deliberately intends to do so.

**"Structural"** means:

- It is not only due to the behavior of individual people
- But because of power relations, economic dependencies, laws, cultural images, role patterns, etc.
- The conditions are systematic and recurring – regardless of individual situations or people

## Examples:

### Laws or institutions

- ➢ If, for example, certain professions were not accessible to women for a long time.
- ➢ If it is impossible for men by law to become equal opportunities commissioners and parity is thus excluded in questions of equality, here would be an example.

### Economical

- ➢ If women earn structurally less (gender pay gap), they are less likely to get into management positions because, for example, childcare is considered their "main job".
- ➢ When men are more often unemployed, long-term unemployed or homeless. In addition, it is not a major social issue and they themselves are to blame.

## Kulturelle Narrative

> Stories, media, language that women primarily portray as beautiful, caring, emotional and less rational/competent.
> There are also for men: e.g. men are perpetrators.

## Structures of violence

> When protective mechanisms for women are weaker in the event of violence or perpetrators often go unpunished (e.g. "victim blaming" in the case of sexual violence).
> Hardly any protective mechanisms and, as already shown, violence by women against men is completely underrepresented in our statistics and is ignored by society. If I had to guess, then the status of men is perhaps comparable to the 60s of women in some respects.

## Education and socialization

> When girls are subtly taught to hold back, while boys are encouraged to be assertive.
> Education for sacrifice for family and state.

# 10. Conclusion: No hate is legitimate

Of course, these are only a few exemplary observations. The fact that around 60% of Gen Z men feel discriminated against is not so much an expression of a supposed loss of privilege, but rather an indicator of a growing visibility of structural disadvantages. Issues such as educational losses, the lack of political representation of male concerns or the lack of recognition of male vulnerability are increasingly coming into public awareness.

In addition, there are phenomena such as misandry in social media or stereotypical narratives within the so-called manosphere, which often reproduce problematic attributions. Both can promote polarization –

whether through pejorative discourses about masculinity or through radical counter-reactions.

As long as social and political institutions trivialize these problems or attach only subordinate importance to them, a vacuum arises that can be filled by extreme positions. For many young men, this ultimately raises the question: Am I being discriminated against – or someone else?

# XV. Dating in the Modern Gender Discourse

## 1. The changed dating behavior

Modern dating culture, shaped by feminist narratives and technological advancements, has fundamentally changed expectations of relationships. While women today enjoy more autonomy and freedom of choice, new insecurities and paradoxical effects are emerging at the same time – for both sexes. The World Health Organization (WHO) now describes loneliness as a global priority,[517] a phenomenon that affects not only men, but also increasingly women. This chapter sheds light on the ambivalent consequences of the new freedoms, in particular the health and psychosocial risks of being single.

## 2. *Hypergamy*

### What is *hypergamy*

*Hypergamy* refers to the social phenomenon that people – especially women – tend to choose a partner with higher social status, more wealth, or better educational and career prospects. The term comes from sociology and evolutionary psychology and is often used in discussions about mate choice, gender roles, and social mobility.

---

[517] https://pm-report.de/gesundheitswesen/2024/who-einsamkeit-als-globale-prioritaet.html

In modern societies, the pattern has changed: women are increasingly reaching high levels of education and careers on their own, which sometimes leads to *homogamy* (partnerships at a similar level) or even *hypogamy* (relationships with a socially or economically "lower" partner).

## Relativizations, attempts at refutation and studies on sexual selection

There are various attempts to refute or relativize the concept – primarily the idea that women tend to date upwards or marry (*hypergamy*).

### Relativizations:

- One explanation is socialization, i.e. that women are socially educated to have certain expectations of a partner.
- On the other hand, there is biology again.

### Refutation attempts:

- A counterexample was cited with Sweden: There, a decreasing *gender pay gap* led to lower *hypergamy*, but also to a higher single rate. In Germany, the *gender pay gap* is larger, but the singles rate is similarly high. Whether there is a correlation or causality here cannot be said unequivocally. Assuming that all women earn more than men and the single rate is 90%, 10% of women live in *hypogamy*, then hypergamy has not been refuted, but has been confirmed in literature to 90%, because that is exactly the fear that is being feared here.
- Sometimes egalitarian societies are used to show that there is no *hypergamy* there. However, there are various statements in the sources: it is claimed that women prefer good hunters, and that

good hunters enjoy a high social status – while at the same time negating this statement. If there is a high status, it is called hypergamy. However, if hypergamy is defined in such a way that the pursuit of a higher social class is in the foreground, it is not technically possible to find hypergamy in egalitarian societies. Nevertheless, the same idea is inherent in this selection principle, namely sexual selection for a better provider. This means that as soon as social classes develop, this behavior becomes visible again as hypergamy.[518] [519] [520] [521]

- I saw another rebuttal argument in Prof. Neil (I didn't find the exact reel). He claimed that women write less selectively, there is statistical data on this from Ok Cupid.

When I heard this for the first time, it didn't seem conclusive to me – after all, women already selectively select when swiping. So why should they suddenly be less selective when writing to someone? I mean, their mailbox is already selective. However, it does not seem to be about the men who have already been matched and their attractiveness, but about the general attractiveness of all users.

However, this also makes little sense: If women already swipe selectively, then the matches are also selective. In order to achieve a "less selective" result, they would have to negatively select the matches she writes.

Then I looked at the whole thing again and came across an interesting Reddit post.[522] Even though the author thinks he's smarter than data science, he makes a good point:

His first objection is, I think, nonsense – he claims that there is a distortion through attractiveness. But this distortion would have to come

---

[518] https://pubmed.ncbi.nlm.nih.gov/21516952/
[519] https://en.wikipedia.org/wiki/Ach%C3%A9#Demography
[520] https://pubmed.ncbi.nlm.nih.gov/23813245/
[521] https://pubmed.ncbi.nlm.nih.gov/26189411/
[522] https://tinyurl.com/55nffmef

from somewhere. Either you would have to have profiles evaluated in a statistically relevant amount (which would be an extreme effort just to distort the informative value), or the app would have to have this distortion built in as a function – which I wouldn't know about.

His second point, on the other hand, is interesting: Who actually writes news? Is it the men without matches or the women whose inbox is so overflowing that they can hardly keep up? No – they are mainly more attractive men and less attractive women. And so the whole thing makes sense again in the typical "Boys Math".

## Sexual selection

- Assessment of attractiveness takes far less than a second[523]
- For women, the following applies: 'The 'external' triumphs over the 'inner values".[524]
- Attractive people are smarter[525]
- 'Intelligence is literally written on men's faces'[526]
- 'Intelligence actually makes you sexy'[527]
- Pretty Privilege: We infer a person's character and abilities from appearance[528]
- Family suitability and social status are important[529]
- Intelligence correlates with higher educational attainment and better career paths[530]

Women, on average, prefer intelligent and attractive men. Studies show a correlation between attractiveness and intelligence. Attractiveness brings social advantages ("Pretty Privilege"), which, however, is associated with certain ideals of beauty, especially in

[523] https://www.uni-bamberg.de/presse/pm/artikel/studie-attraktivitaet-carbon/
[524] https://www.tagesspiegel.de/wissen/frauen-wollen-einen-gut-aussehenden-partner-4924093.html
[525] https://www.oe24.at/madonna/life/deshalb-sind-attraktive-menschen-intelligenter/566686408
[526] https://tinyurl.com/5aztuxbz
[527] https://tinyurl.com/57b36m7x
[528] https://tinyurl.com/2rphwy3f
[529] https://tinyurl.com/yd8xf3dw
[530] https://synaptiqmatch.com/iq-und-erfolg/

Western societies. Intelligence, in turn, correlates with education, higher education with better career prospects and income – and thus with higher social status. Sexual selection has been proven by numerous studies and can explain parts of hypergamy. There are debates about its exact extent and causes, but also whether it might not (almost) completely disappear with equality.

Conversely, this also means that there is hypogamy in men – i.e. the preference for partners whose social characteristics are perceived as inferior. Men feel disturbed more often when their partner earns more.[531] To be honest, I had to laugh when I read the text of the alleged feminist, which I had just cited as a source. In her text, she describes men as highly sensitive beings. If the woman earns 40% or more of the total family budget, psychological stress in men increases significantly. This can lead to a lower life expectancy or even impotence.

As a highly sensitive being, I have directly searched for some studies on the subject of neuroticism, which prove that women have higher neuroticism values and are therefore more sensitive beings.[532] [533] But jokes aside: The gender pay gap seems to be about our potency – I will definitely revise this chapter again. On the other hand, this expectation is also a result of socialization, and recognizing this is a first step towards potency.

Back to the central problem: The more pronounced or rigid both phenomena are in a society, the more financial equality between men and women leads to a growing gap between the sexes — often called the gender gap — if hypergamy and hypogamy aren't addressed at the same time. Maybe the whole "80/20" talk, along with rising numbers of singles, can be seen as a reminder that women don't abandon hypergamy as quickly as they gain equality.

---

[531] https://freizeit.at/lust-liebe/beziehungsstudie-maenner-hauptverdiener/402295841
[532] https://psycnet.apa.org/record/2008-18683-004
[533] https://pmc.ncbi.nlm.nih.gov/articles/PMC3023236/

## Study result from Norway[534]

Although the United Nations has repeatedly named Norway the world's most equal country over the past 15 years, significant gender gaps remain in terms of pay and employment patterns. In this study, we offer theoretical explanations of why gendered employment and income patterns can persist even with full gender equality in the labor market; that is, even in a society where the distributions of income potential are identical, and gender discrimination does not exist. The decisive factor is the choice of partner of men and women and the subsequent division of gainful employment and household work. Hypergamy means that couples get together in such a way that the man has a higher income potential than the woman. This, combined with the standard economic theory of household specialization, provides a rationale for prioritizing one's professional career over theirs.

We have laid out theoretical foundations for the existence of hypergamy and presented overwhelming empirical evidence that hypergamy is an important feature of partner choice patterns in Norway. Households are systematically formed in such a way that the man has, on average, the highest rank within the gender distribution of income potential, and men with very poor income prospects have a high probability of remaining unmarried.

# 3. Gender gap

## 3.1 What is the gender gap?

The **gender gap** describes the social phenomenon that men and women are becoming more and more distant from each other in certain aspects – especially with regard to partnership, career and social dynamics. The term is often used in discussions about hypergamy, gender roles, and demographic developments.

---

[534] https://docs.iza.org/dp12185.pdf

243

## 3.2 Possible causes of the gender gap

### Financial equality and hypergamy

- Women are achieving ever higher educational qualifications and incomes.
- Hypergamy
- The result: More women and men remain single because women are looking "upwards", but fewer and fewer men are above them.

### Shifting gender roles

- Traditionally, men were providers and women took care of the household and family.
- These roles are now dissolved or mixed, but they are not equally accepted in all areas of society.
- Many women want an equal or "better" partner, while some men feel overwhelmed by traditional expectations.

### Different partner choice strategies

- Men tend to choose women based on youth and beauty (evolutionary psychology explanation: fertility).
- Women often prefer status, intelligence and attractiveness (evolutionary psychology: care and protection).
- Since women are increasingly earning well themselves, the pool of "attractive" partners is decreasing.

### Demographic changes

- In many Western countries, there are more well-educated women than men.
- This creates a "mismatch" on the partner market: highly educated women find fewer men with an "equal" status.

## Social Isolation & Digital Developments

- Online dating reinforces existing selection patterns: a small proportion of men get the most female matches, while many men get hardly any attention.
- At the same time, social media reinforces unrealistic expectations of relationships and partners.

## Result

The gender gap is the result of several social, economic and technological developments. It is particularly evident in higher singles rates, a tense partner market and changing gender dynamics.

# 4. The "single epidemic"

The WHO warns of the consequences of social isolation,[535] which is associated with an increased risk of cardiovascular disease, dementia and premature death. But while *male loneliness* is much discussed, the precarious effects of singleness on women often remain invisible or even misrepresented.

## Life expectancy and health

Married women over 65 live an average of **1.5 years longer** than unmarried women and spend **2.0 years more in good health.**[536]

## Mental health

- **Depression**: Unmarried women are more likely to report depressive symptoms, with the quality of the relationship being decisive: conflictual partnerships can even increase the risk.

---

[535]
https://pm-report.de/gesundheitswesen/2024/who-einsamkeit-als-globale-prioritaet.html
[536] https://pubmed.ncbi.nlm.nih.gov/32875051/

- **Suicide risk**: Single women are less likely to commit suicide than men, but the risk is **30% higher** than for married women. Education has a less preventive effect on women – motherhood, on the other hand, significantly reduces the rate.
- **Substance abuse**: In a 15-country study, women who have never been married have twice **the risk** of addiction as married women. Divorced women also suffered from anxiety disorders.

## Social networks: A deceptive advantage?

Although single women are often better at maintaining friendships than men, these rarely replace the emotional security of a partnership. Married women benefit from stable financial security and practical support – factors that reduce stress and increase well-being. At the same time, an ambivalent picture emerges: Financially independent singles value their freedom, but complain more often about loneliness.

"Singles are twice as likely to be affected by loneliness as couples," says Parship,[537] but the longer women stay single, the better it gets. It only gets worse for men. In old age, the trend is reversing again.[538]

# 5. Single women

In the following, I have taken the trouble to show a somewhat extensive overview of the effects.

## Life span

Married women aged 65 and over have, on average, a total life expectancy that is 1.5 years higher and active life expectancy that is 2.0 years higher than unmarried women. This means that singles tend to live fewer years and spend fewer years in good health.[539]

---

[537] https://tinyurl.com/nhfnru5p
[538] https://tinyurl.com/4x2zcn3p
[539] https://pubmed.ncbi.nlm.nih.gov/32875051/

There are also counterclaims, so I have seen several times that it is claimed that there is a Harvard study that claims this, but I could not find it.[540] Another source is Paul Dolan.[541] Since books do not have to be checked by another expert, however, he seems to have made a misinterpretation.[542] He admits his misinterpretation and qualifies his statement by saying that he believes it is fair to claim that men benefit more from marriage than women, but he also accepts if someone interprets the data differently.[543]

Another Harvard study I was able to find says that a long and good life is built on good relationships.[544]

## Risk of death

Single women, especially divorced or widowed women under 40, have a **48% higher risk of dying** than married women – a figure that is similarly high for men.[545]

## Suicide

Single women have a higher risk of suicide than married women, but lower than divorced women. Education protects men, while motherhood is a protective factor for women.[546]

## Depressions

Married women have fewer symptoms of depression compared to unmarried women. This is mainly attributed to the protective effect of a partnership, which comes from better social support, economic stability and positive mutual influences. The quality of the relationship also plays

---

[540] https://www.instagram.com/katara.selflovejourney/reel/DEw7tKENVpi/
[541] https://tinyurl.com/2s3dhpfr
[542] https://tinyurl.com/mr48bnyy
[543] https://en.wikipedia.org/wiki/Paul_Dolan_(behavioural_scientist)
[544] https://www.fitbook.de/mind-body/studie-gluecklich-laenger-leben
[545] https://tinyurl.com/3sfjtksj
[546] https://pophealthmetrics.biomedcentral.com/articles/10.1186/s12963-021-00263-2

an essential role – the more harmonious and stable the partnership, the more pronounced the protective effect.[547] [548]

## Mood, anxiety and substance use disorders[549]

An international study in 15 countries found that women who have never been married have a higher risk of developing mental disorders for the first time than married women. It was particularly striking that they suffered from addictions more often than married women. In addition, it was shown that a previous marriage (i.e. divorce or separation) further increases the risk of mental disorders, especially with regard to substance abuse. These results suggest that the protective effect of marriage plays a role for women, especially in the area of mental health.

## Happy in the context of the family structure[550]

The study shows that our well-being in old age depends heavily on our position within the family structure. In addition to current relationships, previous family transitions – such as births and deaths – also play an important role. Hünteler and Hank identify different generational trajectories that depict the "kinship reservoir" (parents, children, grandchildren). People with a small family network have an increased risk of physical limitations, while people in three-generational structures suffer less often from depression and health problems. The timing of role transitions, such as when childless people experience the loss of a parent at an early age, also influences long-term well-being.

Children usually make you happy[551] [552]

---

[547] https://tinyurl.com/246h3t8x
[548] https://pubmed.ncbi.nlm.nih.gov/9870051/
[549] https://pmc.ncbi.nlm.nih.gov/articles/PMC2891411/
[550] https://tinyurl.com/45t6s4ev
[551] https://wzb.eu/de/pressemitteilung/kinder-machen-gluecklich-meisten
[552] https://tinyurl.com/3k9cawxk

Children make no difference[553] (she also points out that the increased depression of single women may have something to do with socialization.)

Children don't make you happy[554]

Prof. Martin Schröder found out that women are measurably well-off, just as satisfied as men, and if you ask why they live the way they do, the answer is because they decide so. Women are dissatisfied when the man does all the housework. Social contacts increase satisfaction (up to 5 good friends), self-improvement does not[555]

## Women are happier than men as singles[556]

In many of these respects, men have similar results: in some, married men benefit more, in others, married women. When it comes to happiness, there is no consensus. There are also a few studies that show that women derive well-being from the ability to do what they want with their money, or that they build social networks better than men or married women as singles, but overall, women also seem to suffer from being single. It seems to me to be more of a single epidemic.

# 6. Counterpoints: Singleness as empowerment?

Feminist currents emphasize that being single cannot be a deficit, but a conscious choice of life. Women who consciously live alone report greater satisfaction with their autonomy and career.

Nevertheless, the fact remains that society's focus on individual self-actualization weakens collective safety nets. Where families and communities used to take over, today the pressure to meet all the needs

---

[553] https://www.hu-berlin.de/de/pr/nachrichten/dezember-2024/nr-241218-1
[554] https://tinyurl.com/2e85a5re
[555] https://youtu.be/Yt_i98OnTF4?si=mf8z6gwAWhZd0_6g
[556] https://journals.sagepub.com/doi/10.1177/19485506241287960

of life – emotional, financial, social – alone weighs on the individual. This overwhelms many, regardless of gender.

## 7. Conclusion

The "single epidemic" reveals a paradox: despite greater freedoms and options, loneliness and psychological stress are increasing. Although feminist progress has broken down outdated role models, there is still a lack of viable alternatives for coexistence.

# XVI. The Incel Subculture[557]

## 1. Definition and Origin

Incels (short for "involuntary celibate") are part of an online subculture that is predominantly composed of heterosexual men. They define themselves by their inability to find romantic or sexual relationships, even though they wish to. Many advocate a misogynistic ideology that blames women for their situation and justifies violence. The term was coined in 1997 by Canadian student Alana, who created an inclusive platform for people who wanted to discuss social isolation and sexual abstinence. However, from the 2010s onwards, the movement evolved into a community associated with acts of terrorism such as those of Elliot Rodger and Alek Minassian. (That's what Wikipedia claims)

---

[557] https://en.wikipedia.org/wiki/Incel

## 2. Ideology and Core Concepts

### Blackpill

Adherents of the Blackpill ideology assume that appearance and genetics determine the success of a partnership in a biologically determined way, and that any self-improvement is futile.[558] This fatalistic worldview leads to resignation and covert or open hatred of women, as those affected are denied any possibility of influence.[559]

### Enemy images

- **"Femoids"**: A pejorative slang term in which women are portrayed as dehumanized objects.[560] "Female" and "android" can also be understood as a critique of hypergamy behavior, in the sense of: You can't escape your programming, which is a reference to biological determinism.
- **"Chads"**: Attractive, self-confident men are ridiculed and idealized as unattainable, which reinforces the feeling of exclusion.

### Glorification of violence

Some forums celebrate Elliot Rodger as a "Supreme Gentleman" and martyr, glorify his act as an "incel rebellion" and refer to him as a "saint" in hate threads.[561] Calls for violence against "Chads" and "Femoids" are explicitly advocated and propagated as a legitimate countermeasure against a supposedly female-dominated society.[562]

---

[558] https://cujournal.ie/article/id/26/
[559] https://www.crimejusticejournal.com/article/view/2138
[560] https://www.adl.org/resources/backgrounder/incels-involuntary-celibates
[561] https://en.wikipedia.org/wiki/Elliot_Rodger
[562] https://www.bbc.com/news/world-us-canada-43892189

## Networking with other movements

The incel scene overlaps strongly with the manosphere (MGTOW, pickup artists) and draws ideological proximity to right-wing extremist and anti-feminist groups.[563]

## So much hatred has rarely reached me

With Jasmin Gnu − "So much hatred has rarely reached me ... − Rezo confronts me!"[564] you can see what such an incel shitstorm looks like. At one point, Rezo refers to their idea that it could not be their fault (from their point of view) and counters by emphasizing individual responsibility: You can work on yourself.

## Hypergamy, equality and single-rate

While feminists demand equal rights and equal opportunities − as evidenced by the decreasing gender pay gap (16% in Germany in 2024) and nearly equal socio-economic status of the sexes − incels point to the increase in the single rate as evidence of persistent, partly biological hypergamy. A recent Norwegian study actually shows that women in one of the world's most equal societies are still more likely to choose partners with higher status.[565] At the same time, long-term surveys show that hypergamy in Western countries is slowly declining with increasing equality, but not as fast as economic indicators.

## Social critique and limits of the incel narrative

The incel debate raises an important question: How does a society change in which a significant part of the population remains single? The criticism is directed equally at sociologists, feminists and political decision-makers, whose reforms have promoted legal equality and equal

---

[563] https://tinyurl.com/7nvjv3wz
[564] https://youtu.be/tYUCE0uSyrQ?si=nhgTv4B00thN9gHl
[565] https://www.frisch.uio.no/publikasjoner/pdf/2020/Formatert/jhr.58.3.1219-10604R1.full.pdf

opportunities, but have not been able to guarantee the "promised homogamy".

## 3. Structure and online presence

Incel forums such as former subreddits (e.g. r/incels) or specialized platforms serve as retreats. Moderated areas often exclude women and LGBTQ+ people. Despite repeated suspensions of major platforms (e.g., Reddit, 2017), users are migrating to niche sites like 4chan or dark net forums. Discussions revolve around self-hatred, revenge fantasies and pseudo-scientific justifications of one's own situation.

## 4. Study: Levels of Well-Being Among Men Who Are Incel[566]

The study Levels of Well-Being Among Men Who Are Incel reveals profound psychosocial crises among self-identified incel men. Compared to a control group of non-incels, they showed significantly higher levels of depression, anxiety and loneliness: While 75% of incels suffered from moderate to severe depression, this was only true for 33% of non-incels. The difference was similarly serious for anxiety disorders (67% vs. 38%). These burdens are also reflected in radically lower life satisfaction, which is largely attributed to social exclusion, romantic rejection and the feeling of social failure.

A central factor for this is the pronounced tendency towards interpersonal victim role (TIV). Incels are more inclined to see themselves as morally superior, to react to others without empathy, and to mentally chew through past insults again and again. Paradoxically, however, this victim attitude intensified the feeling of loneliness, especially in non-incels – in incels themselves, this effect was weaker, presumably because their already extremely high level of loneliness could hardly be increased ("ceiling effect").

---

[566] https://tinyurl.com/5pyd24tv

The result on sociosexual desire was surprising: Although incels reported a significantly stronger interest in short-term sexual contact than non-incels, this unfulfilled need did not further worsen their mental health – contrary to expectations. This contradicts the assumption that purely sexual frustration decisively shapes their suffering. Instead, the data suggest that deeper factors such as social isolation, identity crises, or the internalized "blackpill" ideology (the belief that their location is genetic and unchangeable) dominate. Incels may have learned to devalue their sexual desire or consider it irrelevant in order to reduce cognitive dissonance.

Demographically, the study refutes common clichés: Incels are by no means a homogeneously white or right-wing group. 36% identified as BIPOC (Black, Indigenous, or People of Color), and politically they were divided (45% on the left, 39% on the right). However, socio-economic disadvantages are striking: 17% of incels were NEETs (not in education, employment or training) and 50% lived with their parents – factors that reduce their attractiveness in the partnership market and increase their marginalization.

## 5. Violence and terrorism

Since 2014, several incel-related acts of violence have been committed:

- **Elliot Rodger** (2014): Killed six people in California and became an icon of the movement.
- **Alek Minassian** (2018): Carried out a car attack in Toronto and called for the "incel rebellion".
- **Jake Davison** (2021): Shot down five people in Plymouth (UK), including his mother.
- Governments such as Canada and the USA are increasingly classifying incel ideologies as a terrorist threat.

However:

- The Federal Government does not see **any concrete relevance** to the danger posed by the incel scene in Germany.[567] [568]
- No murder in Germany can be traced back exclusively to incels
- Violent incels are only a subgroup, and stigmatizing the entire community because of it could do more harm than good[569]

ZDF[570] speaks of at least 58 murders that can be associated with an incel connection. What that means exactly can only be guessed at. To be able to present a case at all, you have to travel to England and even then it is not an incel, but it only has incel parallels.

# 6. Downside

William Costello[571] – who also did the aforementioned study – points out that among incels, about 30% have had suicidal thoughts every day for the past two weeks. In comparison, 5% of the population said they had had such thoughts at least once in the last year. 30% of men are believed to have autism, compared to 1% of the general population.[572] He uses this statistic to illustrate that in order to break the cycle, you have to show incels that society has far more understanding of their problems than they think.

However, this statement does not apply to one particular group – and that is feminists. You don't even have to be an incel to have such experiences; from my own experience, I can say that it is enough if you have a different opinion, and you are quickly labeled as an incel. Instead of discussing objectively, they then like to explain why a woman could never like you – be it because your penis is too small, you are poor, you probably still live with your mother or that you are "not a man". And if you're hurt, vulnerability is also unmanly.

---

[567] https://dserver.bundestag.de/btd/20/006/2000624.pdf
[568] https://www.praeventionstag.de/nano.cms/news/details/5919
[569] https://tinyurl.com/5n6h32cf
[570] https://www.zdf.de/video/reportagen/die-spur-224/incels-amok-frauenhass-toxisch-100
[571] https://www.instagram.com/p/DHduTEjIORw/
[572] https://www.instagram.com/p/DHifrNWI7Rl/

Obviously, feminists know the weaknesses of their image of the enemy and use the existing power imbalance to play them off against the socially weak and marginalized, unstable male group. We don't know how many of the 7,478 male suicides[573] identify as incels, nor how many cases bullying was a major motivation. So when an incel runs amok, we see it all over the news, but when an incel commits suicide due to bullying, it's not even in any statistics. This does not justify misogyny, but differentiates.

Of course, serious feminism would distance itself from such an approach, but feminist discourses usually treat incels as a woman-hating movement without addressing the individual and social causes. Instead of a differentiated view, patriarchy is often named as the main problem, while the specific psychological and social burdens of these men are ignored. Feminist sources that analyze incels as a heterogeneous group with different perspectives are rare.

At the same time, there is no serious attempt to sensitize one's own circles to a differentiated examination of this phenomenon – whether to avoid premature stigmatization or to prevent bullying against this already marginalized group. But this would be an important step towards breaking the cycle of social exclusion and radicalization. Ironically, this is exactly what many incels want and what William Costello calls an essential first step towards improvement.

# 7. Cultural representations

Incel ideology can be found in literature (Michel Houellebecq's *Whatever*) and series such as *Law & Order: SVU* (episode "Holden's Manifesto"). Films like *The Beast* (2023) address radicalisation.

---

[573] https://tinyurl.com/3nbvpe9c

## 8. Conclusion

As some studies emphasize, the complex incel problem requires not only interdisciplinary research, but also a systematic examination of the structural and individual factors – involving all relevant actors from politics, the media and civil society initiatives. This is the only way to promote a transparent culture of debate that defuses radicalization mechanisms and enables solutions beyond stigmatization.

# XVII. Conscription

## 1. Introduction

Conscription is one of the oldest instruments of state authority – and at the same time a magnifying glass for social inequalities. For centuries, almost exclusively men were obliged to serve in the military, while women were exempt from this "duty". Even today, at a time when formal equality is proclaimed, many states adhere to this practice.

## 2. Historical background

Conscription is rooted in an idea of masculinity that idealizes strength, sacrifice and responsibility to protect. Since ancient times, military service has been considered a **rite of manhood**:

- In ancient Sparta, boys were raised to be warriors from the age of seven.[574]
- In the Prussian army of the 18th century, service was both an honor and a duty.
- Even in modern democracies such as Germany, compulsory military service was levied exclusively for men until 2011.

---

[574] https://en.wikipedia.org/wiki/Spartan_army#Training

This tradition reflects a patriarchal barter: men were given social status and power in exchange for their willingness to risk their lives in war.

# 3. Social pressure

Men who evaded service were historically and culturally marginalized:

- **Criminal sanctions**: In the Federal Republic of Germany, conscientious objectors were threatened with prison sentences until 1983.
- **Social stigmatization**: In the USA, "draft dodgers" were considered cowards during the Vietnam War – many fled to Canada.[575]

This dynamic reinforces toxic norms of masculinity: the man as "protector" has to endure suffering without complaining – a narrative that taboos emotional vulnerability.

# 4. Modern paradoxes

While many countries abolished compulsory military service, it remains in place in countries such as South Korea, Israel or Norway (gender-neutral since 2015). But even in "progressive" nations there is an imbalance:

- **Germany**: Although compulsory military service was suspended in 2011, only men are still obliged to do so in the event of tension (§ 3 WPflG).
- **USA:** Although women have been allowed to take on all combat roles since 2015, only men must register for the *Selective Service* – otherwise there is a risk of penalties such as the withdrawal of study grants.

---

[575] https://en.wikipedia.org/wiki/Draft_evasion_in_the_Vietnam_War

# 5. Result

The debate about conscription reveals a fundamental contradiction: How can a society demand equality on the one hand and hold on to gender-specific duties on the other?

**Possible solutions:**

- **Gender neutrality**: Mandatory service for all – whether military or civilian – promotes fairness and a sense of community.
- With equal opportunities comes equality of duty.

Ultimately, it is not just about military policy, but about the question of what kind of society we want to be: one that pushes men into outdated roles – or one that understands protection, responsibility and sacrifice as human, not gender-specific values.

# XVIII. Harsher Penalties for Men

## 1. Introduction

Criminal law is supposed to be neutral and objective – but studies show that gender stereotypes shape judgments. Men receive up to **63% longer prison sentences** than women[576] for comparable offenses. This discrepancy raises questions: Is it a statistical necessity or a structural bias? This chapter examines how social role models influence the judiciary – and why even a supposedly neutral system reproduces inequality.

---

[576] https://repository.law.umich.edu/cgi/viewcontent.cgi?article=1164&context=law_econ_current

# 2. The data situation

Research results worldwide consistently show gender-specific differences:

- Sexual misconduct among teachers resulted in 54% of men with a prison sentence and an average of 2.4 years in prison, and 44% and 1.6 years for women.[577]
- Most studies confirm that there are gender-specific differences in sentencing – and that women tend to receive milder sentences than men (Doerner & Demuth, 2014; Holland & Prohaska, 2021; Koons-Witt et al., 2012; Spivak et al., 2014; Tillyer et al., 2015). Evil Woman Hypothesis – women can also be affected if they violate existing gender roles, for example: being a mother.[578]
- In the study, 98.1% of cases were resolved through plea deals. Women were more likely to receive reduced charges and were less likely to be imprisoned (17% compared to 28% for men). Across all eight main crime categories, the proportion of men imprisoned was consistently higher, with women more likely to be sentenced to prison for robbery and assault, while men were disproportionately imprisoned for property crimes. Although prison sentences did not vary in length between the sexes, men received significantly longer suspended and jail sentences.[579]

Even if previous convictions and crime modalities are taken into account, the gap remains.

# 3. Result

The harsher punishment of men is not a law of nature, but a relic of outdated gender images. An equitable system must:

---

[577] https://tinyurl.com/mr3b6pv3
[578] https://www.crimejusticejournal.com/article/download/3622/1564
[579] https://tinyurl.com/4fc2786m

- **Consider context**: Why do men commit certain crimes? What role does poverty, trauma or socialization play?
- **Decriminalization**: Therapy instead of imprisonment for non-violent offenses.
- **Prioritize humanity**: Punishment should depend on the facts of the case – not on gender.

As long as the judiciary frames men as "born perpetrators" and women as "victims", it will remain a mirror of social double standards. The challenge is not in punishment, but in prevention – and in seeing both genders as *complete human beings.*

# XIX. Abortion

The abortion debate revolves around the fundamental question of when an embryo is considered a "human being" in the sense of human rights – and thus a bearer of its own right to life. This discussion requires a precise distinction between the biological human condition, which is widely recognized by a broad social and scientific consensus, and the ethical-legal attribution of full human rights.

## 1. Social consensus: When does human life begin?[580]

Empirical surveys show that there is no uniform view among the population about the exact beginning of human existence. A study by the University of Freiburg showed that about 30% of those surveyed consider the protection of the embryo to be necessary from the moment of fertilization, while 25% link the beginning of human existence with implantation – about six days after fertilization. More than 40% of the participants use later criteria, such as brain development or pain perception, as a basis. Overall, about 55% of those surveyed consider

---

[580] https://tinyurl.com/mszzuwva

the embryo to be "human" from the sixth day at the latest. This finding indicates that there is a social and scientific consensus that recognizes the humanity of the embryo at a very early stage. (However, the survey is old and not representative with 428 respondents, but it shows in which direction the opinions are moving.)

## 2. Norbert Hoersters Position[581]

Norbert Hoerster emphasizes that an embryo is indisputably a human being from a biological point of view. This fact is recognized by a large part of the population, as the above data suggests. Nevertheless, Hoerster argues that the embryo in the early stages of its existence does not yet have to be regarded as a "human being in the full sense" or as a full-fledged legal person with its own right to life. Certain qualities – such as awareness, self-reflection and the ability to develop future interests – are decisive for the recognition of a full right to life. Since an embryo does not yet possess these characteristics at an early stage of development, it cannot automatically be ascribed the status of a full person from an ethical and legal perspective. This shows that although the embryo is biologically human and is already recognized by many as a human being, being human alone does not fully establish human rights if the normative ethical requirements have not yet been met. Personally, I don't like this argument, it feels like we're introducing the category of a subhuman.

## 3. The potentiality argument

A common approach to embryo protection is the potentiality argument. Proponents claim: "The embryo becomes a human being, so it must be treated like a human being." This argument appeals to the embryo's inherent potential to develop into a fully developed human being and is used by many pro-life advocates as the basis for absolute protection.

---

[581] https://www.bpb.de/themen/umwelt/bioethik/33779/wann-beginnt-das-recht-auf-leben/

## Objections to the potentiality argument:

### Biology versus ethics

It is true that the potentiality argument states that the inherent potential in embryonic development makes the embryo worthy of protection. However, the mere existence of this potential is not sufficient to grant him full human rights at an early stage. A seed that has the potential to become a tree is not protected as a tree from the first moment. Rights should be based on the actually existing, ethically relevant characteristics – not just on potential. However, the analogy doesn't seem to be quite right. Seed and tree are more comparable to embryo and adult than to "human vs. human". Even if the tree belongs to the pine, the seed is still not a lower jaw.

### Logical inconsistency

If the potential alone were decisive, contraception and unfertilized germ cells would also have to be considered worthy of protection – which is not the case in practice. – Neither egg nor sperm alone have potential.

### Practical absurdity

If the potential were to be taken as the only criterion, this would result in the fetus having to be fully protected in emergency situations where the mother's life is at risk – even if this leads to serious consequences for the woman. The mother has the same right to protect her life.

And then there are objections to the objections of objections.

# 4. The Human Argument

Another argument is: "To have human rights, it is enough to be human." So if 55% of the population and 55% of science agree on being human, then the embryo is considered human. This position puts the mere human condition in the foreground – regardless of the potential or whether the individual already possesses all the characteristics of a full-fledged person.

The "German Institute for Human Rights"[582] answers the question "Are human rights universally valid?" with "Human rights apply everywhere in the world and for **every person**. Their universality is not called into question by the diversity of people and cultures. ..." continues to address the question "What does inclusion have to do with human rights?" with "Inclusion means that **every person belongs**, **no matter** what they look like, **what they can do** or **how old** or rich **they are**. Everyone should be able to shape their lives in a self-determined way, **no one** should be disadvantaged, excluded or discriminated against – that is inclusion and that is also a core idea of human rights. For this to be possible, barriers must be broken down and individual support must be provided. When everyone can be there, it's normal to be different."

As the answers show, there is only one condition attached to human rights and that is being human, and then they apply to all people, several times it is pointed out that there is no exclusion, and it is also not linked to characteristics or ability or age.

But is there no way to undermine them? Here, in turn, the "German Institute for Human Rights" answers the question "Is the state allowed to restrict human rights at will?", with "No. Interference with human rights is only permitted under certain conditions: it must be based on a law and justified by a public interest or the protection of the fundamental rights of third parties. In addition, the restriction must be

---

[582] https://tinyurl.com/44y3x79y

"proportionate". ..." – So it works after all? – Legally, perhaps, but morally I refer here again to Norbert Hoerster.

He points out that the constitution ascribes an inalienable right to life to every human being. If this status is granted to the embryo, it follows that any abortion would have to be prohibited in principle – except in cases in which it serves to save life or protect the pregnant woman from serious damage to her health. Hoerster also draws a comparison: If the right to life already applies to a born child, the question arises whether it would then be justifiable to kill such a child, for example due to personal or social stress. And he answers this with: "No, anyone who claims that our current liberalization of early abortion is compatible with the humanity of the embryo and its resulting right to life is deceiving himself and others.[583] For this reason, he later points out that the embryo in the early stage of its existence does not yet have to be regarded as a "human being in the full sense".

In addition, the article that proves the consensus on being human is so old that it is already in the SPIEGEL archive. In addition, human genetics is only one of many specialist groups, and the announced 55% represent only a narrow majority – after all, only 428 people were surveyed, which is by no means representative of Germany or even the world. Perhaps the consensus has already changed again. The fact that this changing consensus has an impact on the assessment of the question also explains why this discussion does not revolve exclusively around being human and instead focuses on women's rights. But should we really subordinate a fundamental biological and philosophical question of the human condition to the political debate about women's rights versus religious dogmas? This is not to question the value of women's rights, but rather whether science should not feel obliged to follow the unbiased search for truth.

---

[583] https://www.bpb.de/themen/umwelt/bioethik/33779/wann-beginnt-das-recht-auf-leben/

## 5. The role of men – a neglected factor

The abortion debate is predominantly conducted as a women's issue, with the co-responsibility and interests of men often remaining in the background. Men are directly involved in the process as partners, fathers and producers, but usually do not have a direct say. This contradiction – shared responsibility without corresponding decision-making authority – leads to the fact that the male perspective is often neglected. This is not primarily about turning the discourse into a purely "male issue", but about recognizing that the right to life of the embryo as such must be evaluated independently of parental interests.

## 6. Future scenario: Artificial wombs

Technological advances in ectogenesis – the development of embryos in artificial wombs – could theoretically represent a compromise between women's right to self-determination and the protection of life. The embryo could be moved out of the womb to continue to thrive under controlled conditions without restricting the woman's bodily autonomy. But this option also raises new ethical and practical questions: Who is responsible for an embryo transplanted into an artificial uterus? Are states allowed to oblige women to use this technology or deny them this option? And how is the fate of the embryo decided, especially when financial, legal and moral interests come into conflict? Historical experience with restrictive reproduction laws, e.g. Romania in 1966 with Decree 770, warns of the danger of neglect. It should also be mentioned that this technology is still in its infancy and will probably not be launched on the market in the coming years.

## 7. Conclusion: Why the debate knows no winners

The discussion about abortion remains a tragedy without clear winners. There is no question that an embryo is a human being from a biological point of view – and the social consensus suggests that many recognize being human early in the developmental process. But this does not automatically mean that he must be regarded as a full-fledged person with comprehensive human rights in an ethical and legal sense – at least according to Norbert Hoerster and others. The abortion debate forces us to continuously negotiate between biological facts, normative ethical considerations and social consensus lines. Anyone who allows abortion must explain why embryos have no human rights; whoever prohibits them must explain why an evolving human being – whose full rights may only be justified by certain ethically relevant qualities – is given priority over the rights of a person who has already been born.

Ultimately, the debate shows that the essence of being human is far more multidimensional than purely biological criteria can express. There are no easy answers, only an ongoing discourse that calls on us to constantly renegotiate the balance between individual rights, social norms and ethical principles.

## XX. Who cares what happens tomorrow?

The birth rate is more than a demographic indicator: it is at the center of an ethical field of tension that sets individual life plans against collective future scenarios. Birth rates are falling worldwide – in some countries far below the reproduction threshold of 2.1 children per woman. While for some this is a sign of progress (emancipation from biological "constraints", self-determination), it raises fundamental questions: Are we as a generation allowed to decide whether the human line of existence will continue? And if so, what moral duties are derived from this?

The debate is marked by paradoxes. On the one hand, liberal societies emphasize the right to reproductive autonomy – no one should be forced to have children. On the other hand, the collective reality shows that a permanent decline in births destabilizes systems based on intergenerational solidarity: pensions, health care, even cultural continuity. Two ways of thinking collide here: individualism, which puts personal freedom above the survival of the group, and collectivism, which sees society as a whole worth protecting.

But how can a low birth rate be morally criticized at all without falling into authoritarian patterns? One starting point is the "right to exist" of future generations – but here you quickly reach your limits. Non-existent people cannot be bearers of rights, since rights are tied to subjects. At the same time, we are part of a cycle of life that has been passed down through thousands of generations. The decision to break this cycle raises existential questions: Are we "guardians" of human continuity, or is this idea a relic of past thought patterns?

From the point of view of critical theory, this reveals a power imbalance: the living have the sovereignty of interpretation, resources and the possibility of enabling – or denying – the existence of future people. In this light, individualism does not appear as neutral freedom, but as a privilege of the present that excludes potential life in the future. But even this analysis does not necessarily lead to an obligation to father children. It only shows that the debate is never purely private, but always political.

Ultimately, the birth rate debate remains a balancing act. Neither can a collective duty to reproduce be enforced without coercion, nor can the consequences of shrinking societies be ignored. Perhaps the answer lies neither in moral appeals nor in state paternalism, but in a structural facilitation of freedom of choice: family-friendly politics, fair distribution of care work and the recognition that children are not a private matter, but a collective project – one that leaves room for doubt, ambivalence and freedom.

# 1. Correlation vs. Causality

A basic rule of statistics is: **correlation is not the same as causation**.

- **Correlation**: Two phenomena occur together (e.g. feminism and declining birth rates).
- **Causality**: One phenomenon directly causes the other (e.g. feminism *leads to* a decline in births).
- A correlation can also be a causality if the causal relationship (cause → effect) is not yet clear or has not yet been discovered.
- The more often a correlation occurs in a certain context, the more likely causality is.

# 2. Factors that can lower the birth rate

### Urbanization

In urban areas, the cost of living is often higher, housing is limited, and it is more difficult to reconcile family and career. These framework conditions mean that couples tend to have fewer children.

### Economic burdens

High rents, rising prices and uncertain labor markets are forcing many young people to postpone or downsize their family planning in order to maintain financial stability.

### Higher level of education and career focus

Women with higher education and career goals often decide to start a family later. Longer periods of education and career ambitions often reduce the number of children you can have.

### Access to contraception and reproductive rights

Improved access to contraception and reproductive health services allows for more effective family planning, leading to a more conscious approach to the number of children.

## Later marriage and partnership formation

In modern societies, people tend to start their families later, which shortens the reproductive window and thus lowers the average number of children.

## Individualism and changed life goals

The trend towards more self-realization and personal freedom means that children are seen as less compelling. The desire to realize oneself often competes with traditional family formation.

## Secularization

As religious ties decline, so does the social pressure to start large families. Secularized societies tend to have fewer children as religious norms and traditions lose influence.

# 3. Birth rates in the West[584]

Here are the birth rates (children per woman) in Western countries:

- **Germany**: 1.46
- **Italy**: 1.22
- **Spain**: 1.12
- **Greece**: 1.43
- **Portugal**: 1,43
- **France**: 1.79 (highest in the EU)[585]
- **Sweden**: 1.52[586]
- **Norway**: 1.41
- **USA:** 1.66
- **Canada:** 1.33

---

[584] https://data.worldbank.org/indicator/SP.DYN.TFRT.IN
[585] https://data.worldbank.org/indicator/SP.DYN.TFRT.IN?locations=FR
[586] https://tinyurl.com/5n6rrxth

- **United Kingdom**: 1.57
- **Ireland**: 1.70
- **Switzerland** 1.39

**Top 5 countries with the highest birth rates**:

- **Niger**: 6.75
- **Chad**: 6.22
- **Somalia**: 6.20
- **Mali**: 5.87
- **Afghanistan**: 4,52

No western country reaches the **conservation limit of 2.1**. The world is at 2.2, falling.

Overpopulation could also be a problem, but the trend is in the opposite direction.

# 4. Feminism and birth rate

While it is difficult to establish a direct causality between feminism and the decline in births, it is hard to deny that certain feminist narratives may not be conducive to a healthy birth rate.

- Missing and erroneous feminist education on the topic.
- Fact-based and repeatedly communicated feminist education can also inadvertently increase fears of men. 155 homicides due to intimate partner violence against women – compared to 1,328 fatal car accidents[587] involving women. Nevertheless, the fear of driving is hardly widespread among women, while male-related threat scenarios appear to be more present. However, a murder is not to be equated with an accident, emotionally or in its social significance.

---

[587] https://tinyurl.com/33bt4fj3

- Feminism discourses that frame relationship successes as *"bare minimum"* : Even happy wives are not interpreted as proof of successful partnerships, but as victims of internalized expectations.
- The abolition of income tax splitting discriminates against the traditional family
- A feminist rhetoric that romanticizes childlessness as "liberation" without naming the consequences for pension systems or society

Here I refer again to the chapter "Single Women". Anyone who knows feminism's contributions to this topic was probably surprised, because feminism usually only emphasizes the positive effects for single women. The prediction that by 2030 about 45% of all women from 25 to 44 will be childless singles is also celebrated by some.[588] [589]

- This trend has a major impact on social media in particular, and the sexes are drifting further and further apart.
- Hate rhetoric on both sides
- Inability to relate on both sides: Trend – women have higher demands,[590] men withdraw – this leads to more singles

# 5. Pension and intergenerational contract

The intergenerational contract is based on a simple premise: the young finance the old. But if the young are missing, the system collapses.

"Currently, there are 1.8 contributors for one old-age pensioner. At the beginning of the 1960s, the ratio was even more solid: here there were six actively insured workers for every old-age pensioner. ... According to forecasts by the IW Cologne, there will be 1.5 contributors

---

[588] https://www.instagram.com/p/DGdDp19zl26/
[589] https://www.morganstanley.com/ideas/womens-impact-on-the-economy
[590] https://www.instagram.com/p/DI_oIiFsZp3/

for every pensioner in 2030. In 2050, there could even be only 1.3 contributors."[591]

The decision not to have children is individually legitimate – but collectively it is an **act of desolidarization**. Those who benefit from infrastructure, pensions and health care that others finance through their children, well I don't know how I could put it nicely, but correctly. We owe our current state to decisions made 20 to 60 years ago. The decisions we make today will be paid for by people in 20 to 60 years.

# 6. Dangers of this development

The falling birth rates in the West are not an abstract forecast – they are already reality. The consequences affect not only pension systems, but society as a whole.

## 6.1 Loss of prosperity and inflation

A shrinking young generation means fewer workers to pay taxes, promote innovation and boost consumption. The consequences:

- **Labour shortage**: According to the German Economic Institute (IW), there will be a shortage of 5 million skilled workers in Germany by 2030.[592]
- **Wage-price spiral**
- The supply-demand ratio is also developing in favor of inflation.
- Stagnation: Without young consumers and founders, economic momentum is declining.

Take Japan, for example: For decades, the country has been struggling with stagnation in growth and a decline in prosperity – directly correlated with its ageing population. (Birth rate: 1.26[593]. Inflation does

---

[591] https://tinyurl.com/3smmz27w
[592] https://tinyurl.com/bdh7fa54
[593] https://tinyurl.com/3z3hkn6n

not apply now, but there are other reasons, such as the fact that the elderly save heavily for fear of poverty in old age and thus money disappears from the economic cycle.)[594]

## 6.2 Poverty in old age

When fewer and fewer young people pay for more and more old people, poverty in old age becomes a mass phenomenon.

According to the German Pension Insurance, the pension level is 48% today, and by 2040 it will fall to 43%. With the rising cost of living, this means that pensioners end up with basic security despite decades of work.

Feminism addresses poverty in old age, but mostly as a purely women's problem, known as the "gender pension gap". The crisis affects everyone, but there are no solutions. The focus is often on redistribution ("more of the pie for women") instead of increasing the size of the pie by more contributors and thus more children.

## 6.3 Political extremes

Economic insecurity and fear of decline create a breeding ground for populist and extremist movements.

**Historical examples:**

- The Weimar Republic collapsed under hyperinflation and mass unemployment – and paved the way for National Socialism.
- Brexit: Many voters decided to leave the EU out of frustration with stagnating wages and overburdened social systems

---

[594] https://www.fr.de/wirtschaft/japan-macht-die-geburtenrate-zur-chefsache-92324022.html

- Trump could also serve as an example. I don't know to what extent her remarks are true (see source[595]), but that is the idea of what could be a reaction to the current development.

Today, we are observing similar patterns: right-wing populist parties in Europe are instrumentalizing the fear of foreign infiltration through migration – an attempt to counteract the decline in births. At the same time, envy of large families is growing ("They also get child benefit!" or today I saw a reel that introduced the business model of single mother of two).

## 6.4 The Call for Responsibility

The debate about pension cuts for the childless is only the beginning. There are already demands such as:

- "Childless tax": An annual levy for people without children to support pension funds.
- Inheritance tax bonus for parents who pass on assets to their children.
- "Demands to reduce the pensions of the childless or to cancel them altogether are popular." it said, for example, in a Stern article. Even if the article as a whole argues against it.[596]

There is a demanding logic behind this: instead of creating incentives, there is punishment. But coercion does not necessarily lead to more births – perhaps only to more resentment. But the more dramatic the situation becomes, the more logical it seems to make responsibilities visible again. So if some pensioners have to live in poverty, then perhaps the one who has contributed to this development.

---

[595] https://www.instagram.com/p/DIzlCPkMiek/
[596] https://tinyurl.com/29surtcr

## 6.5 The romanticization of childlessness

While feminism rightly emphasizes that children are not a duty, it often glorifies childlessness as the ultimate in self-realization. Hashtags like #ChildfreeByChoice or bestsellers like "*No Kid - 40 reasons not to have children*" celebrate freedom - but they conceal the downside:

- Poverty in old age: Many of the single women over 80 in Germany live in poverty
- Social isolation: Without a family, the risk of dying alone in old age increases.

At the same time, it is ignored that many women *remain involuntarily* childless – for fear of career setbacks or financial insecurity.

## 6.6 The worst combination

The worst combination seems to be that collectivism prevails, while women of childbearing age often orient themselves towards Western individualism. This is reflected in values such as South Korea (0.78), Taiwan (0.9), Singapore (1.04) and Japan (1.26). In these countries, men often have very traditional ideas.

## 6.7 South Korea and Japan's actions

South Korea is struggling with the world's lowest birth rate and is now trying to use financial incentives to encourage more people to marry and start a family.

In the city of Busan, there is a pilot project in which singles between the ages of 23 and 43 can participate in events to get to know potential partners. Successful matches will initially receive $604 per person. If the couple falls in love and the families get to know each other, there is another $1,200. If they decide to get married, they will receive $24,000 as a wedding gift. In addition, the city provides a housing deposit of $36,000 or a rent subsidy of $960 per month for five years.

In total, couples can receive between $64,000 and $85,000. If the program is successful, it will also be extended to foreign residents in 2025. The aim is to combat the demographic crisis with a multicultural community.[597] There are many such programs, but the success leaves much to be desired.

Although cities like Seoul organize dating events with attractive incentives such as cash gifts, data shows that out of over 4,000 attendees, only 24 have gotten married in the past three years. Many communities have already discontinued their programs, mainly because of a strong imbalance between male and female participants.

There is a shortage of women in rural areas, as many young women migrate to larger cities, where they see better career opportunities. In some cases, even female government employees were forced to attend the events to make up for the lack of women.

In addition, women in South Korea are generally less interested in partnerships than men: only 18% of young women consider dating programs necessary, compared to 51% of men.[598]

Japan, on the other hand, is relying on a state-owned dating app to counteract this trend. The app is intended to support people who want to get married who have not yet taken any active steps to find a partner. Unlike traditional dating apps, registration requires extensive documents, including proof of income, identity verification, and a declaration of intent to marry.

In addition to the app, Japan also promotes family-friendly measures, such as in the city of Akashi, where parents benefit from free diapers

---

[597] https://tinyurl.com/4swbzrb2
[598] https://www.koreatimes.co.kr/www/nation/2025/03/113_385407.html

and daycare places from the second child onwards. These incentives have already led to an increase in the birth rate there.[599]

Japan's Plan 2025 to address the population crisis combines financial incentives, structural reforms and relaxed immigration policies. With a population declining for 15 years and a record number of deaths – with only 730,000 births last year – there is a risk of a drastic decline from 125 to 87 million by 2070. To counter this, the government is allocating 5.3 trillion yen to support programs for young families and plans to spend an additional 3.6 trillion yen annually on child benefits, as well as increased childcare and education support.

At the same time, more flexible visa regulations are intended to promote the influx of foreign workers – especially in sectors such as care for the elderly and agriculture – in order to compensate for the domestic labor shortage. At the same time, the government is trying to improve the compatibility of work and family life through measures such as the introduction of a four-day week and more flexible parental regulations. It is emphasized that real change can only come about if men are also more involved in raising children.

Another negative factor is the decline in the marriage rate, which is facilitated by traditional gender roles and economic uncertainties. Overall, Japan's approach to tackling the demographic crisis requires comprehensive measures that go far beyond mere financial incentives.[600]

# 7. Conclusion: Individualism vs. Survival

Modern feminism faces a dilemma: on the one hand, it rightly demands equality, but on the other hand, it ignores the demographic consequences of a society that sees children as a private matter. The slogan *"My body, my choice"* is an expression of freedom – but also of short-sightedness.

---

[599] https://tinyurl.com/3vffuhu4
[600] https://tinyurl.com/3hw7n28m

**Part of the answer probably lies in politics:**

- Infrastructure: Free daycare centers, all-day schools and affordable housing for families.
- Financial incentives: tax exemptions for parents, wage subsidies during parental leave.
- Cultural change: Appreciation for parenthood – not as a "sacrifice", but as a social investment.

Sweden and Norway are leading the way. But with limited success: in 2010, the birth rates in both countries were still almost 2, today they are only 1.52 and 1.41 – a sign that social attitudes play a role in addition to politics. But it doesn't help here if the public accepts it and young women stick to their opinion, that makes for the worst combination.

**But it probably takes more than that:**

- Self-determination **and** the common good united,
- making parenting attractive through infrastructure and financial incentives,
- Guys, you probably have to do more care work, otherwise it won't work,
- Feminism – maybe less negative narratives

A society in which everyone thinks only of themselves first has no future – it is inevitably heading for its own collapse.

# XXI. The Future of the Gender Debate

Yes, what can I say? At first, I thought this chapter was a good idea, but at the time I thought 100 pages would be enough for the book. In the meantime, however, I notice that a serious attempt to predict the future is like reading a crystal ball. That's why I prefer to outline only a few central points that could perhaps be improved.

The first thing to do is to reduce the misandry that is anchored in our society to such an extent that it is perceived as a social problem at all. Only then can we work on equality in the sense of empathy and recognize men's lives and problems as equal. Only from here on can this debate be conducted at eye level.

We need a comprehensive index that tries to record gender disadvantages as fairly and objectively as possible. Calculate the adjusted gender pay gap to the end, even an approximate calculation is better than what we have now. The statistics for time could be collected every 24 hours and displayed in more groups in terms of gender view, Singles, Couples, Married, Married with child, singles with child. If you don't know the developments between these groups, you can't really make many of the statements that are made here about care work. More official dark field studies are needed to be communicated. Once a year, which is relevant under criminal law, is quite nice, but it would also be cool if we regularly showed people the reality of life.

Neutral body that checks subsidies and quotas. Is there a need or a disadvantage here? What is the success of the measure? And in the end, the population will be informed transparently. Something similar could be done for violence prevention and aid programs. Men need to become more active in their own soft power structures.

Sexist narratives should be titled as such, if they are according to traditional theory and objective data/theses/studies underpin this. As I said, in traditional theory you can falsify everything with better data/theses/studies/arguments. In critical theory, one can only believe and hope. The same applies in the context of normal discrimination, such as generalizations and demonizations.

Equal research: For every 2.25 studies on women, there is one for men.[601]

# Epilogue

Yes, what else can I say. If you were only half as surprised as I was about some topics, then you were quite surprised – in a positive and negative sense – and that you can take some things from this book with you for your own perspective.

# Source

1. https://youtu.be/6w_96Hnz8JM?si=4aOrJAA19owxvOkt
2. https://blogs.law.columbia.edu/critique1313/files/2019/09/Horkheimer-Traditional-and-Critical-Theory-2.pdf
3. https://en.wikipedia.org/wiki/Positivism
4. https://en.wikipedia.org/wiki/Critical_theory
5. https://plato.stanford.edu/entries/critical-theory/
6. https://opentextbc.ca/introductiontosociology3rdedition/chapter/1-3-theoretical-perspectives/
7. https://en.wikipedia.org/wiki/Critical_theory
8. https://plato.stanford.edu/entries/popper/#BasiStatFalsCon
9. https://papers.ssrn.com/sol3/papers.cfm?abstract_id=3467041
10. https://public.websites.umich.edu/~eandersn/hownotreview.html
11. https://books.google.de/books?id=w2gzw6zz4fIC
12. https://plato.stanford.edu/archIves/sum2023/entries/feminism-epistemology/
13. https://direct.mit.edu/qss/article/3/1/244/108658/Researching-women-and-men-1996-2020-Is
14. https://pmc.ncbi.nlm.nih.gov/articles/PMC5751942/
15. https://pmc.ncbi.nlm.nih.gov/articles/PMC10691233/
16. https://www.cambridge.org/core/journals/behavioral-and-brain-sciences/article/abs/socialization-versus-biology-time-to-move-on/34AD05119B350119A57B9C2D8FE4B8DA
17. https://www.frontiersin.org/journals/psychology/articles/10.3389/fpsyg.2020.00609/full
18. https://www.bundesregierung.de/breg-de/schwerpunkte-der-bundesregierung/75-jahre-grundgesetz/gleichberechtigung-grundgesetz-2262564
19. https://www.bpb.de/kurz-knapp/lexika/das-junge-politik-lexikon/320423/gleichberechtigung/
20. https://www.europarl.europa.eu/about-parliament/de/democracy-and-human-rights/fundamental-rights-in-the-eu/promoting-equal-opportunities

---

[601] https://direct.mit.edu/qss/article/3/1/244/108658/Researching-women-and-men-1996-2020-Is

21. https://www.bmfsfj.de/bmfsfj/themen/gleichstellung
22. https://eige.europa.eu/publications-resources/thesaurus/terms/1059?language_content_entity=de
23. https://www.politische-bildung-brandenburg.de/lexikon/paritaet-parite
24. https://www.welt.de/debatte/kommentare/article188529839/Gender-Debatte-Paritaet-bedeutet-das-Gegenteil-von-Freiheit.html
25. https://de.wikipedia.org/wiki/Sexismus
26. https://youtu.be/ayxgHMu3bwU?si=lPq5KXHjT3273Rj4
27. https://www.bpb.de/themen/gender-diversitaet/frauen-in-deutschland/49418/frauenanteil-im-deutschen-bundestag/
28. https://de.statista.com/statistik/daten/studie/1558420/umfrage/sitzverteilung-im-deutschen-bundestag/
29. https://www.bpb.de/themen/parteien/parteien-in-deutschland/zahlen-und-fakten/140358/die-soziale-zusammensetzung-der-parteimitgliederschaften/
30. https://www.statista.com/statistics/955972/women-share-political-party-members-germany/
31. https://www.bundestag.de/dokumente/textarchiv/2025/kw09-wahlergebnis-statistik-1055550
32. https://de.wikipedia.org/wiki/Liste_fraktionsloser_Mitglieder_des_Deutschen_Bundestags
33. https://www.bundesstiftung-gleichstellung.de/wissen/themenfelder/repraesentanz-und-teilhabe-von-frauen-in-der-politik-2/
34. https://en.wikipedia.org/wiki/Motherhood_penalty
35. https://www.cdu-deutschlands.de/mitglied-werden
36. https://www.spd.de/unterstuetzen/mitglied-werden
37. https://www.gruene.de/mitglied-werden
38. https://en.wikipedia.org/wiki/Gender-equality_paradox
39. https://ifstudies.org/blog/of-boys-and-toys
40. https://pmc.ncbi.nlm.nih.gov/articles/PMC7002030/
41. https://www.hessenschau.de/wirtschaft/frauen-nur-halb-so-oft-in-fuehrungspositionen-wie-maenner-v1,frauen-in-fuehrungspositionen-102.html
42. https://www.nationalgeographic.de/wissenschaft/2022/07/warum-maenner-frueher-sterben-studie-liefert-erste-eindeutige-beweise
43. https://www.welt.de/partnerschaft/article10874913/Maenner-haeufiger-Opfer-von-Gewalt-als-Frauen.html
44. https://www.maennergewaltschutz.de/maennerschutz-und-beratung/bedarf/
45. https://www.bundestag.de/dokumente/textarchiv/2025/kw05-de-sexuelle-gewalt-1042042
46. https://www.deutschlandfunk.de/gewalthilfegesetz-100.html
47. https://www.bundestag.de/mediathek?videoid=7629270#url=L21lZGlhdGhla292ZXJsYXk/dmlkZW9pZD03NjI5Mjcw&mod=mediathek
48. https://www.deutschlandfunk.de/gewalthilfegesetz-100.html
49. https://www.instagram.com/reel/DHA8KrnsQ9O/
50. https://manndat.de/jungen/antidiskriminierungsstelle-fuer-jungen-nicht-zustaendig.html
51. https://jungenleseliste.de/stand-der-jungenleseforderung-in-den-bundeslandern/
52. https://britishbusinessexcellenceawards.co.uk/from-the-awards/new-research-shows-uks-gender-pay-gap-reverses-as-young-women-now-out-earn-men
53. https://manndat.de/geschlechterpolitik/gleichstellungsbeauftragte-verhindern-gleichstellung-teil-1.html

54. https://manndat.de/geschlechterpolitik/gleichstellungsbeauftragte-verhindern-gleichstellung-teil-2.html
55. https://manndat.de/geschlechterpolitik/gleichstellungsbeauftragte-verhindern-gleichstellung-teil-3-der-experte.html
56. https://manndat.de/jungen/antidiskriminierungsstelle-fuer-jungen-nicht-zustaendig.html
57. https://www.researchgate.net/figure/Abbildung-33-Jugendarbeitslosigkeit-15-bis-24-Jahre-in-Deutschland-nach-Geschlecht_fig1_346005254
58. https://www.instagram.com/p/DH_K_MsKUu8/
59. https://journals.plos.org/plosone/article?id=10.1371/journal.pone.0205349
60. https://de.wikipedia.org/wiki/Index_der_geschlechtsspezifischen_Entwicklung
61. https://de.wikipedia.org/wiki/Index_der_geschlechtsspezifischen_Ungleichheit
62. https://de.wikipedia.org/wiki/Global_Gender_Gap_Report
63. https://eige.europa.eu/gender-equality-index/2024/DE
64. https://www.oecd.org/content/dam/oecd/en/publications/reports/2024/09/education-at-a-glance-2024-country-notes_532eb29d/germany_937cfefb/7060bda5-en.pdf
65. https://en.wikipedia.org/wiki/Selectorate_theory
66. https://academic.oup.com/isq/article-abstract/45/1/27/1792550
67. https://bristoluniversitypressdigital.com/edcollchap/book/9781529239492/ch005.xml
68. https://wac.colostate.edu/docs/books/positionality/chapter6.pdf
69. https://academic.oup.com/isq/article-abstract/45/1/27/1792550
70. https://cawp.rutgers.edu/news-media/press-releases/rethinking-womens-political-power
71. https://www.wilsoncenter.org/sites/default/files/media/documents/publication/womens_political_networks_complete_guide.pdf
72. https://academic.oup.com/sp/advance-article/doi/10.1093/sp/jxae019/7900929
73. https://mediarep.org/server/api/core/bitstreams/d1b53c1b-3f8d-4ecd-82a7-44543371b446/content
74. https://www.kas.de/en/single-title/-/content/frauen-maenner-und-kaum-unterschiede
75. https://bristoluniversitypressdigital.com/edcollchap/book/9781529239492/ch005.xml
76. https://academic.oup.com/isq/article-abstract/45/1/27/1792550
77. https://wac.colostate.edu/docs/books/positionality/chapter6.pdf
78. https://www.researchgate.net/publication/284545645_Power_and_social_influence_in_relationships
79. https://www.britishcouncil.org/research-insight/engendering-soft-power-women-representation
80. https://www.eui.eu/Documents/MWP/ProgramActivities/2017-2018/master-classes/Ridgeway-Gender-status-leadership.pdf
81. https://www.researchgate.net/publication/284545645_Power_and_social_influence_in_relationships
82. https://pmc.ncbi.nlm.nih.gov/articles/PMC5680601/
83. https://neurosciencenews.com/power-dynamics-happiness-relationships-18829/
84. https://journals.sagepub.com/doi/10.1177/08912432241230555
85. https://en.wikipedia.org/wiki/Expectation_states_theory
86. https://www.verywellmind.com/understanding-gender-roles-and-their-effect-on-our-relationships-7499408
87. https://nielseniq.com/global/en/insights/analysis/2024/shaping-success-a-deep-dive-into-womens-impact-on-the-cpg-landscape/

88. https://girlpowermarketing.com/statistics-purchasing-power-women/
89. https://www.pewresearch.org/social-trends/2008/09/25/women-call-the-shots-at-home-public-mixed-on-gender-roles-in-jobs/
90. https://www.bundesregierung.de/breg-de/schwerpunkte-der-bundesregierung/75-jahre-grundgesetz/artikel-3-gg-2267592
91. https://www.bmfsfj.de/resource/blob/94418/d666740ce14dd9af4f5cfd0a4882692f/neue-wege-fuer-jungs-broschuere-data.pdf Chapter 5.1
92. https://frauensicht.ch/gesellschaft/geschlechterrollen/diskriminierung-billige-ausreden-von-maennern/
93. https://www.instagram.com/p/DI-6fiyuIIs/
94. https://www.spiegel.de/kultur/gesellschaft/warum-es-keinen-sexismus-gegen-maenner-oder-rassismus-gegen-weisse-gibt-a-1236954.html
95. https://www.derstandard.at/story/3000000243900/werden-mittlerweile-maenner-staerker-diskriminiert-als-frauen
96. https://mads.de/feminismus-als-problem-wieso-sich-maenner-benachteiligt-fuehlen/
97. https://www.spiegel.de/kultur/gesellschaft/warum-es-keinen-sexismus-gegen-maenner-oder-rassismus-gegen-weisse-gibt-a-1236954.html
98. https://www.brigitte.de/aktuell/gesellschaft/studie--45-prozent-der-maenner-fuehlen-sich-vom-feminismus-diskriminiert-13789116.html
99. https://www.20min.ch/story/jeder-zweite-mann-fuehlt-sich-diskriminiert-358528104146
100. https://www.ipsos.com/de-at/millennials-and-gen-z-less-favour-gender-equality-older-generations
101. https://www.amazon.com/WAR-AGAINST-BOYS-Misguided-Feminism/dp/0684849577
102. https://medium.com/@alexandermoreaudelyon/erin-pizzey-the-story-of-the-feminist-who-was-threatened-for-acknowledging-male-victims-a5a810964857
103. https://en.wikipedia.org/wiki/Erin_Pizzey
104. https://search.worldcat.org/de/title/829180547
105. https://www.nationalgeographic.de/geschichte-und-kultur/2023/07/frauen-jagd-geschlechter-mythos-jaeger-sammler
106. https://www.sciencedirect.com/science/article/abs/pii/S1090513824000497
107. https://www.vivekvenkataraman.com/blog/2023/7/5/debunking-a-debunking
108. https://science.orf.at/stories/3220047/
109. https://sportsandmedicine.com/de/2022/08/leistungsunterschiede-zwischen-mann-und-frau-im-sport/
110. https://www.nationalgeographic.de/geschichte-und-kultur/2023/07/frauen-jagd-geschlechter-mythos-jaeger-sammler
111. https://phys.org/news/2023-10-prehistoric-gender-roles-women-hunters.html
112. https://www.sueddeutsche.de/sport/ultralaeufe-frauen-maenner-vergleich-zeiten-lux.XttGSoGctyv32gKnbaydhJ?reduced=true
113. https://www.markus-bussmann.com/2013/07/ausdauerjagd.html
114. https://deutsch.wikibrief.org/wiki/Persistence_hunting
115. https://de.wikipedia.org/wiki/Hetzjagd
116. https://www.biomedcentral.com/about/press-centre/science-press-releases/24-sep-2014-
117. https://de.wikipedia.org/wiki/Hadza
118. https://www.taylorfrancis.com/books/mono/10.4324/9781351329248/ache-life-history-kim-hill-magdalena-hurtado
119. https://johnhawks.net/weblog/high-adult-mortality-in-some-contemporary-hunter-gatherers/

120. https://www.sciencedirect.com/science/article/abs/pii/S030544031200297X
121. https://www.sci.news/othersciences/anthropology/neanderthals-upper-paleolithic-humans-head-trauma-injuries-06612.html
122. https://de.wikipedia.org/wiki/J%C3%A4ger_und_Sammler
123. https://www.cambridge.org/core/books/abs/cambridge-world-history-of-violence/violence-in-palaeolithic-and-mesolithic-huntergatherer-communities/3A47960C35DF4B0246A6436FC1353E87
124. https://johnhawks.net/weblog/high-adult-mortality-in-some-contemporary-hunter-gatherers/
125. https://www.koeblergerhard.de/Fontes/CodexHammurapi_de.htm
126. https://en.wikipedia.org/wiki/Mosuo
127. https://manndat.de/jungen/bildung/was-der-bildungsbericht-verschweigt-teil-5-1-schlechtere-benotung-bei-gleichen-leistungen.html
128. https://www.instagram.com/p/DH_K_MsKUu8/
129. https://www.bpb.de/themen/bildung/dossier-bildung/315992/bildungsungleichheiten-zwischen-den-geschlechtern/
130. https://psycnet.apa.org/record/2014-15035-001
131. https://www.tandfonline.com/doi/full/10.1080/01425692.2022.2122942
132. https://www.bbc.com/news/education-31751672
133. https://srcd.onlinelibrary.wiley.com/doi/10.1111/cdev.12079
134. https://boys-up.de/jungen-im-bildungsabseits/
135. https://youtu.be/ZuAaD33yW5k?si=spUOGGIIiUZ3hJ7-
136. https://pmc.ncbi.nlm.nih.gov/articles/PMC3101894/
137. https://www.bmfsfj.de/resource/blob/94418/d666740ce14dd9af4f5cfd0a4882692f/neue-wege-fuer-jungs-broschuere-data.pdf Chapter 5.1
138. https://op.europa.eu/webpub/eac/education-and-training-monitor/de/country-reports/germany.html
139. https://www.smartick.com/data/charted-high-school-dropout-rates-in-the-united-states/
140. https://www.pewresearch.org/short-reads/2021/11/08/whats-behind-the-growing-gap-between-men-and-women-in-college-completion/
141. https://www.pewresearch.org/social-trends/2011/08/17/iv-by-the-numbers-gender-race-and-education/
142. https://www.statista.com/statistics/184266/educational-attainment-of-high-school-diploma-or-higher-by-gender/
143. https://youtu.be/sABcWG9OHOk?si=l5O1DeWXxfkWn2pV
144. https://youtu.be/FL1c45TDx5I?si=S9dV8cabs9Lznxbc
145. https://youtu.be/7A0ZfAoKPrA?si=4s6SiFGyZyG31EHi
146. https://www.researchgate.net/publication/323197652_The_Gender-Equality_Paradox_in_Science_Technology_Engineering_and_Mathematics_Education
147. https://www.theguardian.com/inequality/2018/feb/16/guilt-over-household-chores-is-harming-working-womens-health-housework
148. https://www.science.org/doi/10.1126/sciadv.adt1646
149. https://ifstudies.org/in-the-news/liberal-women-lonelier-more-unhappy-than-conservative-counterparts-american-family-survey
150. https://www.mlive.com/news/kalamazoo/2012/04/a_closer_look_at_the_gender_ga.html
151. https://www.rsfjournal.org/content/11/1/154
152. https://jbhe.com/2024/12/young-black-women-are-significantly-outpacing-black-men-in-educational-attainment/

153. https://www.pewresearch.org/social-trends/2021/10/05/rising-share-of-u-s-adults-are-living-without-a-spouse-or-partner/
154. https://www.uni-paderborn.de/gleichstellung/genderportal/gender-glossar/leaky-pipeline
155. https://www.destatis.de/DE/Presse/Pressemitteilungen/2024/08/PD24_315_213.html
156. https://www.destatis.de/DE/Themen/Gesellschaft-Umwelt/Bevoelkerung/Geburten/kinderlosigkeit-und-mutterschaft.html
157. https://journals.indianapolis.iu.edu/index.php/advancesinsocialwork/article/download/23220/23016
158. https://ijds.org/Volume15/IJDSv15p089-110Mirick5906.pdf
159. https://www.bzh.bayern.de/fileadmin/user_upload/Publikationen/Beitraege_zur_Hochschulforschung/2021/2021-3-Brandt-Briedis-Schwabe.pdf
160. https://www.womeninstem.co.uk/breaking-stereotypes/is-the-maternal-wall-causing-a-critical-leak-in-the-stem-pipeline/
161. https://www.bu.edu/articles/2019/pregnant-and-phd/
162. https://occrl.illinois.edu/our-products/voices-and-viewpoints-detail/current-topics/2023/06/15/doctoral-student-moms-the-invisible-nontraditional-students-on-campus
163. https://pmc.ncbi.nlm.nih.gov/articles/PMC3939045/
164. https://awis.org/resource/motherhood-causing-critical-leak-stem-pipeline/
165. https://www.sciencedirect.com/science/article/pii/S0277539524001407?#s0120
166. https://ugeo.urbistat.com/AdminStat/de/de/demografia/eta/deutschland/276/1
167. https://en.wikipedia.org/wiki/Variability_hypothesis
168. https://academiainsider.com/iq-phd/
169. https://www.religiournal.com/pdf/ijrr10001.pdf
170. https://www.sueddeutsche.de/panorama/neue-studie-also-doch-maenner-sind-intelligenter-als-frauen-1.859443
171. https://www.deutschlandfunkkultur.de/radikale-foerderung-eine-niederlaendische-uni-will-nur-noch-100.html
172. https://www.uni-due.de/physik/gleichstellung/gleichstellungsmassnahmen.php
173. https://www.spiegel.de/lebenundlernen/uni/us-experiment-frauen-bei-professur-im-vorteil-a-1029276.html
174. https://largescaleassessmentsineducation.springeropen.com/articles/10.1186/s40536-019-0070-9
175. https://www.destatis.de/DE/Themen/Gesellschaft-Umwelt/Bildung-Forschung-Kultur/Hochschulen/Tabellen/personal-hochschulen.html
176. https://unric.org/en/gender-equality-smaller-pay-gaps-in-belgium-italy-and-luxembourg/
177. https://pubmed.ncbi.nlm.nih.gov/19883140/
178. https://journals.sagepub.com/doi/10.1177/0956797617741719
179. https://www.centreforsocialjustice.org.uk/library/lost-boys
180. https://op.europa.eu/webpub/eac/education-and-training-monitor/de/country-reports/germany.html
181. https://www.academics.de/ratgeber/weibliche-fuehrungskraefte
182. https://www.diw.de/documents/dokumentenarchiv/17/diw_01.c.510355.de/20150707_f%C3%BChrungskr%C3%A4ftemonitor_wichtigsteergebnisse.pdf
183. https://statistik.arbeitsagentur.de/DE/Statischer-Content/Grundlagen/Methodik-Qualitaet/Methodenberichte/Beschaeftigungsstatistik/Generische-Publikationen/Methodenbericht-Beschaeftigte-mit-Leitungsfunktion.pdf?__blob=publicationFile

184. https://www.destatis.de/DE/Themen/Branchen-Unternehmen/Unternehmen/Kleine-Unterneh
men-Mittlere-Unternehmen/aktuell-beschaeftigte.html
185. https://www.ifm-bonn.org/fileadmin/data/redaktion/publikationen/ifm_materialien/dokumen
te/IfM-Materialien-253_2017.pdf
186. https://ftp.zew.de/pub/zew-docs/gutachten/Die_volkswirtschaftliche_Bedeutung_der_Famili
enunternehmen_Auflage_6_2023.pdf
187. https://www.kfw.de/PDF/Download-Center/Konzernthemen/Research/PDF-Dokumente-Fok
us-Volkswirtschaft/Fokus-2024/Fokus-Nr.-455-Maerz-2024-Chefinnen.pdf
188. https://www.vgsd.de/selbstständige-frauen-verdienen-44-prozent-weniger-als-selbststaendi
ge-maenner/
189. https://life-online.de/die-auswertung-fuer-den-girlsday-und-boysday-2024-ist-da/
190. https://www.randstad.de/karriere/berufe/frauen-handwerksberufe-maenner-soziale-berufe/#s
ection-title-49661
191. https://donortracker.org/donor_profiles/germany/gender
192. https://www.frauengesundheitsportal.de/aktuelles/aktuelle-meldungen/lost-in-perfection-fast
-jeder-zweite-berufstaetige-haeufig-unter-druck/
193. https://www.cream-migration.org/publ_uploads/CDP_13_23.pdf
194. https://www.destatis.de/EN/Themes/Labour/Labour-Market/Quality-Employment/Dimensio
n1/1_5_GenderPayGap.html
195. https://ec.europa.eu/eurostat/statistics-explained/index.php?title=Gender_pay_gap_statistics
196. https://www.destatis.de/DE/Themen/Arbeit/Verdienste/Verdienste-GenderPayGap/_inhalt.ht
ml#sprg633332
197. https://pubmed.ncbi.nlm.nih.gov/19883140/
198. https://www.researchgate.net/publication/323197652_The_Gender-Equality_Paradox_in_Sci
ence_Technology_Engineering_and_Mathematics_Education
199. https://docs.autismresearchcentre.com/papers/2009_Auyeung_etal_ChildEQSQ_JADD.pdf
200. https://www.pewresearch.org/social-trends/2023/04/13/in-a-growing-share-of-u-s-marriages-
husbands-and-wives-earn-about-the-same/
201. https://docs.iza.org/dp12185.pdf
202. https://www.wmtxlaw.com/divorce-and-custody-statistics-2024/
203. https://melbournefamilylawyers.com.au/news/child-custody-statistics-by-gender
204. https://melbournefamilylawyers.com.au/news/child-custody-statistics-by-gender
205. https://ascentlawfirm.com/are-mothers-more-likely-to-get-child-custody-during-divorce/
206. https://www.complexfamilylaw.com/featured-articles/gender-bias-where-are-we/
207. https://www.linkedin.com/pulse/bias-against-men-child-custody-cases-nbqxe/
208. https://www.micklinlawgroup.com/3-statistics-point-to-men-sabotaging-their-alimony-rights
/
209. https://www.deutschlandfunk.de/ehegattensplitting-abschaffen-nachteile-vorteile-100.html
210. https://www.bls.gov/news.release/pdf/atus.pdf
211. https://www.destatis.de/DE/Themen/Gesellschaft-Umwelt/Einkommen-Konsum-Lebensbedi
ngungen/Zeitverwendung/Tabellen/erwerbsarbeit-unbezahlte-arbeit-geschlecht-zve.html
212. https://www.destatis.de/DE/Themen/Gesellschaft-Umwelt/Einkommen-Konsum-Lebensbedi
ngungen/Zeitverwendung/Tabellen/arbeit-muetter-vaeter-zve.html
213. https://www.apa.org/news/press/releases/2011/12/working-moms
214. https://www.parent.com/blogs/conversations/2023-is-part-time-employment-the-ideal-situati
on-for-working-parents

215. https://www.mother.ly/parenting/maternal-gatekeeping-why-moms-end-up-doing-it-all/
216. https://pmc.ncbi.nlm.nih.gov/articles/PMC9977166/#S17
217. https://scholarsarchive.byu.edu/facpub/4214/
218. https://www.mybestself101.org/blog/encouraging-men-to-open-up
219. https://www.sciencedirect.com/science/article/pii/S175606162300071X
220. https://www.instagram.com/p/DIJCBP7tryr/
221. https://www.gesundheitsforschung-bmbf.de/de/geschlechtersensible-forschung-im-fokus-der-bmbf-forderung-17772.php
222. https://orwh.od.nih.gov/sex-as-biological-variable
223. https://report.nih.gov/funding/categorical-spending#/
224. https://orwh.od.nih.gov/including-women-and-minorities-in-clinical-research-background
225. https://www.appliedclinicaltrialsonline.com/view/women-and-trials-when-gender-consideration
226. https://pmc.ncbi.nlm.nih.gov/articles/PMC10062729/
227. https://www.sciencedirect.com/science/article/abs/pii/S1551714422000441
228. https://trialsjournal.biomedcentral.com/articles/10.1186/s13063-022-07004-2
229. https://www.quarks.de/gesundheit/medizin/gender-health-gap/
230. https://ec.europa.eu/eurostat/en/web/products-eurostat-news/w/ddn-20250314-3
231. https://ec.europa.eu/eurostat/statistics-explained/index.php?title=Causes_of_death_statistics
232. https://ec.europa.eu/eurostat/web/products-eurostat-news/-/edn-20210428-1
233. https://ec.europa.eu/eurostat/statistics-explained/index.php?title=Mental_health_and_related_issues_statistics
234. https://www.theguardian.com/commentisfree/2025/may/07/the-guardian-view-on-bias-in-medical-research-disregard-for-womens-health-belongs-in-the-past
235. https://www.ncbi.nlm.nih.gov/books/NBK612400/
236. https://www.heise.de/en/background/Gender-health-gap-There-is-a-lack-of-basic-research-10308180.html
237. https://cdn.jss.org.au/wp-content/uploads/2024/02/05144735/The-Man-Box-2024-7.1-LR.pdf
238. https://www.destatis.de/DE/Themen/Gesellschaft-Umwelt/Gesundheit/Todesursachen/Tabellen/suizide.html
239. https://de.statista.com/statistik/daten/studie/1353141/umfrage/strafgefangene-im-offenen-geschlossenen-vollzug-nach-geschlecht/
240. https://youtu.be/XBov_16F1GU?si=ymXjMzQI_PAjEsnr
241. https://pubmed.ncbi.nlm.nih.gov/24525762/
242. https://youtu.be/XBov_16F1GU?si=p84IXAviHpYaZ_VY
243. https://www.continuingedcourses.net/active/courses/course040.php
244. https://introspectioncounseling.com/what-are-mens-issues-in-therapy/
245. https://www.centreformalepsychology.com/male-psychology-magazine-listings/are-men-less-willing-to-engage-in-traditional-talking-therapy-because-therapy-has-been-feminised
246. https://pubmed.ncbi.nlm.nih.gov/34959153/
247. https://pubmed.ncbi.nlm.nih.gov/37755928/
248. https://pubmed.ncbi.nlm.nih.gov/38996078/
249. https://www.focus.de/gesundheit/ratgeber/wie-haeufig-hinter-gewalttaten-tatsaechlich-psychische-erkrankungen-stecken_b2d72fce-2520-435b-b8cf-baba38731796.html
250. https://www.vaeter-zeit.de/vaeter-maenner/maennergewalt-gewalt-gegen-jungen.php

251. https://www.tauwetter.de/images/phocadownload/pdf/2021/2021%20Schlingmann%20-%20Sexualisierte%20Gewalt%20gegen%20Manner.pdf
252. https://www.bka.de/SharedDocs/Downloads/DE/Publikationen/PolizeilicheKriminalstatistik/2023/BundesdatenDelikte/03_MordTotschlagToetungAufVerlangenBRD.html
253. https://www.kriminalpolizei.de/ausgaben/2023/september/detailansicht-september/artikel/toetungsdelikte-durch-frauen.html
254. https://www.stern.de/panorama/verbrechen/muetter--die-ihre-babys-toeten--das-sind-keine-monster---stern-lesestueck-am-sonntag-6578280.html
255. https://pubmed.ncbi.nlm.nih.gov/23593128/
256. https://www.sciencedaily.com/releases/2014/02/140225122423.htm
257. https://jamanetwork.com/journals/jama/fullarticle/190980
258. https://publications.aap.org/pediatrics/article-abstract/110/2/e18/64327/Underascertainment-of-Child-Maltreatment?redirectedFrom=fulltext?autologincheck=redirected
259. https://journals.sagepub.com/doi/abs/10.1177/19253621221077870
260. https://www.cdc.gov/mmwr/volumes/69/wr/mm6939a1.htm/
261. https://www.bka.de/SharedDocs/Downloads/DE/Publikationen/PolizeilicheKriminalstatistik/2023/BundesdatenDelikte/04_VergewaltigungSexNoetigungBRD.html
262. https://www.instagram.com/p/DJWXygbIt_K/?img_index=1
263. https://www.cdc.gov/nisvs/documentation/nisvsReportonSexualViolence.pdf
264. https://pubmed.ncbi.nlm.nih.gov/36227317/
265. https://www.tandfonline.com/doi/pdf/10.3402/vgi.v3i0.14834
266. https://nij.ojp.gov/library/publications/sexual-offenders-intellectual-disabilities-exploratory-comparison-study
267. https://en.wikipedia.org/wiki/Sexual_abuse_and_intellectual_disability
268. https://journals.sagepub.com/doi/10.1177/15248380251325210?int.sj-abstract.similar-articles.8
269. https://www.bka.de/DE/UnsereAufgaben/Forschung/ForschungsprojekteUndErgebnisse/Dunkelfeldforschung/SKiD/Ergebnisse/Ergebnisse_node.html
270. https://pmc.ncbi.nlm.nih.gov/articles/PMC10732194/
271. https://pubmed.ncbi.nlm.nih.gov/26934546/
272. https://www.bka.de/DE/UnsereAufgaben/Forschung/ForschungsprojekteUndErgebnisse/Dunkelfeldforschung/SKiD/Befragungsperson/SKiD_Fragebogen.html
273. https://uscholar.univie.ac.at/detail/o:1162297
274. https://www.hilfetelefon.de/aktuelles/weiter-steigende-zahlen-im-bereich-haeusliche-gewalt/
275. https://pmc.ncbi.nlm.nih.gov/articles/PMC1854883/
276. https://www.researchgate.net/publication/259905459_A_Typology_of_Domestic_Violence_Intimate_Terrorism_Violent_Resistance_and_Situational_Couple_Violence_by_Michael_P_Johnson
277. https://www.maennergewaltschutz.de/neuigkeiten/kfn-studie-maenner-partnerschaftsgewalt/
278. https://www.researchgate.net/publication/386189016_Bidirectional_and_Unidirectional_Intimate_Partner_Violence_A_Comprehensive_Review
279. https://www.gewaltinfo.at/themen/geschlechtsspezifische-burschen-und-maennerarbeit/maenner-als-opfer-haeuslicher-gewalt.html
280. https://www.spiegel.de/wissenschaft/mensch/weibliche-uebergriffe-die-verdraengte-gewalt-a-718585.html
281. https://psycnet.apa.org/record/2010-06192-009

282. https://www.researchgate.net/publication/272209909_Motivations_for_Men_and_Women's_Intimate_Partner_Violence_Perpetration_A_Comprehensive_Review
283. https://psycnet.apa.org/record/2012-19696-004
284. https://pmc.ncbi.nlm.nih.gov/articles/PMC3384540/
285. https://pmc.ncbi.nlm.nih.gov/articles/PMC6157722/
286. https://www.researchgate.net/publication/335132754_Meta-analysis_and_systematic_review_for_the_treatment_of_perpetrators_of_intimate_partner_violence
287. https://pmc.ncbi.nlm.nih.gov/articles/PMC10666508/
288. https://pubmed.ncbi.nlm.nih.gov/38506141/
289. https://www.instagram.com/p/DIyLYafIQ-P/
290. https://www.ons.gov.uk/peoplepopulationandcommunity/crimeandjustice/articles/redevelopmentofdomesticabusestatistics/researchupdatedecember2024
291. https://www.frauenhauskoordinierung.de/themenportal/gewalt-gegen-frauen/gewaltformen/femizide
292. https://www.swr.de/swraktuell/baden-wuerttemberg/suedbaden/kommentar-femizide-in-suedbaden-100.html
293. https://de.wikipedia.org/wiki/Femizid
294. https://www.bmi.bund.de/SharedDocs/schwerpunkte/DE/gewalt-gegen-frauen/gewalt-gegen-frauen-artikel.html
295. https://www.euronews.com/my-europe/2021/07/07/nine-out-of-ten-hate-crimes-going-unreported-eu-report-claims
296. https://www.amnesty.eu/news/the-eu-must-act-to-prevent-and-prosecute-homophobic-transphobic-crime-0799/
297. https://www.europarl.europa.eu/RegData/etudes/ATAG/2022/733520/EPRS_ATA%282022%29733520_EN.pdf
298. https://www.justice.gov/crt/hate-crime-laws
299. https://eur-lex.europa.eu/eli/dir/2012/29/oj/eng
300. https://www.unodc.org/documents/data-and-analysis/gsh/2023/GSH23_Special_Points.pdf
301. https://www.spiegel.de/kultur/feminismus-und-strafrecht-warum-der-begriff-femizid-strafrechtlich-unbrauchbar-ist-kolumne-a-2c851939-3e9f-4e90-b324-0d188cc59226
302. https://www.bundestag.de/dokumente/textarchiv/2021/kw09-pa-familie-femizide-822324
303. https://en.wikipedia.org/w/index.php?title=Who_Stole_Feminism%3F
304. https://en.wikipedia.org/wiki/Rape_culture
305. https://www.bmi.bund.de/SharedDocs/schwerpunkte/DE/gewalt-gegen-frauen/gewalt-gegen-frauen-artikel.html
306. https://assets.publishing.service.gov.uk/media/5a81b1c5e5274a2e87dbf034/HO-Domestic-Homicide-Review-Analysis-161206.pdf
307. https://www.researchgate.net/publication/359384749_Mental_Disorders_and_Intimate_Partner_Femicide_Clinical_Characteristics_in_Perpetrators_of_Intimate_Partner_Femicide_and_Male-to-Male_Homicide
308. https://pmc.ncbi.nlm.nih.gov/articles/PMC8977448/
309. https://de.wikipedia.org/wiki/Imperativ_%28Modus%29#Infinitiv
310. https://www.welt.de/kultur/plus250679146/Karriere-Auf-viele-Jobs-brauche-ich-mich-nicht-zu-bewerben-ich-bin-keine-Frau-keine-Minderheit.html
311. https://www.dtv.de/buch/maenner-toeten-14922

312. https://www.nw.de/lokal/bielefeld/mitte/23741262_Maenner-toeten-Irritierende-Slogans-an-Waenden-und-Ladenfassaden-im-Bielefelder-Westen.html
313. https://www.vaeter-zeit.de/vaeter-maenner/maennergewalt-gewalt-gegen-jungen.php
314. https://www.gewaltinfo.at/fachwissen/gewalt-an-kindern-und-jugendlichen-durch-erwachsene.html
315. https://beauftragte-missbrauch.de/fileadmin/Content/pdf/Pressemitteilungen/2020/01_Januar/28/Fact_Sheet_Zahlen_und_Fakten_sexueller_Missbrauch.pdf
316. https://en.wikipedia.org/wiki/Rape_in_Germany#cite_note-16
317. https://www.aktion-tu-was.de/fileadmin/dokumente/infotext-kindesmisshandlung-p.pdf
318. https://www.leuphana.de/news/meldungen/titelstories/mobbingstudie.htm
319. https://girlsschools.org/wp-content/uploads/2019/04/Research-Brief-on-Girls-and-Bullying.pdf
320. https://journals.sagepub.com/doi/10.1177/026975809600400201
321. https://www.researchgate.net/profile/Derek-Chadee/post/Where-would-I-find-research-on-the-following-pre-2000-UK-Is-victimisation-associated-with-heightened-fear-of-crime/attachment/59d62b1a79197b80779897bc/AS%3A341909391331349%401458528959987/download/Hale+1996.pdf
322. https://journals.sagepub.com/doi/10.1177/07340168221088570
323. https://www.instagram.com/p/DH0H1ZsPPru/
324. https://www.mdr.de/nachrichten/deutschland/gesellschaft/kriminalitaet-statistik-sicherheit-grenzkontrollen-migration-100.html
325. https://en.wikipedia.org/wiki/Mean_world_syndrome
326. https://digitalcommons.pace.edu/dissertations/AAI30249838/
327. https://www.nature.com/articles/s41599-020-0430-7
328. https://www.aijssnet.com/journals/Vol_6_No_3_September_2017/11.pdf
329. https://www.instagram.com/p/DJOVsJSCBxj/?img_index=1
330. https://ovc.ojp.gov/about/crime-victims-fund
331. https://www.nursefamilypartnership.org/about/proven-results/prevent-child-abuse-neglect/
332. https://oig.hhs.gov/reports-and-publications/workplan/summary/wp-summary-0000782.asp
333. https://cvg.org/impact/
334. https://national-policies.eacea.ec.europa.eu/youthwiki/chapters/germany/17-funding-youth-policy
335. https://www.hilfetelefon.de/fileadmin/content/04_Materialien/1_Materialien_Bestellen/Jahresberichte/2022/BAFZA_Hilfetelefon_Jahresbericht_Das_Jahr_in_Zahlen_2022_web_bf.pdf
336. https://www.big-berlin.info/sites/default/files/downloads/490_BIG_Projektdokumentation_2013_en.pdf
337. https://stop-partnergewalt.org/stop-wirkt-erfolgsgeschichten/
338. https://www.demokratie-leben.de/dl/foerderung/wen-wir-foerdern
339. https://www.who.int/publications/i/item/9789241564793
340. https://pubmed.ncbi.nlm.nih.gov/26689979/
341. https://en.wikipedia.org/wiki/Child_discipline
342. https://www.bka.de/DE/UnsereAufgaben/Forschung/ForschungsprojekteUndErgebnisse/Dunkelfeldforschung/SKiD/Ergebnisse/Ergebnisse_node.html
343. https://de.wikipedia.org/wiki/Intersektionalit%C3%A4t
344. https://de.wikipedia.org/wiki/Standpunkt-Theorie
345. https://committees.parliament.uk/writtenevidence/18973/pdf/

346. https://www.canada.ca/en/correctional-service/corporate/library/research/research-brief/24-08.html
347. https://www.focus.de/gesundheit/ratgeber/wie-haeufig-hinter-gewalttaten-tatsaechlich-psychische-erkrankungen-stecken_b2d72fce-2520-435b-b8cf-baba38731796.html
348. https://pmc.ncbi.nlm.nih.gov/articles/PMC3154094/
349. https://familyconflict.eu/wp-content/uploads/BatesFrankfurt-DEU.pdf
350. https://ijfrp.journals.yorku.ca/index.php/ijfrp/article/view/39581
351. https://pmc.ncbi.nlm.nih.gov/articles/PMC3154094/
352. https://de.wikipedia.org/wiki/D%C3%A4monisierung
353. https://en.wikipedia.org/wiki/Mean_world_syndrome
354. https://en.wikipedia.org/wiki/Cognitive_dissonance
355. https://merionwest.com/2021/09/02/the-psychology-of-critical-social-justice/
356. https://en.wikipedia.org/wiki/Social_justice
357. https://newdiscourses.com/2020/02/naming-enemy-critical-social-justice/
358. https://en.wikipedia.org/wiki/James_A._Lindsay
359. https://www.youtube.com/watch?v=kVk9a5Jcd1k&ab_channel=MichaelNayna
360. https://nycmuseumgallery.org/1196/entertainment/how-has-social-media-affected-cancel-culture/
361. https://www.dailymail.co.uk/news/article-14066353/sexual-encounter-Oxford-student-Alexander-Rogers-cancelled.html
362. https://www.stuff.co.nz/world-news/360483365/alexander-rogers-wasnt-just-cancelled-he-was-bullied-death
363. https://www.bbc.com/news/articles/cdd0gyjlqyvo
364. https://freespeechunion.org/i-lived-in-fear-of-being-cancelled-as-an-oxbridge-student-we-all-did/
365. https://www.kosmo.at/frau-angestarrt-blinder-mann-aus-fitnessstudio-geworfen/
366. https://youtu.be/o84rnYTuunQ?si=TtnvKGYobl-szpmY
367. https://newsroom.iza.org/en/archive/research/gender-bias-on-social-media-women-face-unequal-scrutiny/
368. https://www.degruyter.com/document/doi/10.12987/9780300235029/html
369. https://de.wikipedia.org/wiki/D%C3%A4monisierung
370. https://pmc.ncbi.nlm.nih.gov/articles/PMC1854883/
371. https://www.researchgate.net/publication/386189016_Bidirectional_and_Unidirectional_Intimate_Partner_Violence_A_Comprehensive_Review
372. https://www.kriminalpolizei.de/ausgaben/2023/detailansicht-2023/artikel/toetungsdelikte-durch-frauen.html
373. https://www.vaeter-zeit.de/vaeter-maenner/maennergewalt-gewalt-gegen-jungen.php
374. https://en.wikipedia.org/wiki/Mean_world_syndrome
375. https://www.presseportal.de/pm/64713/5540659
376. https://bjs.ojp.gov/press-release/criminal-victimization-2022
377. https://www.statista.com/statistics/251923/usa-reported-forcible-rape-cases-by-gender/
378. https://youtu.be/6w_96Hnz8JM?si=sMGvMQw9lzedSWCA
379. https://youtu.be/lxeEI_tnKkw?si=CWvzllF_Jgacd21X
380. https://youtu.be/KwLNSAn1AAo?si=t1VYsc_mvNMOHXxI
381. https://youtu.be/ZuAaD33yW5k?si=Hg-YOgRiWV9S1P31

382. https://www.zdf.de/comedy/bosetti-will-reden/bosetti-will-reden-vom-15-mai-2024-100.htm l Available until 14.05.2026

383. https://de.wikipedia.org/wiki/Generalverdacht

384. https://www.wienerzeitung.at/a/mann-oder-baer

385. https://www.glamour.de/artikel/mann-oder-baer-auf-tiktok-kommentar

386. https://www.spiegel.de/netzwelt/web/tiktok-baer-oder-mann-auf-wen-allein-im-wald-lieber-t reffen-a-e33ea737-3284-4982-b320-29cc2bc983f8

387. https://www.morgenpost.de/vermischtes/article242308280/Baer-oder-Mann-TikTok-Trend-d eckt-Aengste-junger-Menschen-auf.html

388. https://tu-dresden.de/bu/der-bereich/chancengleichheit/fun/news/mann-oder-baer-tiktok-tren ds-als-gesellschaftlicher-spiegel-1

389. https://weisser-ring.de/gewalt_gegen_maenner

390. https://www.bionity.com/de/lexikon/Misandrie.html

391. https://docs.iza.org/dp17493.pdf

392. https://youtu.be/0uZFHpEh5So?si=r3NI1qYl5FmLYZuT

393. https://youtu.be/OEPsqFLhHBc?si=er6Yb1rVwS8jYCQG

394. https://youtu.be/m9keJhpRG5o?si=gLHOievzUGYuoH6J

395. https://www.instagram.com/p/DITkT4qo-ze/

396. https://www.amazon.co.uk/Aileen-Wuornos-Shirt-American-Serial/dp/B0CS3K54KC

397. https://www.amazon.com/How-Piss-Off-Men-Shatter/dp/1728291925

398. https://www.amazon.de/Ich-hasse-M%C3%A4nner-Pauline-Harmange/dp/3499006758

399. https://youtu.be/Lxpe5vYL5Ks?si=zQVJOKoxE0TI5afB

400. https://www.instagram.com/p/DKckannNxIe/

401. https://www.instagram.com/p/DIGotktOcbP

402. https://www.instagram.com/p/DC9VLMEpsRX/

403. https://www.instagram.com/p/DIHjhvFpqp7/

404. https://www.instagram.com/p/DH855jfpw44/

405. https://www.instagram.com/p/DH84GXMJ2Za/

406. https://www.instagram.com/p/DI-5sM-uRbv/

407. https://www.instagram.com/p/DI3xclMotWj/

408. https://www.instagram.com/p/DJmtvogMqUG/

409. https://www.instagram.com/reel/DJkIPg_yHlb/

410. https://www.instagram.com/p/DI4gmH-pTmM/

411. https://www.instagram.com/reel/DIpWrvDTmJY/

412. https://www.instagram.com/p/DIAEF5Zhwsc

413. https://www.instagram.com/p/DJuP1Duv1BD/

414. https://www.instagram.com/p/DJUkv92sYD4/

415. https://www.instagram.com/p/DI0w22esKuG/

416. https://www.instagram.com/p/DH_ARIYgtJj/

417. https://www.instagram.com/p/DH9Mx_upKUU/

418. https://www.instagram.com/p/DJEGzDDO9QR/

419. https://www.instagram.com/p/DJBst4-ItAR/

420. https://www.instagram.com/reel/DJFZBXRvIfw/

421. https://www.instagram.com/p/DI0EwKuRV9H/?img_index=2

422. https://www.instagram.com/p/DJTZTRjgZBg/

423. https://www.instagram.com/reel/DJm1oP4owTj/

424. https://www.instagram.com/p/DJog_lRv2cZ/
425. https://www.instagram.com/p/DJb14APMjKH/
426. https://www.instagram.com/p/DJUNVbGsLrv/
427. https://www.swr.de/swraktuell/rheinland-pfalz/kaiserslautern/urteil-landgericht-kaiserslautern-prozess-toedlicher-messerstich-im-hauptbahnhof-nach-sexueller-belaestigung-102.html
428. https://www.instagram.com/p/DJbKyizPhSY/
429. https://www.instagram.com/p/DJTp2dAKn8X/
430. https://www.instagram.com/p/DKZ3Pi9R4k7/
431. https://www.instagram.com/p/DJT0n7bIavc/
432. https://www.instagram.com/p/DJFSGk9z1LE/?img_index=1
433. https://www.instagram.com/p/DJKU5ivyZ-O/?img_index=2
434. https://www.instagram.com/p/DI4SLRJRXBi/
435. https://www.instagram.com/p/DI-I0U_ozIk/
436. https://www.instagram.com/p/DIuvxgooEzZ/
437. https://www.instagram.com/p/DJKDl11KS7v/
438. https://www.instagram.com/p/DI9pKBiouMd/
439. https://www.instagram.com/p/DI4hJQ-InVq/
440. https://www.instagram.com/p/DJALGe7TUIv/?img_index=1
441. https://www.instagram.com/reel/DImITufRDuV/
442. https://www.instagram.com/p/DJSvB18pHy_/
443. https://www.instagram.com/p/DJKfFvCJ-km
444. https://www.instagram.com/p/DJgx4MftBi6/
445. https://www.instagram.com/p/DJMj3PcSYaA/
446. https://www.instagram.com/reel/DJHuK-7pUGi/
447. https://www.esanum.de/blogs/onkologie-blog/feeds/today/posts/in-guten-und-in-schlechten-zeiten-in-gesundheit-und-krankheit
448. https://www.forum-gesundheitspolitik.de/artikel/artikel.pl?artikel=1669
449. https://www.sbs.com.au/news/article/does-winning-the-lottery-lead-to-divorce-its-different-for-women-and-men/o110o00tb
450. https://www.instagram.com/p/DJimxDASMeK/
451. https://www.instagram.com/p/DJSuSAtJeLI/
452. https://www.instagram.com/p/DJCH1FDh9VO/
453. https://www.instagram.com/reel/DI_exaBBDiz/
454. https://www.instagram.com/p/DI8M4-LAR0H/
455. https://www.instagram.com/p/DJBFXCeAsnv/?img_index=1
456. https://www.instagram.com/p/DH9KsxzJEza/
457. https://www.instagram.com/p/DI1Tigvquyj/
458. https://www.instagram.com/reel/DJCUT2YtRRF/
459. https://www.instagram.com/p/DH59LT4IErl/
460. https://www.instagram.com/reel/DI9X6pCTqb2/
461. https://www.instagram.com/p/DJj0dIrS7-N/?img_index=1
462. https://www.instagram.com/p/DJEHDpZu2hd/
463. https://www.instagram.com/p/DHuMzWXtadQ/
464. https://www.instagram.com/p/DHrTHUBoW9W/
465. https://www.instagram.com/p/DJEmiDTI8B2/
466. https://www.instagram.com/p/DHlpeiJo3-m/

467. https://www.instagram.com/p/DHHoYWapKLw/
468. https://www.instagram.com/p/DHjPCDOpEKD/
469. https://www.instagram.com/reel/DDIWYmqp1hs/
470. https://www.instagram.com/reel/DIyRWcJR3G4/
471. https://www.instagram.com/p/DJKN7oOMC09/
472. https://www.instagram.com/reel/DIG8JZcp6rM/
473. https://www.instagram.com/p/DHOdyx0pLTH/
474. https://www.instagram.com/p/DGuAGW3IhzW/
475. https://www.instagram.com/reel/C8ahOcLSnTl/
476. https://www.instagram.com/p/DJPNJ_IIxle/
477. https://www.instagram.com/p/DHMna1Vp3yL/
478. https://www.instagram.com/p/DIoXrJtvQv0/?img_index=1
479. https://www.instagram.com/p/DIExC9kstm9/?img_index=2
480. https://www.instagram.com/p/DJbwLsmARbW/
481. https://www.instagram.com/p/DHMIcMRp00T
482. https://www.instagram.com/reel/DIJxyEFpQy5/
483. https://www.instagram.com/reel/DIKmhIFvEpM/
484. https://www.independent.co.uk/student/news/university-of-york-s-decision-to-cancel-interna
tional-men-s-day-frankly-looks-rather-silly-says-mp-in-parliamentary-debate-on-male-suicid
e-a6741811.html
485. https://www.bbc.com/news/uk-england-york-north-yorkshire-34857143
486. https://www.york.ac.uk/news-and-events/news/2015/events/mensday-gender-equality/
487. https://www.washingtonexaminer.com/red-alert-politics/2195937/despite-male-suicide-scho
ol-cancels-mens-health-day-after-feminists-complain/
488. https://www.instagram.com/p/DIK4Gq_xFxy/
489. https://www.instagram.com/p/DJgqgeDict8/?img_index=2
490. https://www.instagram.com/reel/DJ2wMU8JZrr/
491. https://www.instagram.com/p/DJFMURoIygV/
492. https://youtu.be/4kf8RcpX82U?si=li7dbj46jxocMniz
493. https://youtu.be/_ShWaIErHP4?si=mWEIY1K1CSvVlucL
494. https://www.instagram.com/p/DJIQ1WIoZQ7/
495. https://www.instagram.com/p/DKPKthbMQOw/?img_index=1
496. https://www.instagram.com/p/DJJcuXRM8mv/
497. https://www.iccl.ie/news/82-of-the-irish-public-wants-big-techs-toxic-algorithms-switched-o
ff/
498. https://www.instagram.com/p/DIJAMJqtqpw/
499. https://de.statista.com/statistik/daten/studie/1295284/umfrage/einstellung-der-deutschen-geg
enueber-feminismus/
500. https://www.gesetze-im-internet.de/gg/art_3.html
501. https://youtu.be/OObJmnsjnsY?si=v4jYONe1bMoG0O5m
502. https://www.kriminalpolizei.de/ausgaben/2024/dezember/detailansicht-dezember/artikel/gew
altkriminalitaet-durch-kinder-und-jugendliche.html
503. https://de.statista.com/statistik/daten/studie/167208/umfrage/kinder-und-jugendliche-mordop
fer-unter-18-jahren-in-deutschland/
504. https://www.uniklinikum-dresden.de/de/das-klinikum/kliniken-polikliniken-institute/pso/fors
chung-und-lehre/forschergruppen/filizid-aufarbeitung
505. https://www.nature.com/articles/s41467-018-04773-w

506. https://en.wikipedia.org/wiki/Male_warrior_hypothesis
507. https://www.deutschlandfunk.de/uno-analyse-70-prozent-der-toten-sind-frauen-und-kinder-1 04.html
508. https://unric.org/de/berichte-ueber-massengraeber-in-gaza-un-hochkommissar-fuer-mensche nrechte-tuerk-fordert-untersuchung/
509. https://www.researchgate.net/publication/328004056_Insights_From_fMRI_Studies_Into_In group_Bias
510. https://en.wikipedia.org/wiki/Susan_Fiske
511. https://royalsocietypublishing.org/doi/10.1098/rsbl.2024.0381
512. https://pubmed.ncbi.nlm.nih.gov/19254100/
513. https://www.sciencedirect.com/science/article/abs/pii/S0749597820303630
514. https://lup.lub.lu.se/luur/download?func=downloadFile&recordOId=9186735&fileOId=918 6737
515. https://www.researchgate.net/publication/232558222_A_meta-analytic_review_of_the_relati onship_between_gender_and_belief_in_a_just_world
516. https://www.artofmanliness.com/character/behavior/male-expendability/
517. https://pm-report.de/gesundheitswesen/2024/who-einsamkeit-als-globale-prioritaet.html
518. https://pubmed.ncbi.nlm.nih.gov/21516952/
519. https://en.wikipedia.org/wiki/Ach%C3%A9#Demography
520. https://pubmed.ncbi.nlm.nih.gov/23813245/
521. https://pubmed.ncbi.nlm.nih.gov/26189411/
522. https://www.reddit.com/r/PurplePillDebate/comments/ot4qzd/what_the_okcupid_data_really _says/
523. https://www.uni-bamberg.de/presse/pm/artikel/studie-attraktivitaet-carbon/
524. https://www.tagesspiegel.de/wissen/frauen-wollen-einen-gut-aussehenden-partner-4924093. html
525. https://www.oe24.at/madonna/life/deshalb-sind-attraktive-menschen-intelligenter/56668640 8
526. https://www.welt.de/vermischtes/article160308431/Was-das-Gesicht-ueber-die-Intelligenz-v erraet.html
527. https://www.augsburger-allgemeine.de/panorama/US-Studie-Intelligenz-macht-Maenner-sex y-id4276291.html
528. https://www.oe24.at/madonna/life/pretty-privilege-darum-haben-es-schoene-menschen-leich ter-im-leben/555925590
529. https://www.focus.de/gesundheit/news/mann-kaempft-frau-waehlt-partnersuche_id_2436636 .html
530. https://synaptiqmatch.com/iq-und-erfolg/
531. https://freizeit.at/lust-liebe/beziehungsstudie-maenner-hauptverdiener/402295841
532. https://psycnet.apa.org/record/2008-18683-004
533. https://pmc.ncbi.nlm.nih.gov/articles/PMC3023236/
534. https://docs.iza.org/dp12185.pdf
535. https://pm-report.de/gesundheitswesen/2024/who-einsamkeit-als-globale-prioritaet.html
536. https://pubmed.ncbi.nlm.nih.gov/32875051/
537. https://innofact-marktforschung.de/parship-studie-immer-mehr-junge-menschen-fuehlen-sic h-einsam-ganz-besonders-singles/
538. https://www.barmer.de/gesundheit-verstehen/psyche/einsamkeit/einsame-frauen-und-maenn er-1140290

539. https://pubmed.ncbi.nlm.nih.gov/32875051/
540. https://www.instagram.com/katara.selflovejourney/reel/DEw7tKENVpi/
541. https://www.focus.de/gesundheit/neue-studie-frauen-leben-laenger-und-gluecklicher-wenn-sie-ehe-und-kinderlos-bleiben_id_201367960.html
542. https://www.vox.com/future-perfect/2019/6/4/18650969/married-women-miserable-fake-paul-dolan-happiness
543. https://en.wikipedia.org/wiki/Paul_Dolan_(behavioural_scientist)
544. https://www.fitbook.de/mind-body/studie-gluecklich-laenger-leben
545. https://read.dukeupress.edu/demography/article-abstract/27/2/233/171206/Mortality-Differentials-by-Marital-Status-An
546. https://pophealthmetrics.biomedcentral.com/articles/10.1186/s12963-021-00263-2
547. https://www.theguardian.com/lifeandstyle/2024/nov/04/moving-in-with-someone-cuts-chances-of-being-depressed-finds-study
548. https://pubmed.ncbi.nlm.nih.gov/9870051/
549. https://pmc.ncbi.nlm.nih.gov/articles/PMC2891411/
550. https://www.demogr.mpg.de/de/news_events_6123/news_pressemitteilungen_4630/news/gluecklich_und_gesund_im_familiengefuege_13274
551. https://wzb.eu/de/pressemitteilung/kinder-machen-gluecklich-meisten
552. https://www.demogr.mpg.de/de/news_events_6123/news_pressemitteilungen_4630/presse/elternschaft_langzeitinvestition_ins_glueck_1863
553. https://www.hu-berlin.de/de/pr/nachrichten/dezember-2024/nr-241218-1
554. https://www.spiegel.de/wissenschaft/mensch/weltweite-umfrage-eltern-sind-nicht-gluecklicher-als-kinderlose-a-943490.html
555. https://youtu.be/Yt_i98OnTF4?si=mf8z6gwAWhZd0_6g
556. https://journals.sagepub.com/doi/10.1177/19485506241287960
557. https://en.wikipedia.org/wiki/Incel
558. https://cujournal.ie/article/id/26/
559. https://www.crimejusticejournal.com/article/view/2138
560. https://www.adl.org/resources/backgrounder/incels-involuntary-celibates
561. https://en.wikipedia.org/wiki/Elliot_Rodger
562. https://www.bbc.com/news/world-us-canada-43892189
563. https://icct.nl/sites/default/files/2023-01/Mapping-the-Ideological-Landscape-of-Misogyny%20%282%29.pdf
564. https://youtu.be/tYUCE0uSvrQ?si=nhgTv4B00thN9gHl
565. https://www.frisch.uio.no/publikasjoner/pdf/2020/Formatert/jhr.58.3.1219-10604R1.full.pdf
566. https://www.researchgate.net/publication/363484489_Levels_of_Well-Being_Among_Men_Who_Are_Incel_Involuntarily_Celibate
567. https://dserver.bundestag.de/btd/20/006/2000624.pdf
568. https://www.praeventionstag.de/nano.cms/news/details/5919
569. https://home-affairs.ec.europa.eu/system/files/2021-08/ran_cn_incel_phenomenon_20210803_de.pdf
570. https://www.zdf.de/video/reportagen/die-spur-224/incels-amok-frauenhass-toxisch-100
571. https://www.instagram.com/p/DHduTEjIORw/
572. https://www.instagram.com/p/DHifrNWI7Rl/
573. https://www.destatis.de/DE/Themen/Gesellschaft-Umwelt/Gesundheit/Todesursachen/Tabellen/suizide.html#119324

574. https://en.wikipedia.org/wiki/Spartan_army#Training
575. https://en.wikipedia.org/wiki/Draft_evasion_in_the_Vietnam_War
576. https://repository.law.umich.edu/cgi/viewcontent.cgi?article=1164&context=law_econ_current
577. https://www.mcgrathtraining.com/post/offenders-and-sentencing-by-gender-are-females-treated-differently
578. https://www.crimejusticejournal.com/article/download/3622/1564
579. https://www.ojp.gov/ncjrs/virtual-library/abstracts/gender-differences-sentencing-felony-offenders
580. https://www.spiegel.de/wissenschaft/wann-ist-ein-embryo-ein-mensch-a-e2367d1d-0002-0001-0000-000040525890
581. https://www.bpb.de/themen/umwelt/bioethik/33779/wann-beginnt-das-recht-auf-leben/
582. https://www.institut-fuer-menschenrechte.de/themen/menschenrechtsbildung/was-sind-menschenrechte
583. https://www.bpb.de/themen/umwelt/bioethik/33779/wann-beginnt-das-recht-auf-leben/
584. https://data.worldbank.org/indicator/SP.DYN.TFRT.IN
585. https://data.worldbank.org/indicator/SP.DYN.TFRT.IN?locations=FR
586. https://datacommons.org/place?utm_medium=explore&dcid=country/SWE&mprop=fertilityRate&popt=Person&cpv=gender,Female&hl=en
587. https://www.destatis.de/DE/Themen/Gesellschaft-Umwelt/Verkehrsunfaelle/Publikationen/Downloads-Verkehrsunfaelle/unfaelle-frauen-maenner-5462407207004.pdf?__blob=publicationFile
588. https://www.instagram.com/p/DGdDp19zl26/
589. https://www.morganstanley.com/ideas/womens-impact-on-the-economy
590. https://www.instagram.com/p/DI_oIiFsZp3/
591. https://de.statista.com/infografik/25320/verhaeltnis-von-altersrentnern-zu-beitragszahlern-in-der-gesetzlichen-rentenversicherung/
592. https://www.csp-sw.de/news/alarmierende-prognose-deutschland-droht-massiver-fachkraeftemangel-5-millionen-arbeitskraefte-bis-2030-gesucht/
593. https://datacommons.org/place/country/JPN?utm_medium=explore&mprop=fertilityRate&popt=Person&cpv=gender,Female&hl=en
594. https://www.fr.de/wirtschaft/japan-macht-die-geburtenrate-zur-chefsache-92324022.html
595. https://www.instagram.com/p/DIzlCPkMiek/
596. https://www.stern.de/politik/deutschland/rentensystem--wie-kinderlose-zu-suendenboecken-einer-falschen-politik-gemacht-werden-7351738.html
597. https://www.nzherald.co.nz/lifestyle/south-korean-city-offering-64000-for-people-to-get-married-and-have-children/3FRFCBSL3BC6DH6OGWYJNVUX54/
598. https://www.koreatimes.co.kr/www/nation/2025/03/113_385407.html
599. https://www.watson.ch/international/daten/325131486-japan-mit-staatlicher-dating-app-wegen-des-starken-geburtenrueckgangs
600. https://www.vietnam.vn/de/ke-hoach-nam-2025-cua-nhat-ban-nham-giai-quyet-khung-hoang-dan-so
601. https://direct.mit.edu/qss/article/3/1/244/108658/Researching-women-and-men-1996-2020-Is